'David Brown helps us regard art and imagination as truly and irreducibly constructive (though not beyond criticism), and as potentially part of genuine critique – even when ignored almost completely by much of academic theology. There is no one I would rather be reading, or have students of theology and the arts be taking into full consideration. In fact, I've never read a theologian more informed – and more "generous" – in insisting on the integral connection between theology, the arts, and imagination.'
    Frank Burch Brown, Frederick Doyle Kershner Professor Emeritus of Religion and the Arts, Christian Theological Seminary, USA

'In this important volume of essays David Brown works to widen the avenues of exchange between theology and the arts, getting the traffic between the two to move more freely in both directions and to carry heavier freight in the process. Brown's writing is irenic and erudite, drawing insights from an astonishing range of biblical, theological and art historical studies into new, mutually enriching dialogue.'
    Jonathan A. Anderson, Associate Professor of Art, Biola University, USA

'An excellent introduction to the work of David Brown, these essays offer great insight into the theoretical principles and criteria undergirding his writings on human creativity and the imagination. The central idea in Brown's work, which is the intrinsic, sacramental relationship of revelation and imagination, will prove to be a significant starting point for new theological developments in the years to come.'
    Stephan van Erp, Professor of Fundamental Theology, KU Leuven, Belgium

Divine Generosity and Human Creativity

Partly in a desire to defend divine freedom and partly because it is seen as the only way of preserving a distinctive voice for theology, much contemporary theology has artificially restricted revelation and religious experience, effectively cutting off those who find God beyond the walls of the Church. Against this tendency, David Brown argues for divine generosity and a broader vision of reality that sees God deploying symbols (literary, visual and sacramental) as a means of mediating between the divine world and our own material existence. A sustained argument for divine interaction and more specifically the ways in which God speaks in the wider imaginative world, this volume calls for a careful listening exercise since symbols are richer and more open in their possibilities than their users often suppose. Not only is this true of the imagery of Scripture, even inanimate objects like buildings or hostile but creative artists can have important things to say to the believing Christian. An ideal introduction that also moves the conversation forward, this volume addresses foundations, the multivalent power of symbols, artists as theologians and meaning in religious architecture.

David Brown retired from the University of St Andrews as Professor of Theology, Aesthetics and Culture in 2015, having previously held positions at Oxford and Durham. Five major volumes on relations between theology and the arts were published with OUP between 1999 and 2008, with a large edited volume on *Durham Cathedral: History, Fabric and Culture* (Yale, 2015) his most recent contribution. He was elected a Fellow of the British Academy in 2002 and of the Royal Society of Edinburgh in 2012.

Christopher R. Brewer is Manager of Publishing and Strategic Partnerships at The Colossian Forum on Faith, Science and Culture in Grand Rapids, Michigan, USA, and Visiting Scholar at Calvin College. He has edited or co-edited two other volumes, including *Art that Tells the Story*.

Robert MacSwain is Associate Professor of Theology at the School of Theology of the University of the South in Sewanee, Tennessee, USA. The author of *Solved by Sacrifice: Austin Farrer, Fideism, and the Evidence of Faith*, he has edited or co-edited six other volumes, including *Theology, Aesthetics, and Culture: Responses to the Work of David Brown*.

Divine Generosity and Human Creativity
Theology through Symbol, Painting and Architecture

David Brown

Edited by Christopher R. Brewer and Robert MacSwain

Routledge
Taylor & Francis Group
LONDON AND NEW YORK

First published 2017
by Routledge
2 Park Square, Milton Park, Abingdon, Oxon OX14 4RN

and by Routledge
711 Third Avenue, New York, NY 10017

Routledge is an imprint of the Taylor & Francis Group, an informa business

© 2017 David Brown

The right of David Brown to be identified as author of this work has been asserted by him in accordance with sections 77 and 78 of the Copyright, Designs and Patents Act 1988.

All rights reserved. No part of this book may be reprinted or reproduced or utilised in any form or by any electronic, mechanical, or other means, now known or hereafter invented, including photocopying and recording, or in any information storage or retrieval system, without permission in writing from the publishers.

Trademark notice: Product or corporate names may be trademarks or registered trademarks, and are used only for identification and explanation without intent to infringe.

British Library Cataloguing in Publication Data
A catalogue record for this book is available from the British Library

Library of Congress Cataloguing in Publication Data
Names: Brown, David, 1948 July 1– author. | Brewer, Christopher R., editor.
Title: Divine generosity and human creativity: theology through
symbol, painting and architecture; edited by
Christopher R. Brewer and Robert MacSwain.
Description: New York : Routledge, 2017. |
Includes bibliographical references and index.
Identifiers: LCCN 2016037771| ISBN 9781472465603 (hardback: alk. paper) | ISBN 9781472465634 (pbk.: alk. paper) | ISBN 9781315577807 (ebook)
Subjects: LCSH: Christianity and the arts. |
Architecture and religion. | Christian art and symbolism.
Classification: LCC BR115.A8 B759 2017 | DDC 246–dc23
LC record available at https://lccn.loc.gov/2016037771

ISBN: 978-1-4724-6560-3 (hbk)
ISBN: 978-1-4724-6563-4 (pbk)
ISBN: 978-1-315-57780-7 (ebk)

Typeset in Sabon
by Out of House Publishing

Contents

Editor's Introduction
Christopher R. Brewer   ix

PART I
Foundations   1

   Introduction   3
1 In the Beginning Was the Image   7
2 Why Theology Needs the Arts   23
3 Learning from Pagans   37

PART II
The Power of Symbols   49

   Introduction   51
4 Understanding Symbol   53
5 Baptism and Water as Cosmological Symbol   65
6 'The darkness and the light are both alike to
    thee': Finding God in Limited Light and in Darkness   81

PART III
Artists as Theologians   99

   Introduction   101
7 The Annunciation as True Fiction   105

8	Why the Ascension Matters	113
9	Artists on the Trinity	130

PART IV
Meaning in Religious Architecture   151

	Introduction	153
10	Architecture and Theism	156
11	Interfaith Dialogue through Architecture	167
12	Tensions between Politics and Religious Symbolism in Architecture	178
13	Worshipping with Art and Architecture	190
	Index	204

Editor's Introduction

Christopher R. Brewer

David Brown's career is most often divided into two halves: the early Brown, who was concerned with matters of philosophical theology, and the later Brown, more interested in the arts and culture. The fact that, with the publication of this volume, two volumes of essays have now been published – the first comprising essays on philosophical theology,[1] and this second volume essays on the arts and culture – might seem to reinforce this division of Brown's work into two halves.[2] I intend to argue, however, that while there is some truth to this two-halves characterisation, there is a more fundamental unity underlying Brown's corpus, which might be described from one side as a sustained argument *against* deism and for a generous God or, from the other side, a sacramental vision of reality that is mediated through inspired human creativity.[3] Admittedly, to sustain this claim I will need to use 'deism' in a more extended meaning than is commonplace (and indeed more widely than Brown himself) but the continuities are nonetheless remarkable. I begin, then, with Brown's sustained argument *against* deism before discussing his related notion of theology through symbol, painting and architecture.

While Brown's argument no doubt has its roots in Bishop Butler's response to seventeenth-century deism,[4] the deism against which Brown now argues is, from his perspective, the result of theologians excluding from divine activity a wide range of human experience once thought significant. Previously concerned with the proponents of explicit forms of contemporary deism (e.g. Maurice Wiles, John Hick), Brown is now rooting out implicit forms of deism rife in contemporary theology (as seen in Karl Barth and his heirs). Whereas he once argued for divine 'intervention', against an explicit deism's non-interventionist stance, he now argues for a continuing process of divine 'interaction',[5] and this against an implicit deism's restrictive notion of revelation. In its current form, then, Brown's argument *against* deism has less to do with some abstract philosophical notion of non-intervention than it does with a very real pastoral concern for those negatively affected by the Church and its theologians' unwillingness to recognise God at work more broadly. 'There is', according to Brown, 'too much of a mismatch between what the Church takes to be significant and the actual experience of the wider population.'[6] The result is that the unchurched either think God irrelevant (i.e. functional deism) or opt for their experience of God outwith the Church (i.e. spiritual but not religious). Brown thinks this a sad state of affairs, and one that is completely unnecessary given that the Church once took seriously a wide range of human experience, and could do so once more.[7] Drawing upon Augustine's analogy, Brown wants to acknowledge 'God ... already everywhere in the world like the water in a sponge.'[8]

In his earlier work, Brown was thus seeking to argue, *against* deism, that a general pattern of divine interventionism applies, and that, as he puts it, 'the debate with deism must take account of the whole range of religious experience and its interpretations'.[9] This desire to 'take account' – with reference to religious experience as *revelation* – is, I argue, the thread connecting the so-called early and later Brown. Ever the accountant of religious experience, Brown's hyper-empirical method is concerned with 'the whole range of data',[10] i.e. as relevant to constructive theology,[11] and more specifically, 'a satisfactory counter-case to deism's view of the material'.[12]

Getting down to the details, Brown's fundamental desire to 'take account' has 'four important consequences'.[13] These consequences are significant in supporting my argument for continuity rather than evincing any real discontinuity of method, so much so that, frankly, I wonder how anyone could think Brown's more recent work a departure from his earlier commitments. The four consequences are as follows: first, 'the question of evidence for intervention and the nature of the theistic model cannot be disentangled'. Second, 'the philosophical theologian will need to engage very closely with the material in question'.[14] Third, 'the traditional procedures of the philosopher will need to be reversed... [W]e will have to assume in advance that the material under investigation is ... most likely to fall under the rubric of "revelation", without the application of any proposed tests for revelation being made in advance.'[15] Fourth, 'no precise signification can be attached to the term "revelation" until the investigation is complete'.[16] One need only compare these four consequences from *The Divine Trinity* in 1985 with the Introduction to Brown's 2004 monograph, *God and Enchantment of Place*, to see my point. Brown has consistently sought to draw attention to 'the evidence', and not only as a means to the proximate end of rethinking the theistic model, but, more importantly, as a sustained and pastoral argument *against* deism. As Brown writes: 'People still find God in the great range of human experience that their ancestors once did. It is just that serious consideration is no longer given to such experience within the Church. Instead, an intellectual system is offered that now hangs free of the once universally shared assumptions on which it was based: the divine reality available everywhere to be encountered.'[17] Put simply: the Church and its theologians have failed to account for the evidence, and in so doing dismiss not only the experience, but also the claimant. The same could be said with reference to many theologians' response to Brown: i.e. that theology has been guilty not only of the sin of ignoring the wide range of material to which Brown seeks to draw attention, but also the sin of killing, or in any case attempting to kill, the messenger in the form of calls for criteria.[18] These calls – most often for christological criteria – are, however, less than clear, for as Brown notes, 'there is the whole question of what is meant by a christological criterion'.[19] There is, one might say, an impatience in theology that masquerades as a desire for clarity vis-à-vis criteria. Against this tendency, Brown calls for 'a careful listening exercise, the final result of which cannot be predetermined in advance'.[20]

This brings us to the present volume, in which Brown argues that theology, in narrowing its focus to systematics, has neglected a wide range of religious experience beyond the walls of the Church. Against this tendency – what might be described in the words of the Irish Catholic philosopher William Desmond as a 'dogmatic skepticism' – Brown advocates 'an open tradition that is willing to learn from approaches beyond the narrow compass of the Christian community itself', and in particular from the work of artists, musicians and architects, regardless of their own religious convictions.[21] Exhibiting what Desmond refers to as a 'fertile skepticism that opens thought to otherness',[22] Brown speaks of 'learning from pagans',[23] and 'the "correction" of biblical perspectives'.[24] While many find this language troubling, it should be noted that Brown's concern throughout is to maximise meaning, drawing attention to the ways in which God speaks, as well as 'the need for continuing development',[25] and this has everything to do with symbol, painting and architecture.

Symbol, for the sake of context, is the lens through which Brown sees painting and architecture. As previously noted, he is committed to divine interactionism and human freedom, but balancing God's agency with human freedom is challenging, to say the least, as God's intervention might well encroach upon human freedom, or, if one gives priority to human freedom, frustrate the divine purpose.[26] Brown's solution is to explore the role of symbols with reference to divine dialogue.[27] He argues 'that symbols exercise a crucial role in God's dialogue' with humanity,[28] and this for three reasons, the third of which is most relevant here. Symbols have to do with the subconscious, and this is 'important because it makes it a medium through which God can act upon us, without destroying our freedom in the process'.[29] Put simply: symbols are the means by which God interacts with humans while preserving their freedom, and this whether the context is ecclesiastical (i.e. the sacraments) or beyond the walls of the Church (i.e. the sacramental).

Turning now to theology through painting and architecture, it should be noted that, unlike Jeremy Begbie, who uses similar language,[30] Brown is seeking to draw attention to innovative and corrective rather than merely illustrative potential.[31] More like Brown in this sense is George Pattison, who advocates a 'dialogue between art and religion … with each partner seeking to appreciate the specific contribution of the other'.[32] This approach to theology through painting and architecture is, I suggest, in many ways like Desmond's approach to 'philosophy and its others'. Desmond argues: 'philosophy cannot just hold a conceptual monologue with itself in which it rests satisfied to merely reformulate

xii *Editor's Introduction*

the voices of its others in its own terms. It must listen to the voices of the others. Wherever appropriate it must let its own voice be reformulated under the impact of their otherness.'[33] For Brown, this means that painting and architecture, as well as culture more generally, might trigger development through 'imaginative re-engagement'.[34] He thus speaks of artists as theologians (in Part III of this volume), and elsewhere encourages us 'to listen even where [God] seems most distant',[35] in the work of Francis Bacon, for example.

To speak of theology *through* symbol, painting and architecture is, then, to speak of the case for divine interaction and sacramental presence. This case, however, is no argument (i.e. in the sense of the traditional arguments for the existence of God), but, rather, an education, and this is desperately needed, for as Brown writes, 'in our own day we lack the education to attend to the signs that speak of divine immanence, and so instead see only humanism'.[36] This volume seeks to redress this lack – what the Cambridge theologian Howard E. Root referred to as 'a state of imaginative impoverishment'[37] – and this in an effort to nourish not only theology, but also faith. This, as Root said, though it might just as easily have been said by Brown, 'is only another way of saying that the enterprise of theology cannot come to life until it takes to heart the principle of the Incarnation'.[38] It is to such an exercise in listening that the reader is now invited.

Notes

1 David Brown, *God in a Single Vision: Integrating Philosophy and Theology*, ed. Christopher R. Brewer and Robert MacSwain (London and New York: Routledge, 2016).
2 Brown himself has commented: 'Those familiar with my academic history will be aware that my career divides effectively into two halves, the first primarily concerned with relations between theology and philosophy and the second with the arts and culture more generally.' David Brown, 'In the Beginning was the Image: Why the Arts Matter to Theology', a paper presented at the Society for the Study of Theology conference in Manchester, 12–14 April 2010. That said, he continues: 'Not that I have abandoned interest in philosophy but I have come to see some of the issues raised by the arts as more fundamental' (ibid.).
3 See David Brown, 'Sacramentality', in *The Oxford Handbook of Theology and Modern European Thought*, ed. Nicholas Adams, George Pattison and Graham Ward (Oxford: Oxford University Press, 2013), 615–631; David Brown, 'A Sacramental World: Why It Matters', in *The Oxford Handbook of Sacramental Theology*, ed. Hans Boersma and Matthew Levering (Oxford: Oxford University Press, 2015), 603–615. For an excellent introduction to Brown's work along these lines, see Robert MacSwain, '"A Generous God": The Sacramental Vision of David Brown', *International Journal for the Study of the Christian Church* 15 (2015), 139–150. See also Patrick Sherry, 'The Sacramentality of Things', *New Blackfriars* 89 (2008), 575–590.
4 Brown acknowledges Butler in the Preface to *The Divine Trinity*, noting that 'his earlier refutation of deism has helped to inspire my own'. David Brown, *The Divine Trinity* (London: Duckworth; LaSalle, Ill.: Open Court, 1985), vii. See also David Brown, 'Butler and Deism', in *Joseph Butler's Moral and Religious Thought: Tercentenary Essays*, ed. Christopher Cunliffe (Oxford: Clarendon

Press, 1992). 7–28. Brown there suggests that 'despite the passage of time he still offers the best strategy of response to deism' (ibid., 27).
5 David Brown, 'Wittgenstein against the "Wittgensteinians": A Reply to Kenneth Surin on *The Divine Trinity*', *Modern Theology* 2 (1986), 264.
6 David Brown, *God and Enchantment of Place: Reclaiming Human Experience* (Oxford: Oxford University Press, 2004), 2.
7 See Brown, *God and Enchantment of Place*, 6. See also David Brown, 'Experience Skewed', in *Transcending Boundaries in Philosophy and Theology: Reason, Meaning and Experience*, ed. Kevin Vanhoozer and Martin Warner (Aldershot: Ashgate, 2007), 159–175.
8 David Brown, 'In the Beginning was the Image', this volume, 7–22. See also David Brown, *Through the Eyes of the Saints: A Pilgrimage through History* (London and New York: Continuum, 2005), 165; Brown, 'Experience Skewed', 165; David Brown, 'Response: Experience, Symbol, and Revelation: Continuing the Conversation', in *Theology, Aesthetics, and Culture: Responses to the Work of David Brown*, ed. Robert MacSwain and Taylor Worley (Oxford: Oxford University Press, 2012), 269.
9 Brown, *The Divine Trinity*, 52–53
10 Ibid., 53; cf. Brown, *God and Enchantment of Place*, 1–3.
11 Brown, *God and Enchantment of Place*, 1.
12 Brown, *The Divine Trinity*, 53.
13 Ibid.
14 Ibid.
15 Ibid., 54.
16 Ibid.
17 David Brown, *God and Mystery in Words: Experience through Metaphor and Drama* (Oxford: Oxford University Press, 2008), 271.
18 For one example, see Jeremy Begbie, 'Openness and Specificity: A Conversation with David Brown on Theology and Classical Music', in *Theology, Aesthetics, and Culture*, ed. MacSwain and Worley, 145–156, 152–154 in particular. For Brown's response to Begbie, see Brown, 'Response', in *Theology, Aesthetics, and Culture*, ed. MacSwain and Worley, 285. Begbie repeats this criticism in 'Natural Theology and Music', in *The Oxford Handbook of Natural Theology*, ed. Russell Re Manning (Oxford: Oxford University Press, 2013), 567–569; Jeremy Begbie, *Music, Modernity, and God: Essays in Listening* (Oxford: Oxford University Press, 2013), 93.
19 Brown, *God in a Single Vision*, 75; cf. Brown, *Discipleship and Imagination*, 400–402.
20 Brown, *God and Enchantment of Place*, 2.
21 Brown, *Tradition and Imagination*, 7. Desmond defines 'dogmatic skepticism' thus: 'skepticism in regard to others, dogmatism in regard to yourself'. William Desmond, *Philosophy and Its Others: Ways of Being and Mind* (Albany, N.Y.: State University of New York Press, 1990), 19.
22 Desmond, *Philosophy and Its Others*, 19.
23 David Brown, 'The Glory of God Revealed in Art and Music: Learning from Pagans', in *Celebrating Creation: Affirming Catholicism and the Revelation of God's Glory*, ed. Mark Chapman (London: Darton, Longman & Todd, 2004), 43–56, Chapter 3 in this volume.
24 Brown, *Tradition and Imagination*, 1; Brown, 'Response', in *Theology, Aesthetics, and Culture*, ed. MacSwain and Worley, 284–285.
25 Brown, *Tradition and Imagination*, 1.
26 David Brown, 'God and Symbolic Action', in *Divine Action: Studies Inspired by the Philosophical Theology of Austin Farrer*, ed. Brian Hebblethwaite and

xiv *Editor's Introduction*

   Edward Henderson (Edinburgh: T&T Clark, 1990), 107. (Also available in *Scripture, Metaphysics, and Poetry: Austin Farrer's* The Glass of Vision *with Critical Commentary*, ed. Robert MacSwain (Farnham: Ashgate, 2013), 136.
27 Ibid., 110–122, 115–117 in particular. For the corresponding sections in MacSwain, ed., *Scripture, Metaphysics, and Poetry*, 139–147, in particular 142–143. Brown first addressed 'Revelation through the World and its Symbols' in 1989 in his *Invitation to Theology* (Oxford: Basil Blackwell, 1989), 27–31; cf. Brown, *God and Enchantment of Place*, 33. He has more recently returned to the theme, discussing the visual arts (as visual symbols) in *Discipleship and Imagination: Christian Tradition and Truth* (Oxford: Oxford University Press, 2000), 373–384, 380–381 in particular. See also Brown, *God and Enchantment of Place*, 91–92, 98–104, 105; David Brown, *God and Mystery in Words: Experience through Metaphor and Drama* (Oxford: Oxford University Press, 2008), 18–21. More recently still, Brown has spoken of a 'natural theology of symbolism' with reference to the architecture of Durham Cathedral in 'Durham Cathedral as Theology', a paper presented at the Society for the Study of Theology conference in Durham, 4–6 April 2016. This paper has now been published as 'Durham Cathedral and the Jerusalem Temple: Let Sacred Buildings Speak', *International Journal for the Study of the Christian Church* 16 (2016), 93–107. For a more general introduction to 'Symbolic Mediation', see Avery Dulles, *Models of Revelation*, rev. edn (Maryknoll, N.Y.: Orbis, 1992), 131–154.
28 Brown, 'God and Symbolic Action', 115; 142 in MacSwain, ed., *Scripture, Metaphysics, and Poetry*.
29 Ibid., 116; 143 in MacSwain, ed., *Scripture, Metaphysics, and Poetry*. Brown continues: 'For in speaking thus he speaks without us being fully or even at all aware of who it is at work, addressing us. The crucial decision thus becomes clearly ours and not God's, in the sense that what finally matters in determining whether the dialogue continues to develop is whether we choose to bring these images to conscious awareness so that they can be creatively used and communicated to others.' Brown, 'God and Symbolic Action', 116–117; 143 in MacSwain, ed., *Scripture, Metaphysics, and Poetry*.
30 Jeremy Begbie, 'Introduction', in *Beholding the Glory: Incarnation through the Arts* (Grand Rapids, Mich.: Baker Academic, 2001), xi–xv. Begbie there argues: 'It [i.e. 'theology through the arts'] means that unfamiliar theological themes are uncovered, familiar topics exposed and negotiated in fresh and telling ways, obscure matters clarified, and distortions of truth avoided and even corrected' (xiii.) That said, Begbie later criticises Brown for suggesting that the arts might function correctively in relation to biblical insights.
31 For Brown's critique of Begbie's approach, see David Brown, *God and Grace of Body: Sacrament in Ordinary* (Oxford: Oxford University Press, 2007), 245. For Begbie's response to Brown, see Begbie, 'Openness and Specificity', in *Theology, Aesthetics, and Culture*, ed. MacSwain and Worley, 153.
32 George Pattison, *Art, Modernity and Faith*, 2nd edn (London: SCM, 1998), 8. Jonathan A. Anderson has described this kind of dialogue as 'theological art criticism'. Jonathan A. Anderson, 'The (In)visibility of Theology in Contemporary Art Criticism', in *Christian Scholarship in the Twenty-First Century: Prospects and Perils*, ed. Thomas M. Crisp, Steve L. Porter and Gregg A. Ten Elshof (Grand Rapids, Mich.: Eerdmans, 2014), 68.
33 Desmond, *Philosophy and Its Others*, 5.
34 Brown, *God and Enchantment of Place*, 1. See also George Pattison, *Crucifixions and Resurrections of the Image: Christian Reflections on Art and Modernity* (London: SCM, 2009), 19–20.
35 Brown, *Tradition and Imagination*, 374.
36 Brown, *God and Enchantment of Place*, 80.

37 Howard E. Root, 'Beginning All Over Again', in *Soundings: Essays Concerning Christian Understanding*, ed. A. R. Vidler (Cambridge: Cambridge University Press, 1962), 19.
38 Ibid., 18. For additional essays by Brown not included in this volume which address theology through symbol, art and architecture, see David Brown, 'God in the Landscape: Michael Ramsey's Vision', *Anglican Theological Review* 83 (2001), 775–792; David Brown, 'The Incarnation in Twentieth-Century Art', in *The Incarnation: An Interdisciplinary Symposium on the Incarnation*, ed. Stephen T. Davis, Daniel Kendall and Gerald O'Collins (New York: Oxford University Press, 2002), 332–364; David Brown, 'Images of Redemption in Art and Music', in *The Redemption: An Interdisciplinary Symposium on Christ as Redeemer*, ed. Stephen T. Davis, Daniel Kendall and Gerald O'Collins (New York: Oxford University Press, 2004), 295–319; David Brown, 'The Role of Images in Theological Reflection', in *The Human Person in God's World: Studies to Commemorate the Austin Farrer Centenary*, ed. Brian Hebblethwaite and Douglas Hedley (London: SCM Press, 2006), 85–105; David Brown and Ann Loades, 'Learning from the Arts', in *Who is This Man? Christ in the Renewal of the Church*, ed. Jonathan Baker and William Davage (London: Continuum, 2006), 67–102; David Brown, 'Sinai in Art and Architecture', in *The Significance of Sinai: Traditions about Sinai and Divine Revelation in Judaism and Christianity*, ed. George J. Brooke, Hindy Najman and Loren T. Stuckenbruck (Leiden and Boston: Brill, 2008), 313–331; David Brown, 'Symbol, Community and Vegetarianism', in *Eating and Believing: Interdisciplinary Perspectives on Vegetarianism and Theology*, ed. Rachel Muers and David Grumett (London: T&T Clark, 2008), 219–231; David Brown, 'Body as Graced or Vile: Tensions in the Christian Vision', in *The Body and the Arts*, ed. Corinne Saunders, Ulrika Maude and Jane Macnaughton (Basingstoke: Palgrave Macmillan, 2009), 25–38; David Brown, 'Science and Religion in Nineteenth- and Twentieth-Century Landscape Art', in *Reading Genesis after Darwin*, ed. Stephen C. Barton and David Wilkinson (New York: Oxford University Press, 2009), 111–124; David Brown, 'From *Elijah* (1846) to *The Kingdom* (1906): Music and Scripture Interacting in the Nineteenth-Century Oratorio', in *Music and Theology in Nineteenth-Century Britain*, ed. Martin Clarke (Farnham: Ashgate, 2012), 181–195; David Brown, 'Theatre as a Source of Religious Insight and Revelation', in *Theatrical Theology: Explorations in Performing the Faith*, ed. Wesley Vander Lugt and Trevor Hart (Eugene, Ore.: Cascade, 2014), 263–278; David Brown, 'Scotland: Religion, Culture and National Identity', *International Journal for the Study of the Christian Church* 14 (2014), 88–99; and David Brown, 'Context and Experiencing the Sacred', in *Philosophy and Museums: Ethics, Aesthetics and Ontology*, Royal Institute of Philosophy Supplements 79, ed. Victoria S. Harrison and Gary Kemp (Cambridge: Cambridge University Press, forthcoming).

Part I
Foundations

Introduction

In contemporary teaching of Christian doctrine in seminaries and universities the earlier term 'dogmatic theology' has been largely replaced by 'systematics' or 'systematic theology', with the emphasis clearly on the notion of Christian belief as a series of interconnected ideas that can be seen as an overall, coherent system for viewing the world and God's relation to it. This move has brought undoubted benefits but there has also been a price to pay, in the uncoupling of any tight connection with other parts of the discipline of theology and, more relevant here, with questions of impact on actual Christian living and practice. Thus it is surely no accident that the rise in systematics has gone with a corresponding decline in study of worship and preaching, with liturgy now almost unknown as an academic discipline in British universities, though the history of spirituality fares somewhat less badly. Where the situation has changed for the better in both British and American universities is in an increasing interest in the arts, with a number of centres focusing sometimes on the arts in general but, more commonly, on one or another in particular (for example, literature, film or the visual arts).

Yet to my mind the process has still not gone far enough, for the assumption still prevails that the role of the arts can be at most illustrative and not innovative, that is, with their contribution perceived as entirely subject to conclusions that have been reached elsewhere. This is no doubt why some of my friends or erstwhile colleagues judged my move to writing about the arts as also a move to the margins of theology. As Brian Hebblethwaite kindly, though revealingly, observed of a recent book of mine on the incarnation, 'Brown's return to mainstream Christian theology is greatly welcomed.'[1] But it is precisely that assumption that I wish to challenge in this book, not only with regard to contemporary reflection but also in terms of how the entire history of divine interaction with the world should be viewed. Even in the period prior to the growth of modern scholarship about origins of Scripture, there were clear signs of the divine address being wider than the people of Israel or the later Church. Why else does the Bible open with the creation of the world, while periodically we find interactions extending well beyond the community of faith, as in the stories of Balaam's ass and Job, or again in the rebuke to Jonah for his attitude to the people of Nineveh.[2]

Equally, in the New Testament Jesus is shown engaging with those of quite different cultural and religious assumptions, among them Roman soldiers and other foreigners, while the declaration that 'God so loved the world …' suggests a generosity of concern that might well see in those wishing to confine the divine address to Scripture a similar misuse of the keys to knowledge condemned by Jesus.[3] That said, such considerations are surely greatly strengthened by the discoveries of modern scholarship, where Israel is seen developing its faith not in isolation from surrounding cultures but in interaction with them.[4] In other words, it was by listening, however implicitly, that perspectives were broadened and new discoveries made, in everything from monotheism to life after death.[5] This is not to suggest simple dependence. The community of faith then shaped such beliefs to their own experience and understanding of God. But it is to acknowledge a debt, and in large part that seems to have been mediated imaginatively. That is to say, it was through the myths and metaphors and ritual practices of the surrounding cultures being adapted and transformed that our own particular inheritance of faith was created. It therefore behoves us as present-day Christians to continue to pay heed to how God might be speaking to us not only through the Bible and Church but also in the wider imaginative world where God continues to be at work, even if seldom adequately acknowledged.

To see how such claims might be worked out in practice, the reader could turn either to my five volumes written for Oxford University Press between 1999 and 2008,[6] or, more quickly though on a narrower range of issues, to Parts II through IV of this work, where examples from the power of symbols (Part II), artists as theologians (Part III) and meaning in religious architecture (Part IV) are all addressed. The essays in each section derive from a number of different sources. Some could have been easily accessed elsewhere, but for the most part they consist of papers published in some specialised forum, invited lectures appearing here for the first time, or material specially written for the occasion. All have been revised to ensure an integrated volume that can be read consecutively. In deciding what to include and in ensuring a form suitable for publication I have been greatly helped by the two editors, Chris Brewer and Rob MacSwain, former research students of mine now working in the United States, who have made what could have proved a rather tedious task a delight as friendly critique and alternative directions were proposed. I am most grateful to them both.

Two-thirds of Part I is published here for the first time, a matter of some importance as it is here that the question of foundations is most directly addressed. While the third essay seeks to provide specific examples of the divine at work beyond the explicitly Christian, the first two are more theoretical. The second is perhaps the more ambitious of the two in that it seeks to replace customary philosophical groundings of theology with various artistic and imaginative arguments. However, the essay 'In the Beginning was the Image' is placed first because it presents more conventional types of foundation, in appeals to Bible and experience. I hasten to add that this title is not intended to challenge one of the most profound verses in the Bible but rather how it has so often been interpreted, for it cannot be denied that in its long history there has been no shortage of theologians ready to declare that Christianity is essentially a religion of the word. While primarily true, the actual strength of the contention is easily exaggerated. So that essay begins by pointing out the various ways in which all the arts can lay claim to a biblical foundation, with even 'word' itself in a scriptural context closer to a form of art than to the sort of words that find their proper place in philosophical or scientific treatises.[7] The second half of the essay then goes on to indicate what Christianity has lost by retreating from the once intimate connection between religion and the arts, where Christian belief found fresh grounding in the experiences of almost every aspect of life. Consideration is also given to the question of what can be done to reactivate some of the power to nourish and inspire the community of faith that such experience once brought.

The second essay then turns to still deeper questions about the nature of doctrine as such, and offers four arguments for believing that, so far from any art, insofar as it is legitimate, being entirely dependent on theology, theology itself actually needs the arts, if it is adequately to secure its own intellectual foundations in the changed climate of modernity. Four changes in particular are discussed: the collapse of the traditional arguments for God's existence, decline of belief in dualist accounts of an immaterial human soul, acceptance of cultural conditioning and strict limits to human knowledge. The final essay then returns to a theme already implicitly raised in the opening essay, the question of whether what is fed back from the arts need also in itself always be explicitly Christian. Perhaps 'Learning from Pagans' is an unnecessarily provocative title but its choice was intended to draw attention to the issue of what implications may be drawn from the openness of divine action as mediated through the arts. If the divine intention was to open people to the possibility of experiencing God or, if not that, at the very least some form of related aesthetic experience, then it would seem reasonable to expect that, even where God remains unacknowledged, something of his mind and purposes might still shine through. So I end this part of the book as I began, with a generous God seen at work in human creativity that always bears the potential to speak of the divine, and sometimes does indeed do so.

Notes

1 In his generous endorsement of *Divine Humanity* (London: SCM; Waco, Tex.: Baylor University Press, 2011).
2 Balaam was probably a prophet from Ammon (so the Samaritan Pentateuch for Numbers 22:5), while the Uz of the opening verse of Job is sometimes identified with Edom but perhaps more commonly as existing beyond the Euphrates, as in the Dead Sea War Scroll.
3 Luke 11:52; Matthew 23:13.

4 See, for example, Kenton L. Sparks, *Ancient Texts for the Study of the Hebrew Bible: A Guide to the Background Literature* (Peabody, Mass.: Hendrickson, 2005); or for the much later influence of Greek culture, Erich S. Gruen, *Heritage and Hellenism: The Reinvention of Jewish Tradition* (Berkeley: University of California Press, 1998).
5 Both notions occur elsewhere in the Middle East before their first appearance in Israel.
6 *Tradition and Imagination* (Oxford: Oxford University Press, 1999); *Discipleship and Imagination* (Oxford: Oxford University Press, 2000); *God and Enchantment of Place* (Oxford: Oxford University Press, 2004); *God and Grace of Body* (Oxford: Oxford University Press, 2007); and *God and Mystery in Words* (Oxford: Oxford University Press, 2008). For commentary on and critique of these five volumes, see Robert MacSwain and Taylor Worley, eds, *Theology, Aesthetics, and Culture: Responses to the Work of David Brown* (Oxford: Oxford University Press, 2012).
7 And so appropriate justifications extend well beyond traditional appeals to Bezalel and Oholiab: Exodus 31:1–6 and 35:30 to 36:1.

1 In the Beginning Was the Image

This essay proceeds by two stages. The first is concerned to challenge the common Protestant assumption that the role of the arts within Christian faith cannot pretend to any deep basis in the biblical foundations upon which such faith is based. So used are we to hearing the claim that Christianity is a religion of the word that it is very easy to assume that this is the only lens through which scripture should be read, not least when we recall the attack on images in the second commandment and the apparent abandonment of refined architecture and music with the move away from the Jewish Temple. But such assertions, as we shall see, conceal a more complex and interesting reality that fully legitimates a biblical foundation to whichever of the arts we may wish to consider.

The first part of my discussion will have argued for a much deeper foundation for the arts in biblical revelation than is commonly acknowledged even among the arts' advocates, with the Bible now seen as itself a literary work of art, the incarnation functioning as a visual image for God, and music a potential vehicle for divine presence. That perspective is then widened to detect similar patterns across all of human experience, with the arts containing real sacramental potential for such encounters. Admittedly, over the centuries theology gradually retreated from any proper consideration of such possibilities. While noting some of the reasons for this retreat (good as well as bad), I shall argue that the move was decidedly on balance a mistaken one. I end, therefore, by exploring what it might mean for theology once more seriously to re-engage with the arts.

Foundations in Revelation

Visual Art

The way in which the title of this essay modifies the introductory verse of John's Gospel may seem to those unfamiliar with the writings of St John Damascene (d. 750) unduly provocative, but in fact all it does is draw attention to the strategy employed by defenders of icons at the time of the first major iconoclastic controversy. The counterargument ran that God had in effect violated the second commandment by offering a self-portrait in Christ and so thereby legitimated all subsequent representation.[1] So it is no less a doctrine than the incarnation itself that legitimates the visual arts. Of course it does not follow from this that religious visual art is thereby given carte blanche to pursue its own ends. Although not always observed in practice, Orthodoxy has always been much stricter about this than the Western tradition. Prayerful preparation was still to be required of icon painters, and certain subjects were precluded: depictions of the Father, for instance, and extremes of suffering in Christ.[2] Although the West in the end decided to live more dangerously, it was in my view the wiser course. Piety does not guarantee insight, while a wider range of images ensured that art too was able to contribute to theological reflection, for example in challenging subordination of the Spirit.[3]

Literary Art

Those early apologists for the arts, though, it seems to me, stopped well short of where the argument might have carried them, that is, into a reconsideration of what exactly is meant in John by Logos. New Testament scholars continue to disagree about whether the primary inspiration was Hebraic or Hellenistic, but those debates can all too easily mislead us into interpreting the meaning far too narrowly, with precedents used to closely circumscribe the meaning, as, for example, with the Hebrew *dabar* used to put all the stress on divine act or with the Greek *logos* on definition.[4] But not only is the actual Greek term much broader in meaning than its English equivalent, earlier contexts also hint at wider possibilities. Thus Genesis opens with Word as so much more than a divine fiat, in the overflowing generosity of divine creativity in creating a good world. Similarly, as scholars are increasingly acknowledging, Plato's pursuit of definition can only be understood properly against its wider backdrop in a philosopher equally concerned with image, metaphor and style.[5] So, in looking back to those models, we need also to look forward in the gospel to see Logos operating as 'new creation' and 'perfect expression', terms of art that encourage us to find in what follows a gospel largely mediated through literary devices. This is not to deny that the Synoptics also use the literary arts in order to convey better Christ's significance, but it is to claim that in John it has reached a very fine art indeed. Even in the opening miracle to focus on whether it happened or not would be to miss John's primary point. The 180-gallon-hangover of those intoxicated by the divine wine is the rich life promised to believers as contrasted with the watery imperfection of any other alternative.[6]

None of this is to deny that the Christian faith stands or falls on its historical foundations, and so not everything can be symbolic rather than literal. But it would be a mistake to oppose fact and symbol, as though the latter could never actually strengthen Christianity's historical claims.

Take, for instance, Christ stilling the storm and walking on the water.[7] To the modern mind it speaks only of control over natural forces, but in the imaginative context of the time the action would surely have meant so much more, in effect an indisputable claim to divinity. Central to understanding of the original act of creation was God pushing back the waters of chaos, and under restraint they remained even now by the great vault of heaven. Yet here was someone exercising that primal power. Or again, according to the Septuagint it is a fountain that waters Eden, and Jesus promises to be just such living water for humanity at the well in Samaria, at the feast of Tabernacles with its water rituals, and finally on the cross itself.[8] That Word might entail the symbolic without thereby robbing us of strong ontological claims, is, not surprisingly perhaps, a claim often better perceived by poets than by theologians.[9]

One aspect of the literary that I have not hitherto mentioned is what has in fact dominated recent theological discussion of Scripture, and that is the element of story or narrative.[10] While I would wish to endorse fully the notion that salvation is about incorporating our own life story into that of Christ, where I would differ from much of what is written on the subject is in two respects: first, in seeing the need for this often to be mediated through other narratives that bear more directly on the sort of life situation faced by the contemporary Christian; and second, in wanting to acknowledge the basic idea as one that has in fact run through much of post-biblical history. Conspicuous examples of the latter would include Pseudo-Bonaventure's *Meditations* and the *Exercises* of St Ignatius Loyola.[11] On the former, what I have in mind is the way in which the lives of the saints helped Christians in the past to see how the values of Christ might be applied under different circumstances, such as marriage or war.[12] In the contemporary world such a role is often usurped by the novel and even television dramas. In other words, the method of reflection remains the same, even when divorced from Christianity.[13]

In this connection it is worth observing that visual and literary images are not quite the same thing. While literary metaphors and symbols do sometimes also function visually, this is by no means always so, and indeed it is sometimes the case that the literary can be made distinctly comic by being subsumed under the visual. A case in point is some of the images to be found in the last book of the Bible. Fortunately, most modern translations leave the Book of Revelation's figures in the original measurements but what we are in effect offered is a city dwarfing Manhattan at 1,500 miles high, but with surrounding walls of only 140 feet, or again a great tree arching over its solitary street that has a river flowing through its middle but yet is able to sustain the tree's roots on either side.[14] Although bemused smiles are I think inevitable if such images are treated visually, my intention in mentioning them here is not to mock. It is simply to observe that for the author his images were clearly intended to function verbally rather than visually, as a way of integrating competing similes and metaphors from the Hebrew Scriptures, and so need

10 *Foundations*

to be judged that way rather than through their portrayal in, say, the Angers tapestry or Dürer's woodcuts (neither successful in my view).

Music

Here at one level reference might be made to actual use, to the singing of hymns and psalms in the New Testament and to the extensive use of song and orchestra in the Temple.[15] But a much stronger case is in fact available, if appeal is made to the Chronicler's approach to Temple worship. Nowadays lectionaries almost wholly ignore the Chronicler in favour of the Deuteronomic historian, presumably on grounds of greater historical accuracy. Yet it could well be the case that Kings' claim about the extent of the empire under David and Solomon is equally a distortion in terms of a favoured ideal rather than historical reality. Certainly, the Chronicler brushes out some more conspicuous sins such as David's adultery with Bathsheba, but in its place comes a prominence for the Temple that may well reflect historical reality even for the earlier period, given the way in which music, song and dance often assume greater significance in pre-literate cultures. At all events, the important point to note here is that God's presence to his people is actually seen by the Chronicler as mediated through music, a perspective that was to influence no less seminal a figure for Christian music than Johann Sebastian Bach.[16] In 2 Chronicles 5 singing and playing inaugurate the Temple rather than the arrival of the Ark (as in Kings), with all this music culminating in the glory of the Lord's presence (5:15). That glory is then renewed once more after Solomon's prayer (at 7:3).

Architecture

However, even those sympathetic to such a status for music sometimes remain hesitant because of the disappearance of the possibilities for such sacred music in the New Testament dispensation with the loss of the Temple. The point, though, is still more forcibly put with respect to architecture. The familiar story is told of Christ now being our temple, and the eventual adaptation of secular buildings for worship, first houses and then the basilica or law courts. However, that secular story proves on examination much less securely based than is commonly supposed, with a number of key points capable of being made on the other side. First, the early Christians had no alternative but to move to a different sort of building given their chosen form of worship since all ancient temples, including the Jerusalem Temple, presumed sacrificial worship outside and not inside the building. Temples, whether Jewish or pagan, were simply not built for community gatherings. But, second, in any case it is quite misleading to characterise their new first choice – people's homes – as 'secular'. Jews prayed in their homes, while most ancient cultures, including the Roman, went one stage further and had statues of household gods at a central point in the building, where certain key religious acts also took place.[17] So to substitute Christian worship was to offer an alternative form of sacralisation, not to resort to the secular. The earliest adapted house of which we are aware in fact already displays an elaborate programme of imagery on its walls.[18] Admittedly, distinctive types of architecture took time to develop, but it is interesting to observe how often across the styles appeal is repeatedly made to the Jerusalem Temple as the divine model for a perfect building, even if the character of that building is more commonly than not misunderstood until modern times.[19]

Foundations in Human Experience

Philosophers and anthropologists have often seen the arts and religion as closely allied in experience. Indeed, among contemporary philosophers the suggestion is common that so-called 'religious experience' is simply aesthetic or moral experience inappropriately described. However, historically the more generous, and to my mind more intelligible, assumption has been acknowledgement of closely related roots. That, for example, was the position adopted by two eighteenth-century German philosophers, J. G. Hamann and J. G. Herder. The former was a contemporary of Kant in Königsberg, whose writing is often difficult to follow, but he did produce one of the best-known quotations about the primitive social origins, as with religion, of the arts: 'poetry is the mother-tongue of the human race; as gardening is older than agriculture; painting than writing; song than declamation; parable than deduction; barter than trade'.[20] It was a position taken up in the twentieth century by the Dutch historian of religion and politician, Gerard van der Leeuw (d. 1950). In his massively erudite *Sacred and Profane Beauty*,[21] he argued that primitive creativity in the arts was always directed towards symbolising and interpreting the holy, and that it is only in modern times that religion and art have pursued different paths. Against his fellow Dutch Calvinist Abraham Kuyper, he argued that words, and especially the scriptures, are inherently the bearer of images, and as such religion and art can expect a new eschatological convergence.

In a similar way child psychologists like Bettelheim and Piaget have made the imagination central to individual child development,[22] while, more recently, the neurologist Iain McGilchrist in his highly praised best-seller *The Master and his Emissary* has postulated a battle between the left and right hemispheres of our brains in which the instrumental rationality of the left ('the emissary') is attempting through contemporary education and other means to usurp the more imaginative approach of the right hemisphere ('the master') where both the arts and religion have their deepest roots.[23] In two brief paragraphs I can scarcely do justice to such complex considerations. Nonetheless, I have introduced them simply to provide some sort of wider setting for the comments that follow on theology's own continuing retreat from real involvement with the arts, despite occasional hopeful signs to the contrary.

Evaluating Theology's Retreat

In the incarnation God disclosed the divine desire to redeem every aspect of our existence, body no less than soul, social interdependency no less than individual identity. So, given such a holistic perspective, it comes as something of a shock to note how far theology has retreated from areas of human activity that would once have been thought also to be major areas for its concern. Even as recently as the nineteenth century arguments could still rage among Christians about whether there was a pre-eminent Christian architectural style, just as the revival of Gregorian chant in that same century repeated some of the arguments that had emerged in both Reformation movements over the possible negative effects of polyphony.[24] If those two examples suggest interests narrowly confined to worship, go a little further back and you soon find almost every human activity explored in its religious dimensions, including what might now seem remote topics such as food, fashion or even gardening.[25]

Yet, ironically, that range is now most likely to be found in the subject where I first began my academic studies, classics. The threat of the subject's almost total collapse resulted in a wider range of professional interests that is well reflected by the sort of topics now discussed at the annual Classical Association conference. Here are some examples from one I attended in 2010: the social construction of priests in Athenian decrees; *Doctor Who* and historiography; Classical ruins in Neapolitan cribs; fantasising fathers in the Christian physiology of dreams; laughing at the unknowable past in Herodotus; the Irish *Antigone* complex; appropriating the divine gaze in epic; the influence of Nero's Rome on the writings of Oscar Wilde. My point is simply that in marked contrast to when I first studied classics, now everything that touches on the Classical world is seen to be of interest. Yet, despite its central doctrine of divine embroilment in the messiness of our world, theology still places arts and culture at its margins.

Reasons for that retreat are many and varied. Let me here focus on just one, the issue of how theology should approach such spheres of human endeavour. What I want to suggest went wrong in the past was failure to listen and dialogue, and that is a problem that continues into our own day. Take music, for instance. Historically, Christian discussion was dominated by the view (ultimately stemming from Augustine and Boethius) that music's intelligible, ordered character reflected the rationality of the divine mind.[26] So, not surprisingly, when confronted by problematic issues such as the *diabolus in musica* or still more so by the Pythagorean comma, the whole basis of the relationship came to be called into question.[27] But surely a more appropriate response would have been, not retreat, but to consider whether the relationship between music and the divine was sometimes, or perhaps even usually, of a quite different kind.

Sadly, however, equally today theological discussion of the arts is more often than not plagued by prior presuppositions, as though theologians knew themselves to be already in possession of criteria for judging the arts rather than having first to enter into creative dialogue with them. So, for example, is it really the case that all great art must be in some sense redemptive or transformative in order to be great art? Might it not sometimes be just enough to portray truthfully key elements in the human condition, as in the paintings of Francis Bacon? Admittedly, images derived from the crucifixion are used in his case to deny any ultimate meaning to the world, but is it not precisely from the stark awfulness of such negativity that Christ came to deliver us? And so that perspective benefits from being given such clear and powerful articulation.

Again, it will not do to speak of all modern art as indicative of post-Christian decline. That is at the very least to fail to take seriously the conditions of its emergence: the way in which, for instance, the invention of the camera called into question the usefulness of representational art, or realism in film the relevance of 'naturalism' on stage, since it now looked as though other media could achieve such objectives very much better.[28] But, equally, even once this point is acknowledged, the temptation must still be resisted of identifying with what seems the most obviously Christian. So it is not just Peter Brooks's 'holy theatre' that should meet with our approval because of the way issues of transcendence are raised.[29] A Marxist playwright like Bertolt Brecht may appear remote, but his strategy of *Verfremdung* could be seen to have clear parallels with Jesus' strategy in parables, in 'estranging' or dislocating our conventional assumptions. Or, to give an artistic example, while using elephant dung in a depiction of the Virgin Mary may seem obviously disrespectful, as was claimed in a very public debate in New York in 1999, that is not only to ignore the high value given to the commodity in African culture but also the challenge implicitly set to the Western tradition of painting in its use of blue pigment for Mary's robe, extracted as it is from expensive lapis lazuli.[30]

In other words, theology needs to cease to regard the arts as only appropriate when illustrative of truths already known through Scripture or tradition and instead carefully explore meanings first and with the expectation that the arts too can operate as independent vehicles of truth. Even fiction can include truth claims (about character or society for example) as Honoré de Balzac, Charles Dickens and Henry James all affirmed.[31] Indeed, in the past paintings sometimes encapsulated a whole series of major Christian truth claims in a single painting, as, for example, in Piero della Francesca's *Baptism of Christ*.[32] If nowadays, on the whole, the visual arts make less extensive claims, that partial character does not mean that there is no truth there at all, or that the truth to which they draw attention is unimportant. But perhaps the most important difference from the past is the invitation to explore rather than simply assent (as Emily Dickinson urges, things are told 'slant'). Yet, is that not also the position into which biblical criticism has thrown the Church, with competing interpretations of biblical texts now almost the norm rather than the exception?

14 Foundations

Re-engaging with Human Experience of God

Looking at the history of the twentieth century as a whole, it would be hard to deny the conclusion that in the long battle that raged over Schleiermacher's inheritance and in particular his claims regarding the importance of religious experience it was Karl Barth who finally won and not those profoundly influenced by Schleiermacher such as Karl Rahner or Paul Tillich.[33] Most theologians came to believe that Tillich's resolution in God of polar tensions in human experience and Rahner's talk of a divine beckoning from an infinite horizon just seemed too naïvely optimistic about God's communication with the world. Indeed, some writers went further and questioned whether it was meaningful even to talk about experience of God at all, not just in Bonhoeffer's sense of a world where the appropriate conditions no longer held but in the stronger sense of logical incoherence: God was just not that sort of being.[34]

But if in one obvious sense it was a victory, in another it was not, for in effect what happened over the same time period was the rise of 'spirituality' and with it the resultant widespread conviction among artists that a vaguer deity now operated in their world whose precise relationship to the Christian God remained unclear. Turn to the history of dance in that same century, for instance, and one finds a surprisingly large number of famous choreographers who insisted on a religious dimension to dance, though with Christianity, if used at all, usurped to give a more universal reference.[35] Again, Vincent van Gogh's move from Evangelical Christianity to pantheism could almost be said to anticipate the pattern for major artists of the following century, as, for instance, among those influenced by Theosophy such as Kandinsky, Klee and Mondrian. Nor is the pattern different with architects, as can be seen in many of the writings emerging from the Bauhaus or in specific individuals such as Frank Lloyd Wright.[36]

Inevitably, some theologians will take exception to even considering the possibility of experience of God in such contexts. It is all too far removed from the specifics of Christianity to count, they may well say. But why should the vagueness of an experience make it less connected to God? Nor need apparent conflict with other such experiences necessarily be ultimate. So, for instance, we might say that the characteristic feature of Gothic architecture is to draw us towards transcendence, of the Classical to order, of Baroque to exuberance, of Modernism to simplicity, and yet they all say something of the nature of God. Not that everything will be simply a matter of aping some aspect of God's handiwork in creation. To revert to Brecht for a moment, it could be that the definitive moment of conversion will come for some through such an experience of dislocation or estrangement in the theatre, just as with music the delay in its resolution could be what first entices the musician towards Christ, as expectation leads to reflection on hope and its eschatological resolution.[37]

Yet, however argued, it is that step from God active in the natural world to human creativity also mediating the divine to which exception is most likely to be taken. It will be said that God is now subject to human manipulation. Put crudely, it looks as though the divine can now be summoned at will, simply by artists obeying the right set of rules to evoke the corresponding divine attribute or feature of revelation. Nor are objectors likely to be mollified by talking of the need also for the right frame of mind. I suspect that on this issue two fundamentally different perceptions of the nature of God are on a collision course. For some, divine freedom is more important than divine generosity, and so they would resist allowing God to be exposed to all and sundry. But for the more sacramentally minded that is how God in any case operates, not only pre-eminently in the incarnation but also today, not least with respect to the more intimate aspects of Christ's presence in the Eucharist. So as such a similar relation to the wider creation occasions no surprise. Not that this means one has to envisage an endless series of divine acts. Rather, as in Augustine's familiar analogy, God is already everywhere in the world like the water in a sponge, and so it is more a case of tapping into that presence than it having to be brought directly to bear upon the world.[38]

Not that every spiritually uplifting aesthetic experience thereby has also to be seen as an experience of God. As in more obviously 'religious' cases, perceptions can advance, for example in listening to a sermon, without us wanting necessarily on each occasion to speak of a divine address. Equally, however, at the other extreme it would be important to acknowledge that God's address need not always correspond narrowly either to high art or to orthodox Christian belief. As both Nick Cave and Al Green have argued, ordinary pop love songs can have precisely this kind of dimension.[39] Even heavy rock might sometimes work in this way, as with the much analysed example of Led Zeppelin's 'Stairway to Heaven'.[40] God, as we all know, is no respecter of persons, and so it makes no sense to suppose the great mass of the population are excluded from religious experience simply through pernickety concerns with good taste![41]

In none of this do I underestimate the difficulties in characterising what might legitimately be described as such an experience of God and what might not. Much work on criteria remains to be done.[42] But I do want to protest against the alternative, which is either to shunt God into the ghetto of more obvious religious experience such as prayer and worship or to get rid of the notion altogether. Of course all such experience is sullied with other extraneous factors. But those who prefer to deny, for example, architecture any such power and instead to focus on the presence of centuries of prayer need to be reminded that prayer is no more or less pure than the architecture itself. Take Durham Cathedral (where I served as a canon for seventeen years). Certainly, the major reason for its erection was the Normans' desire to assert their absolute superiority over the local Anglo-Saxon population, but however devoutly the monks prayed their motives were just as mixed, in, for example, using Cuthbert to increase the income of the monastery.[43] Nor did things change at the Reformation or since.[44] Ordinary human motives, wherever found, cannot escape being tainted by sin.

Barth's great strength is his insistence that God as the transcendent Other should never be seen as subject to human manipulation, but his weakness in my view is his failure to engage adequately with the messiness of the world. Perhaps the point can best be made by considering the work of a recently deceased novelist who greatly admired him, the American John Updike. In his earlier career he found in Barth's assertion of the otherness of God a vehicle that was to salvage his own faith.[45] Nonetheless, in his novel *Roger's Version* (1986) he observes how both the Barthian and the natural theologian can be corrupted.[46] So his final view was that, while Barth's stress on the otherness of God must be maintained, no less important is our encounter with God in the everyday, and in his case in fact through the golf course.[47] A similar view is taken by Robert Redford in his film *The Legend of Bagger Vance* (2000). But more important than such specifics remains my challenge about the messiness of the incarnation, of God's kenotic embroilment in becoming part of our world in the process of which misunderstandings would seem inevitable. Whether it be golf or Led Zeppelin, Bach or Rembrandt, the transcendent Other is also constantly there in the messiness, awaiting human response.

I might add that it is also here that I find real possibilities for the future direction of natural theology, in engagement with where our contemporaries tend to find their residual sense of God rather than in the now largely redundant traditional arguments. Theology needs to take much more seriously the ten times as many people in Britain who express belief in God as attend church regularly, as well as conspicuous cases of religious experience formed outside of contact with those of faith, as in the moving story of Etty Hillesum during the Second World War.[48]

Renewing the Address of Revelation

Earlier I suggested that John's Gospel is the most literary of all the gospels. But in a sense all of Scripture must be a form of art, since of necessity its writers must use literary devices such as metaphor, simile and symbol to convey meaning, given that its primary subject of discourse is not of this world. Yet, although Paul Ricoeur and numerous others have done valuable work in bringing out such general features, there is surprisingly little reflection on what might be required for adequate translation in detail, either, more basically, from one artistic medium to another or with the added complication of those metaphors and symbols now moved to new cultural contexts, as is inevitably the case if one attempts to span the centuries. The temptation is to suppose that faithfulness means literal correspondence, but that is to make oneself open to failure on at least two counts: first, in supposing that metaphors retain their power whatever the context; and, second, in treating all forms of art as essentially bound by the same rules. Thus, on the latter it needs but a moment's thought to realise that in the history of art great painters were aiming at something rather different from simply the representation of a biblical scene. Not only had they necessarily to supply details lacking in the original narrative if they were to provide an image at all, equally, in order to avoid stultifying the imaginative process, their account had now to be open in new ways, for example of conveying divine otherness or in encouraging engagement.[49] Even where the narrative element is retained, as in film or stage, more connections turn out to be required, and also quite commonly humour, partly to set the tragic elements in greater relief but also to 'incarnate' or humanise the story.[50] The latter is surely one of the great strengths of the medieval mystery plays, an element significantly retained in the impressive 1996 South African version, even as song was given much greater prominence in order to better suit that same context.[51]

However, it is likely to be changes that are seen to arise from new cultural contexts that will occasion most controversy. Certainly, it cannot be denied that theology operates successfully at times through the recovery of biblical insights, as for instance with Liberation theology. But I would disagree profoundly if it were insisted that such backward glances are always how legitimate new insights originate. Essentially, my contention would be that some perceptions about the divine will and nature only become possible at certain specific periods of history, and so revelation is not just a matter of looking back (vitally important though that is) but also of understanding how the revelatory process continues in the engagement of the Church with the present cultural context in which it is set. That way new insights may emerge that could not have been derived so easily, if at all, from Scripture on its own. God has thus in effect also spoken through the wider culture. Two earlier works of mine were devoted to this issue,[52] and so I will offer no major fresh examples here. But it is worth noting that the issue is essentially no different from the history of biblical revelation itself. The stimulus toward new ideas sometimes also came from the wider cultural context, as, for example, in debts to Babylonia, Egypt and Persia.[53] None of this is deny that changing culture can also have a bad influence. So discrimination is obviously necessary.

Even so, I shall end with a relatively small instance that nonetheless illustrates well how things can go badly wrong when theology fails to take seriously the need for an adequate imaginative and artistic account to accompany its more pedestrian assertions. Take the growth of the cult of the largely legendary St Margaret of Antioch.[54] One's first reaction may well be to smile when one first hears her story of a battle with a dragon in which victory is only secured thanks to the cross around her neck. But a more sympathetic judgment, it seems to me, is demanded as soon as the reasons for the growth of her extraordinary popularity in the Middle Ages as patroness of childbirth become known.[55] Arguments about the reversal of the Fall in Christ had already determined that Mary should give birth painlessly, and so an alternative figure was required in order to lead us to sympathise not just with female pain in pregnancy but also its high mortality rate. It was as bad as battling with a dragon, we are being told. Protestants may well object

18 *Foundations*

that, however interesting such a development this might be, it has nothing to do with developing understandings of Scripture. Mary's painless birth was simply a mistake. But the failure of the Reformation to substitute even Mary in Margaret's role could be said to have effectively secularised childbirth. The price was thus quite high in terms of Christianity's future involvement in the suffering of women.

Conclusion

What these reflections suggest to me is a more open-ended way of pursuing systematic theology: not, that is, the denial of the search for system as such but rather the recognition of a richer resource upon which theology can draw in respect of divine action in the world. So far from the scriptures offering simply a set of propositions, they paint images and tell narratives whose significance is not readily reducible to easily formulated conclusions. They are there to inspire the human imagination, and so, while reason and analysis undoubtedly have a role to play, something will always be lost if there is not frequent return to those original resources. But, second, because such a way of working also reflects how God relates to humanity elsewhere in the world he has created, there can be much to learn from such activity. Thus, so far from being suspicious of what the arts may offer, we ought to listen in expectation that God may be speaking through them. This is not to deny that given the universality of sin corruption is likely to exist there as elsewhere, but it is to reject any recommendation that the primary attitude for the Christian should be one of suspicion. To discover more clearly why that must be wrong, the reader should turn to the essay that follows.[56]

Notes

1 *Orations on the Holy Icons*, esp. I, 15; II, 5; III, 8; III, 26. Theodore the Studite adopted a similar position.
2 For rules formulated at the Councils of Trullo (692) and Stoglav (1551) that 'correct' Western tendencies, see Leonid Ouspensky, *Theology of the Icon* (Yonkers, N.Y.: St Vladimir's Press, 1992), I: 91–100; II: 283–323.
3 Although depictions of the dove proceeding from the Father and Son are quite common, so too are ones of the Spirit coming from the Father to the Son, and, more intriguingly, of the Spirit presiding in the middle between Father and Son (e.g. Dürer's *Adoration of the Trinity*, Titian's *Trinity in Glory*). For a discussion of some of these issues, see my 'The Trinity in Art', in *The Trinity: An Interdisciplinary Symposium on the Trinity*, ed. Stephen T. Davis, Daniel Kendall and Gerald O'Collins (Oxford: Oxford University Press, 1999), 329–356; also in Part III of this volume.
4 For the former, e.g. Isaiah 55:11; for the latter, note Plato's use of *didonai logon* to mean 'to give a definition'.
5 As in Christopher Rowe, *Plato and the Art of Philosophical Writing* (Cambridge: Cambridge University Press, 2007); Richard Rutherford, *The Art of Plato* (London: Duckworth, 1995); and Martin Warner, *Philosophical*

Finesse: Studies in the Art of Rational Persuasion (Oxford: Clarendon Press, 1989).
6 Although curiously omitted from many modern lectionaries, the fact that John 2 opens with 'on the third day' already provides a symbolic clue. The six water jars (short of the perfect seven) together held between 120 and 180 gallons.
7 John 6:15–21; cf. Mark 4:35–41 and 6:45–52.
8 Genesis 2:6 (but a 'mist' according to the Hebrew text). For fountains of 'living' or flowing water in John: 4:10; 7:2, 37–38; 19:34; explored at great length in Part II.
9 A thought I pursue jointly with Ann Loades in the essay 'The Divine Poet', in *Christ: The Sacramental Word*, ed. David Brown and Ann Loades (London: SPCK, 1996), 1–25. Among those quoted are Emily Dickinson, Les Murray and Kathleen Raine.
10 Most obviously in Hans Frei and George Lindbeck but also of course in many others.
11 Both enjoin the imaginative exercise of readers envisaging themselves part of Christ's own life-story.
12 Although only with difficulty. Being royal helped in both cases, e.g. Elizabeth of Hungary and Margaret of Scotland in the one case, and Oswald of Northumbria and Louis of France in the other. For an analysis of how saints helped to bridge such gaps, see David Brown, *Discipleship and Imagination: Christian Tradition and Truth* (Oxford: Oxford University Press, 2000), 62–101.
13 If such a divorce is usual in the case of the soap, this is not always so with the modern novel. Graham Greene often used his novels to explore the difficulty of maintaining absolutes in Roman Catholic belief, while for a more recent example, one might note Michael Arditti on the theme of homosexuality.
14 Revelation 21–22. For further implications, see David Brown, *God and Mystery in Words: Experience through Metaphor and Drama* (Oxford: Oxford University Press, 2008), 131–138.
15 For a more detailed discussion, see David Brown, *God and Grace of Body: Sacrament in Ordinary* (Oxford: Oxford University Press, 2007), 225–236.
16 The passage is singled out by Bach in his copy of the *Calov Bible Commentary*.
17 Including rites of passage, such as the giving of the *toga virilis*. For a more extended discussion, see David Brown, *God and Enchantment of Place: Reclaiming Human Experience* (Oxford: Oxford University Press, 2004), 170–176.
18 At Dura Europus in Syria (*c.* 235); also reconstructed at Yale.
19 For some details of this extraordinary history, see *God and Enchantment of Place*, 196–208. Under the Templars even the Dome of the Rock came to be identified as *Templum Domini*.
20 Johann Georg Hamann, *Sämtliche Werke*, ed. J. Nadler (Vienna: Verlag Herder, 1957), II: 197.
21 First published in Dutch in 1932; first English edition: New York: Holt, Rinehart and Winston, 1963: republished 2006 by Oxford University Press.
22 Bruno Bettelheim, *The Uses of Enchantment: The Meaning and Importance of Fairy Tales* (New York: Knopf, 1976); Jean Piaget, *The Moral Judgment of the Child* (London: Kegan Paul, 1932); Jean Piaget, *Plays, Dreams and Imitation in Childhood* (New York: Norton, 1962).
23 Iain McGilchrist, *The Master and his Emissary* (New Haven: Yale University Press, 2009).
24 In the former with the arguments of Pugin and Ruskin; in the latter, with Guéranger, Pothier and Mocquereau at Solesmes, and, more generally, with the Cecilian movement, based initially at Regensburg. Palestrina's *Missa Papae Marcelli* is often quoted as the ideal intended by Trent, while Luther singled out

20 *Foundations*

    Josquin des Prez as his own ideal. In the case of music the ideal was seen as the enhancement of the words such that they remained distinct and audible.

25 For my own observations on food, see *God and Grace of Body*, 120–184. For a valuable, more extended discussion, see David Grumett and Rachel Muers, eds, *Theology on the Menu: Asceticism, Meat and the Christian Diet* (Abingdon: Routledge, 2010). Although the Reformation put an end to many forms of symbolism once associated with gardens such as the *hortus conclusus*, new forms did emerge, as can be seen for instance in the writings of John Evelyn.

26 Boethius' *De institutione musica* is more accessible than Augustine's *De musica*. Great influence was exercised by Wisdom 11:21 ('thou hast ordered all things by measure and number and weight') and by the naturalising of the Greek notion of the harmony of the spheres through appeal to Job 38:7: 'the morning stars sang together, and all the sons of God shouted for joy'.

27 Debates over the former (a dissonant tritone) begin with Guido of Arezzo c. 990. A tritone is an interval of three whole tones such as C to F sharp or G flat. The expressive potential of such dissonance is well exploited by Benjamin Britten in his *War Requiem* to intensify the uneasy relationship between Wilfred Owen's poems and the Ordinary of the Mass. The 'Pythagorean comma' refers to the fact that Pythagorean divisions of the octave are not in practice always compatible with each other or the octave. From the seventeenth century onwards artificial corrections to instruments are introduced, known as 'equal temperament'.

28 The invention of the camera is usually attributed to Daguerre in 1839. Naturalism on stage is particularly associated with the late nineteenth-century dramatists Anton Chekhov, Henrick Ibsen and August Strindberg, but lasted much longer in lesser names.

29 Described in his book, *The Empty Space* (Harmondsworth: Penguin, 1968), 47–72.

30 Imported from Afghanistan, and used in this way till a synthetic version was developed, usually known as French ultramarine. The painting in question was Chris Ofili's 1999 work exhibited at the Brooklyn Museum of Art, to which Mayor Rudy Giuliani took such exception.

31 Usually in the prefaces to their novels. For the references and some discussion, see *Discipleship and Imagination*, 357–360.

32 To be found in the National Gallery in London. A series of symbolic devices are used to indicate that Jesus is the new Joshua who will lead his people to the promised land, through a cross whose hard exterior not only hides health within but also a reference to the people for whom the painting was first intended. There are even subtle allusions to the other two liturgical associations of Epiphany (the Wise Men and Cana). For more detailed consideration, see the discussion in 'Baptism and Water as Cosmological Symbol' in Part II.

33 Though there were of course other influences as well, most obviously Maréchal in the case of Rahner and Schelling in the case of Tillich.

34 For Dietrich Bonhoeffer, *Letters and Papers from Prison: An Abridged Edition*, trans. Reginald Fuller *et al.* (London: SCM, 1953), e.g. 30 April 1944. The latter type of objection can be illustrated from Brian Davies and Denys Turner: in brief, how can infinity be experienced? See also Ben Quash, 'The Density of Divine Address: Liturgy, Drama, and Human Transformation', in *Theology, Aesthetics, and Culture: Responses to the Work of David Brown*, ed. Robert MacSwain and Taylor Worley (Oxford: Oxford University Press, 2012), 241–251, and my response, 270–272.

35 Among them Alvin Ailey, Frederick Ashton, George Balanchine, David Bintley, Isadora Duncan and Martha Graham. For my discussion, see *God and Grace of Body*, 61–119. See also Kimerer L. LaMothe, '"I am the Dance": Towards an Earthed Christianity', in *Theology, Aesthetics, and Culture*, ed. MacSwain and Worley, 131–144.

36 The second director of the Bauhaus, Mies van der Rohe, insisted upon spiritual dimensions to his architecture, and this is found reflected in other members of the Bauhaus, including Lyonel Feineger's iconic images and Johannes Itten's colour theories.
37 The eschatological dimension is a major theme in Jeremy Begbie's analysis of the significance of music.
38 *Confessions* 7.5.
39 'The actualising of God through the medium of the love song remains my prime motivation as an artist': Cave, 'The Secret Life of the Love Song', in *The Complete Lyrics* (London: Penguin, 2001), 2–19, esp. 6.
40 As in Susan Fast, *In the Houses of the Holy: Led Zeppelin and the Power of Rock* (Oxford: Oxford University Press, 2001).
41 Acts 10:34. For my own attempt to approach pop music sympathetically, see *God and Grace of Body*, 295–347.
42 Though the alleged difficulty in distinguishing from aesthetic experience seems to me often exaggerated. Even non-believers sometimes readily admit the difference, e.g. Wilfred Mellers, *Celestial Music? Some Masterpieces of European Religious Music* (Woodbridge: Boydell, 2002).
43 See e.g. David Rollason, 'The Anglo-Norman Priory and its Predecessor', in *Durham Cathedral: History, Fabric and Culture*, ed. David Brown (New Haven: Yale University Press, 2015), 27–38.
44 This is to express disagreement with the contrast drawn in Susan White's essay 'The Theology of Sacred Space', in *The Sense of the Sacramental*, ed. David Brown and Ann Loades (London: SPCK, 1995), 31–43.
45 See his 'Faith in Search of Understanding', in *Assorted Prose* (New York: Knopf, 1965).
46 Both in its Barthian narrator, Roger Lambert, and in the young Dale Kohler, convinced that he can use the Big Bang to prove God's existence.
47 'It is of games the most mysterious, the least earthbound, the one wherein the wall between us and the supernatural is rubbed thinnest': *Golf Dreams* (Harmondsworth: Penguin, 1996), 151.
48 Both the 2000 and 2011 census put the figure at around 70 per cent. Although sent to Auschwitz as a Jew, Hilversum's conviction that she was summoned to speak for God came to her as a wholly secularised individual: Patrick Woodhouse, *Etty Hilversum: A Life Transformed* (London: Continuum, 2009), e.g. 51, 135.
49 For the former, see my attempt to identify the various tactics employed by modern artists to hint at Christ's divinity in 'The Incarnation in Twentieth-Century Art', in *The Incarnation: An Interdisciplinary Symposium on the Incarnation of the Son of God*, ed. Stephen D. Davis, Daniel Kendall and Gerald O'Collins (Oxford: Oxford University Press, 2002), 332–372. For the latter, think of the use of the central tree in Titan's *Noli me tangere* (National Gallery, London) to encourage meditation on the significance of Jesus' rebuke, or the use of gates in Perugino's Galitzin Triptych (National Gallery, Washington, DC) to point through and beyond the crucifixion.
50 Sometimes such imaginative interconnections are large, as in Michel Tournier's novel *The Four Wise Men* (1980 – it briefly elevated him to France's leading novelist), and sometimes quite small, as in the telling of the parable of the Prodigal Son in the context of the objections to including Matthew among the disciples in Franco Zefferelli's film *Jesus of Nazareth* (1978).
51 *The Mysteries* (Heritage Theatre DVD 1996). Humour is at its most effective in the medieval originals in the Wakefield or Townley treatment of the shepherds, especially Mak.

52 *Tradition and Imagination: Revelation and Change* (Oxford: Oxford University Press, 1999) and *Discipleship and Imagination*.
53 Perhaps even in respect to monotheism itself.
54 Discussed in *Discipleship and Imagination*, 83–93.
55 With no need to display her prominently for her significance to be appreciated, as in Van Eyck's *Arnolfini Marriage*.
56 This previously unpublished essay was first presented as one of the principal papers at a conference on theology and the arts, the theme in 2010 for the annual conference of the SST (Society for the Study of Theology). I am grateful for the numerous comments and critiques offered on that occasion which have helped shape the essay's present form.

2 Why Theology Needs the Arts

Before I address the specific issue, some more general comments on the current state of academia may be helpful in providing some sort of wider context. Although some academics attempt to cross disciplines and do so with real enthusiasm, most have an understandable preference for the simpler course, of truly mastering the areas they know best. Indeed, in a world of increasing specialisation it is common for such boundaries to be set within particular disciplines, with historians, for example making the familiar response that 'It's not my period' or theologians observing that doctrine and not Bible is their own area of competence. Equally, with the increasingly conceptually precise nature of philosophy, it often sounds like a terrain excluded even to those who once read the subject, so difficult is it to break easily into understanding the new, more technical kinds of argument. Indeed, so austere are some specialisms that one is tempted sometimes to speculate whether the student starting out on a particular subject has a better sense of the overall state of their chosen discipline than the learned teachers who address them!

However, in the case of theology such natural inclinations towards self-containment are aided and abetted by a unique feature of the discipline: that it claims in some sense to speak on behalf of God. As custodians of divine revelation it would seem that nothing could possibly come from outside and stand as a corrective to what has been unveiled or disclosed by God. While such a stance might have been expected from conservative theologians, in actual fact often even otherwise quite liberal theologians take a similar position, insisting that what they say, for instance, on sexual morality is derived from biblical principles rather than at least in part through influence from the secular culture. That way, of course, the supreme authority of Scripture is maintained but one wonders at what cost in terms of a realistic appreciation of how change has in fact come about.

But those wider issues are not my concern here. Rather in this essay I want to focus on Christian theology's relation to the arts. The last couple of decades has seen a real blossoming of literature on the subject, especially in relation to poetry, visual art and music. Yet, whether the writer be Catholic or Protestant, liberal or conservative, there has been a repeat of the phenomenon described above, what seems to me a surprising reluctance to admit that traffic might go, as it were, in both directions. Instead, discussion has been dominated by what might be labelled exemplarism, the use of criteria drawn from theology to pronounce a particular work of art as good of its kind or not. Its role is thus seen to be at most to enhance belief, not help create it. It is that position which I wish to challenge in this essay by exploring four commonly held philosophical assumptions about the world in which we now live. All four are widely believed to undermine the reasonableness of religious belief, whereas I shall contend that if theologians were to pay more attention to the arts in light of these assumptions they would soon see the arts as natural allies. Inevitably, not everything can be covered in a single essay. So, for simplicity's sake, in what follows I will without further ado assume the truth of these four widely held positions. Although I write primarily as a theologian, the point is equally applicable to philosophers who write on religion. A wider vision that includes the arts could ensure a more balanced assessment of the appropriate relation between contemporary philosophical writing and the arts.

The Collapse of Dualism and Appeal to Metaphor

One major problem that contemporary philosophical reflection poses for any attempt to bridge the gap between God and ourselves is the fact that few intellectuals now believe in the conception of human nature that dominated most of Christian history and which we inherited from Platonism, and that is the sense of us already inhabiting two worlds. Technically known as dualism, it spoke of human beings as consisting of two substances, mortal bodies and immortal souls, and thus of us inhabiting the visible earth as the home of matter and an invisible reality that is the home of minds, ours and God's. Instead we have been returned to what is also the more common biblical picture, of us as psychosomatic unities, mind and body entirely interdependent with us only surviving death, if at all, thanks to divine action and not because of anything inherent in the way we have been made.[1]

If such a conclusion excludes any sense of us already linked to heaven (the invisible world that is God's), the question then of course becomes acute of whether there might be any alternative way of making the connection. I would suggest that reflection on the world of the arts provides just such a possibility through appeal to the imagination, that is, an appeal no longer to the fundamental nature of our minds as such but rather to how those minds work.

Human beings learn the use of words in application to the sensible world. So clearly, if the jump to the divine is to be made, language will need to be stretched in analogies, images and metaphors, what are in effect the common tools of the imagination. Perhaps the relevance of the point to all the imaginative arts can be expressed most clearly by making explicit the parallel between symbol in action, metaphor in writing and image in the visual arts, and how the theological notion of sacramentality is based on a similar structure. Consider first the traditional sacraments. Each involves an action that by doing one thing intends another: the consecration of bread and wine to become the body and blood of Christ, the exchange of rings to establish a permanent relation between two individuals, the anointing of a dying person's body to prepare for life in another world, and so on. Works of the imagination, irrespective of the medium, appear very similarly founded. The metaphors of the poet are intended to take us from one sphere of discourse to another, the images of the artist from one visual image to another (or sometimes quite outside the visual altogether), while a medium like ballet is full of symbolic acts under which gestures of the body are intended to imply acts performed quite differently in ordinary life.

Even prior to his conversion to Anglo-Catholicism in 1927, T. S. Eliot had already detected the importance of metaphor in helping to interconnect what might otherwise seem a non-integrated, un-created world. Thus in a famous essay on 'The Metaphysical Poets' he observes:

> When a poet's mind is perfectly equipped for its work, it is constantly amalgamating disparate experiences; the ordinary man's experience is chaotic, irregular, fragmentary. The latter fails in love, or reads Spinoza, and these two experiences have nothing to do with each other, or with the noise of the typewriter or the smell of cooking; in the mind of the poet these experiences are always forming new wholes.[2]

In other words, as symbol is to action, metaphor to language and image to art, so sacrament is to religion. Each is trying to move us analogically, to take us to a different place, and so establish new wholes. Of course in most uses of the imagination, that other place remains firmly in our present world. Nonetheless, the imagination has already accepted the principle of a move elsewhere, and so it may well be asked, why not then to a vastly different world? As Jesus' use of parables illustrates, or some of the extraordinary imagery and word play found in the prophets,[3] similes and metaphors when well used can draw us from the material world into quite a different order of existence. As already noted, this is not at all to claim that every exercise of the imagination even implicitly evokes God but it is to observe that the imagination is deploying precisely the same kind of tools that make talk of God possible. So, however hostile to faith individual artists may be, they are at least moving humanity onto the same terrain that legitimates talk of God.

The sacramental can thus be seen to build upon the symbolic and metaphorical inasmuch as, though the latter are not sacramental as such, it is not hard to see how the process which they utilise might extend to the more explicitly sacramental participation of one thing in another where too there is both similarity and difference, as in earthly light and heavenly light, running water and Living Water,[4] and so on. Indeed, that very fact of difference that is opened up in analogical language and action helps identify another key contribution that the imagination can make towards an encounter with the divine, and that is in the essentially open-ended character of all imagery and symbol. That is to say, the interpretation of such devices can be pulled in quite a number of different directions, and so the question of an alternative religious world can be raised even when such a thought was far removed from the intention of artist or speaker. This is because once we move beyond the literal the multivalent character of possible comparative allusions cannot be strictly controlled, and indeed one might argue that it is the mark of a great poet or artist to welcome such allusive richness. So the transition to the immaterial can sometimes be imaginatively made even where such thoughts were far from the mind of the creator and perhaps even from most of that of his audience or viewers.[5]

To some this might suggest a purely 'subjective' viewpoint but, while obviously some interpretations might be 'strained', this is hardly to concede that this inevitably happens whenever there is deviation from the majority view. Perhaps one might be allowed to use a poem on the relation between 'Poetry and Religion' to itself express this view, one by the contemporary Australian poet, Les Murray:

> Full religion is the large poem in loving repetition …
> and God is the poetry caught in any religion,
> caught, not imprisoned. Caught as in a mirror
> that is attracted, being in the world as poetry
> is in the poem, a law against closure.[6]

So recent proposals to restore the right hemisphere of the brain to the more central place that is its by nature, as in the neurologist Iain McGilchrist's influential book *The Master and his Emissary*, might suggest something quite deep about how God has made us, with the poetic and the imaginative at the heart of who we are because it makes possible this strong link with divine non-material reality.[7]

The Collapse of Theistic Arguments and the Appeal to Religious Experience

When precisely the need for proofs of God's existence came to dominate philosophical discussion and what were the main impulses for such a way of seeing things is a matter of some contention among intellectual historians. Three significant books in this connection are Michael Buckley's *At the Origin of Modern Atheism*, Charles Taylor's *A Secular Age* and Michael Gillespie's *The Theological Origins of Modernity*.[8] Although they differ greatly over when precisely change set in, their common contention is that the problem begins when religious belief comes to be seen as an *inference* from something else rather than itself directly experienced as part of the air we breathe, as it were. Charles Taylor wants to blame the Reformation when there ceased to be a common culture, but one might equally well go back as far as Aquinas with his five proofs for God's existence. Although modern attempts to disengage Thomas from later Neo-Thomism of the kind typified by Réginald Garrigou-Lagrange are largely successful,[9] the new influence from Aristotle that Aquinas made possible did after all have considerable impact, in generating demands for a rational structure whereby God in effect became an inference rather than part of immediate human experience. Surprisingly, such a view even became part of the official teaching of the Catholic Church in the nineteenth century.[10] Yet even many Christian philosophers would now concede that such contentions were considerably overblown. Bridging the gap between the empirical world and the divine in this way (by strict, deductive argument) was simply not the right way of going about things.[11]

Inevitably, the decline in acceptance of the traditional proofs has brought with it much interest in religious experience, with appeal to such experience now itself sometimes structured as a new form of proof. Indeed, I myself have engaged in such presentations.[12] Here, however, I want my focus to be somewhat different. Almost all such discussion has kept well clear of potential overlaps with aesthetic experience, and it may seem that this was a wise intuition. But I would like to suggest otherwise, not only because much religious experience is thereby unnecessarily excluded but also because much of the appropriate terminology for religious experience is first learnt in aesthetic contexts. Of course the analysis of experience would be much simpler if religious experience always occurred in contexts quite separate from the aesthetic. But in actual fact quite frequently there are interconnections, with initial religious responses, for example, clarified and deepened by subsequent aesthetic encounters and the kind of language and increased perceptivity that they now make possible. So, for example, one thinks of the increased awareness that paintings such as those of Constable or Friedrich make available in their landscapes: Constable with his sensitivity to divine immanence in scenes such as those surrounding Dedham church or Salisbury Cathedral, or Friedrich with his so-called *Rückenfiguren* that invite us to a similar perception to those figures with their backs to us of the divine transcendence implicit in the majestic landscapes that they observe.[13]

Equally, one can see the process at work in the opening lines of familiar poems such as Gerard Manley Hopkins's 'God's Grandeur'.

> The world is charged with the grandeur of God.
> It will flame out, like shining from shook foil;
> It gathers to a greatness, like the ooze of oil
> Crushed. Why do men then now not reck his rod?
> Generations have trod, have trod, have trod;
> And all is seared with trade: bleared, smeared with toil.

Hopkins's suggestion is of an immediate experience, and as such this is contrasted with the effect of trade, under which trees come only to be valued for their timber and not in their own right. So nature is viewed purely instrumentally (i.e. with some further purpose in mind) and not intrinsically, just as it is in itself, as a divine creation. It is that alternative perception to which Hopkins is trying to restore us, and which, arguably, was lost when sacramentality's connection with Platonism was abandoned with its two primary metaphors of participation and imitation that suggest nature and humanity already in some sense bridging the two domains of earthly and heavenly realities. To the objection that all such connections are imposed and not discovered there is of course a long tradition of an alternative explanation, of a learnt culture blinding us to the link. It is to culture's wider deceptive power that Hopkins is here pointing, an insight that he shared with Britain's greatest art critic of the nineteenth century, John Ruskin, part of whose counter-strategy was to bring nature and art into closer relation.

In Ruskin's view human art was at its best when imitating nature, principally because nature as a divine creation itself brought us closer to the ultimate source of all creativity. Indeed, despite his Calvinist roots he insists that nature does not merely point to God but can itself provide experience of the divine nature.[14] So, for example, a seascape stretching to infinity is said not just to point to the possibility of a similar infinity in God, it allows us the actual possibility to experience such infinity as one of the divine's own distinctive attributes. In Ruskin's own words, 'light receding in the distance is of all visible things the least material, the least finite, the farthest withdrawn from the earth … the most typical of the nature of God, the most suggestive of the glory of his dwelling place'.[15] While that makes him sound very similar to many of his predecessors writing on the sublime, in fact six different 'types' of beauty are distinguished in his writings, each of which has the capacity, he suggests, to mediate a particular divine attribute: infinity or incomprehensibility, unity or comprehensiveness, repose or permanence, symmetry or justice, purity or energy, and moderation or restraint.

It is often said that such attitudes to nature cannot survive the discoveries of Darwin. But even though the strength of Ruskin's certainty of such an intimate connection between nature and God was severely tested by Darwin's new theories, it is by no means clear why this should have been so. Strange creatures that had anticipated human beings were already known to the biblical authors in the form of Behemoth and Leviathan and, so far from finding them repulsive, an author like Job can detect God's delight in such variety of forms (Job 40:15 to 41:34).

More recently, a poetic writer like Annie Dillard in her classic meditation of 1976, *Pilgrim at Tinker Creek*, well illustrates how even direct confrontation with 'nature red in tooth and claw' need not undermine such a sense of divine presence within nature. While frankly confessing her perplexity at nature at its most brutal and wasteful, as with the giant water bug and praying mantis,[16] she insists on refusing such encounters decisive sway. Instead, they are held in creative tension with how nature appears elsewhere, with its author a 'spendthrift genius' displaying 'extravagance of care'.[17] In other words, argument remains in her view the wrong category in which to view the symbols of creation. We can experience God directly in nature, even if at times our encounters are quite the reverse. And of course it is not only nature that can be experienced sacramentally in this way. Much of human experience can function similarly, as, for example when human love acts as a cipher for divine love.

In such ideas on nature Ruskin was almost certainly influenced by Wordsworth, even his favoured term 'types' being one such borrowing. But it is important to note that it was not just aesthetic experience of nature that he saw as helping to engender religious experience, he also makes much the same point about works of art, such as poetry, painting and architecture, with expression of infinity in a painting, for example, capable of occasioning a similar experience of divine infinity. At this point objections are likely to come from both sides of the religious divide, questioning the possibility of such experience but for quite different reasons.

Thus on the one hand some Catholic philosophers of religion such as Brian Davies and Denys Turner have queried what it could possibly mean to say that an individual has had an experience of God, given the kind of attributes divinity is supposed to possess.[18] But worries on this score seem to me exaggerated, since even in our ordinary human encounters with one another most experience is aspectival and cumulative; that is to say, we build up interpretative frames rather than receive them in a single, all-encompassing instance.

Equally misconstrued in my view is the objection from the other side that such alleged religious experiences through the arts are merely questionable inferences drawn from the more basic aesthetic experience. Not only is such an inferential way of talking not how the religious experience is characteristically described, but also even non-believers exploring such experience often find themselves identifying a further layer where a religious interpretation is seen as in some way the more natural reading, even though for them it must be resisted. A good case in point is the distinguished music critic Wilfrid Mellers in his exploration of the sort of music that he saw as engendering such descriptions. Intriguingly, his view is not that religious believers have confused the aesthetic and the religious. Rather, it is that a distinctive type of experience beyond the aesthetic has indeed been correctly identified but that it is deceptive if its pull to any sense of an objective encounter with divine reality is accepted. At most, what is on offer is spiritual uplift.[19]

Social Conditioning and Communication through Images

The third area I want to mention involves a claim that is perhaps more prominent in those influenced by continental rather than British analytic philosophy, namely the whole issue of cultural conditioning, of the way in which even despite ourselves we are caught up in the cultural assumptions of our time. Among the works of analytic philosophers, perhaps best known are those of Richard Rorty and Alasdair MacIntyre.[20] More characteristic perhaps, though, would be the contribution of the Frankfurt School (Horkheimer, Adorno and Benjamin) or French philosophers such as Michel Foucault and Jacques Derrida. However that may be, the dominant response for claims to such cultural conditioning in any form from many of the twentieth-century's most important theologians has been strongly hostile: to insist on the radical otherness of biblical revelation, as in the language of the early Barth, of the Bible being 'like a flash of lightning ... as the dissolution of all relativity'.[21] It was a position Barth modified in later life with his talk of 'secular parables' but even then he was cautious, as his correspondence with the writer Carl Zuchmayer indicates.[22] But the problem in any case with such an answer is twofold. First, it flies in the face of the facts. We are now all too aware of the wider cultural influences upon ourselves, and of a similar pattern holding in Scripture. But, second, unless God in his revelation builds on the way human beings are actually situated, it is hard to see why its message should be relevant to socially conditioned beings like ourselves.

From that concession it would be all too easy to draw a purely negative inference: that we are thereby bound to adopt some form of determinism, and with it the relativism of all ideas. But conditioning emphatically does not mean that human beings cannot take any steps beyond the times in which they live (otherwise how would new ideas be possible?). What it does mean is that any such overstepping must bear some relation to where the society as a whole has already reached in its reflections. Even so, the most common response from theologians remains one of anxiety, that to speak of the Bible in this way, however, qualifiedly, is to undermine its claim to contain a divine message that transcends particular times and places. Equally, philosophers have more often than not concluded on the opposite side, as with Jürgen Habermas, that such severe conditioning reduces the possibility of theology making any significant contribution to any wider attempt at Enlightenment convergence of ideas.[23]

It is here that the contribution of the imagination and of its accompanying images can once more come to the rescue, for it is important to note that no particular biblical text stands on its own but rather is part of a continuing tradition of interpretation. Thus, as the existence of duplicate narratives demonstrates,[24] new ways of telling foundational stories arise, as do fresh treatments of particular metaphors and symbols. It is thus quite untrue that present context alone shapes meaning. Instead, what we have is a meaning that as prior to present context and subsequent to it can also be, at least to a degree, transcendent of a particular place and time. Indeed, this can also help explain why close attention to earlier strands of tradition can bring its own distinctive spiritual rewards. The interest lies not in the fact that those earlier strands somehow as already transcendent realities escaped conditioning but rather that because of being part of a tradition they can preserve insights that may have been distorted or lost through later handling of the same images or symbols.

Equally, such an appeal to a tradition of imaginative symbols can also help us deal with the more limited or kenotic understanding of Christ's consciousness that has been forced on us by conclusions in biblical scholarship. Here again it might look initially as though the new way of seeing things presents a major challenge to the transcendence of Jesus and his message. But another way of reading that same evidence is to say that he now becomes more effectively a saviour by sharing in precisely the same sort of conditioning that humanity in general endures. Moreover, although Jesus was born into such a very specific culture and time, because it was part of a developing tradition a whole host of imaginative ideas were available to him as he was growing up that would not have been present, or not present to the same degree in earlier generations and in other parts of the world; among them, for example, the suffering servant, the kingdom of God, the Passover lamb and so on. One theologian who made much of this fact was Austin Farrer in his pioneering 1948 work, *The Glass of Vision*.[25] For Farrer such imagery became the primary vehicle of revelation, with Jesus creatively shaping the imagery he had inherited to his own unique sense of mission. If that is so, then to adopt post-Vatican II's talk of Christ as sacrament is to speak of him drawing on the images and metaphors of his time to help bridge the two worlds (human and divine) in a way that allowed not only his own real creative participation in both but also a similar participation to those who came after him as the images acquire new resonances and meaning.

Limits of Human Knowledge and Complementary Imagery

The final modern change of perspective to which I wish to draw attention where the arts might be relevant to theology is on the question of limits to human knowledge. Kant provided a famous positive spin on his assertion of such limits by asserting that he was 'abolishing knowledge to make room for faith'.[26] Many theologians who have followed Kant have ended up with what can only be described as a very minimal version of Christianity. That is not my intention here, not least since Kant's standards for knowledge can themselves be questioned. Instead, I want to set side by side the continuing theological search for a very tight conceptual system enshrined in the terminology that has now largely replaced Christian doctrine such as dogmatic or systematic theology (or its most recent variant, analytic theology), and how poets and artists have treated the stories and metaphors that they have inherited from the Christian tradition.[27]

The aim, I must emphasise, is not as a way reducing ontological commitments. Christ's divinity, for example, can in my view be proclaimed no less effectively in a powerful metaphor or in the symbolism of a particular painting as in some more straightforward assertion of the fact. Rather, my point is that not all elaboration into system is necessarily an advantage. Implausible premises may be required to keep the whole thing together, whereas left at the level of complementary metaphors mutual enrichment may be the net result. That is to say, put more bluntly, sometimes there may well be a category mistake involved in pushing the language of the imagination, the metaphors and other images of revelation, too far in the direction of more narrowly defined concepts, and that is what may well explain some of the less profitable disputes that have occurred in the history of theology.

Take, for example, the doctrine of the atonement, how we are reconciled to God through Christ. Conventional histories talk of the dominance of different theories at different periods of history, but do so still on the assumption that one must necessarily give place to another since that is how theories operate. But why should we think of the *Christus Victor* approach of Luther necessarily as an alternative to Athanasius' sacrificial account, or even of Anselm's satisfaction theory as requiring to be placed in opposition to Calvin's penal view? Admittedly, in some cases there is a formal logical structure, most obviously so in the past in the case of Anselm's *Cur Deus homo* as well as numerous examples from more recent times in the work of both philosophers and theologians.[28] But the more interesting question in my view is whether the defensible element lies in that formal structure or in the imagery appropriately applied. If the latter, then it could be the case that the apparently opposing elements of imagery could actually be used to complement one another rather than be brought into conflict. After all, the key thing about metaphor is that not every aspect of it is true and so apparent conflict need not imply actual, and that is one way also to read the New Testament, where a range of images are used without any apparent sense of opposition. These include, for example, penalty, ransom, rescue, sacrifice, salvation, satisfaction, substitution and victory. Indeed, that very variety is one reason why this approach was adopted the last time the Church of England's Doctrine Commission was asked to report on the atonement.[29] Nor, it should be noted, is this to say that necessarily we now know less about the atonement than was once thought. In terms of tight, formal argument this is no doubt true but, so far from the metaphors cancelling each other out, one has every reason to believe that an enrichment of understanding would be the net result from their mutual complementarity: thus, sacrifice and satisfaction, judgment and moral stimulation, and so on. As a matter of fact, no particular version of the atonement was ever officially sanctioned by the Church. Even so, the attempt by theologians to advance particular theories did generate major problems, as for instance with the penal approach. So retreat from formal argument to complementary image could certainly lead not only to an enrichment of vision but also to a more eirenic debate.[30]

One further example may help. Much post-war discussion of the doctrine of the Trinity has been dominated by two rival models for understanding, one structured in terms of a society of persons, the other a matter of internal relations within a single person. Early in my career I wrote in favour of a social model but as the years have advanced I have also shown some sympathy for the other model.[31] However, later writing on artistic images for the Trinity led me to question whether either model could offer the complete truth.[32] More recently, Sarah Coakley has written also on artistic images but at somewhat greater length.[33] However, our two approaches are quite different. Coakley comes to the images with certain advance expectations and measures the images in their light, as for instance in her insistence on images of the Spirit being of comparable size to the other two persons, and the Father–Son relationship being less obviously gendered so as to more effectively include women.[34]

My interest was rather in what the artists did with the existing tradition, and so the related possibility that they might actually have something useful to teach theologians. Like Coakley, artists were often concerned to produce a more adequate image for the Spirit, but their desire to remain loyal to the existing tradition of representation meant that in general they adopted an alternative solution to the problem of presenting the Spirit's equality visually. Instead, the Spirit remained as dove but was now allowed to preside either in the centre with the other two persons on either side, or else floating above them both.[35] As a result the order of begetting and processing may well have been forgotten but in defence one may observe that a single image is unlikely to be able to say everything about the Trinity within a single frame.

More pertinent here, though, is how artists have approached the two rival models mentioned above, for what one soon discovers is that any accurate matching of one model against one particular form of representation is impossible. Thus, consider first paintings in which the three trinitarian persons are represented as some kind of society. What quickly becomes apparent is that what is actually being expressed is their relations to one another rather than them simply as three. So, for example, in the famous *Gnadenstuhl* or Mercy Seat images that were hugely popular over several centuries we find the Father sitting on the Mercy Seat of the old covenant as he holds the exposed, crucified Son lovingly in his arms with the Spirit as dove hovering between them as the indispensable link between both.[36] While thus failing to correspond completely with the creedal version of their relations, it is nonetheless clearly on relations that the image is primarily focused; that is, not their separate roles but their interaction and interdependency.

Equally, in cases where a single identity is stressed, as in the comparable verbal repetition of the same attributes in the Athanasian Creed,[37] more often than not what we find is that single image actually pulling towards a more corporate or societal form. Certainly, this seems the intention where three identical, mysterious human forms are presented but it is equally true where there is only one single human form but with three heads.[38] Such images are frequently misunderstood, and not only in our own day. In fifteenth-century Florence St Antoninus, the bishop of the time, led a campaign against them on the grounds that they were *contra naturam*.[39] He did not quite succeed, as some have survived to this day even from his own city,[40]

34 *Foundations*

but a greater irony lies in the fact that their advocates, so far from being worried by the *contra naturam* objection, would almost certainly have taken the comment as a compliment since that was precisely their primary aim: to assert the Trinity as going beyond anything that we can learn from nature. Perhaps the point can be made clearer by looking at comparable images in the pre-Christian pagan world. There it is not just gods in human shape to which this reduplication of form is applied but also those of animal appearance, an additional horn, for example, being provided. The aim was thus, I suggest, primarily intended to indicate intensifying power: that is, more than animal, more than human. So similarly, then, in the Christian context, the attempt was meant to imply the more than purely human, the inadequacy of any analogue with a single human mind. Of course, that does not necessarily entail more than one mind, but it does call into question any notion that the divine mind and human minds are in any obvious sense comparable.

In short, it looks as though reflection on artistic images for the Trinity might lead one to question whether there is any absolute opposition between the two types of approach that have dominated discussion since the Second World War. Rather, neither is adequate on its own to the task. Both analogies will inevitably fail at some point because that is precisely what analogies do. But, rather than lamenting the fact, we should acknowledge some merits in each of the two alternative approaches, for the divine mind does not quite follow either pattern. Instead, whichever analogy we start with, it will still need complementing by its alleged opposite.

Conclusion

What I have sought to argue in considering these four common assumptions in contemporary philosophy is that theology need not be afraid of any alleged consequences, provided, that is, it takes seriously the arts as one of its potential partners. And in making that claim I also intend to suggest that philosophers who write about religion also need to be more widely alert to such a potential contribution since God is mediated not just through the revelation that is inherent in Scripture and in formal philosophical reflections but also in the way our minds work, that is, in the imagination and the undoubted contribution that it can bring.[41]

Notes

1 Although it was certainly the more common view, the biblical pattern is now acknowledged to be more varied than was once thought. See George W. E. Nickelsberg, *Resurrection, Immortality and Eternal Life in Intertestamental Judaism* (New York: Oxford University Press, 1972); and James Barr, *The Garden of Eden and the Hope of Immortality* (London: SCM, 1992).
2 T. S. Eliot, 'The Metaphysical Poets', in *T. S. Eliot, Selected Prose*, ed. F. Kermode (London: Faber & Faber, 1975), 59–67, esp. 64.

3 For example, a basket of fruit (*qayis*) moves Amos to think of the end (*qes*) of Israel (8:1–3).
4 John 4:1–26, esp. 10, 11. 'Living' means literally running water.
5 For two examples – from Francis Bacon and A. E. Housman – see my 'A Sacramental World: Why it Matters', in *The Oxford Handbook of Sacramental Theology*, ed. Hans Boersma and Matthew Levering (Oxford: Oxford University Press, 2015), 603–615.
6 From 'Poetry and Religion', in Les Murray, *Collected Poems* (Manchester: Carcanet, 1998), 267. Used with grateful permission.
7 Iain McGilchrist, *The Master and his Emissary* (New Haven: Yale University Press, 2009).
8 Michael J. Buckley, *At the Origins of Modern Atheism* (New Haven: Yale University Press, 1987); Charles Taylor, *A Secular Age* (Cambridge, Mass.: The Belknap Press of Harvard University Press, 2007); Michael A. Gillespie, *The Theological Origins of Modernity* (Chicago: University of Chicago Press, 2008).
9 See e.g. Fergus Kerr, *After Aquinas: Versions of Thomism* (Oxford: Blackwell, 2002).
10 H. Denzinger and A. Schönmetzer, eds, *Enchiridion symbolorum*, 36th edn (Freiburg: Herder, 1976), 3026.
11 Some notable contemporary philosophers of religion continue to defend one or more of these proofs, among them Brian Davies, Alvin Plantinga, Richard Swinburne and Denys Turner. But, despite the technical brilliance of some of their efforts, few have been convinced.
12 See my 'Realism and Religious Experience', *Religious Studies* 51 (2015), 497–512, now reprinted in David Brown, *God in a Single Vision: Integrating Philosophy and Theology*, ed. Christopher R. Brewer and Robert MacSwain (London: Routledge, 2016), 46–60.
13 See my *God and Enchantment of Place: Reclaiming Human Experience* (Oxford: Oxford University Press, 2004), 84–152, esp. 120–122 and 113–115.
14 John Ruskin, *Modern Painters* (London: George Allen, 1906), II: 3, v–x.
15 Ibid., II: 3, v. 45.
16 Annie Dillard, *Pilgrim at Tinker Creek* (London: Picador, 1976), 18–20, 60–67.
17 Ibid., 70, 117.
18 Brian Davies *Introduction to the Philosophy of Religion* (Oxford: Oxford University Press, 1982); Denys Turner, *The Darkness of God* (Cambridge: Cambridge University Press, 1995).
19 Wilfrid Mellers, *Celestial Music? Some Masterpieces of European Religious Music* (Woodbridge: Boydell Press, 2002).
20 Richard Rorty, *Philosophy and the Mirror of Nature* (Princeton: Princeton University Press, 1979); Alasdair MacIntyre, *Whose Justice? Which Rationality?* (Notre Dame, Ind.: University of Notre Dame Press, 1988).
21 Karl Barth, *The Epistle to the Romans* (London: Oxford University Press, 1933), 331.
22 Carl Zuchmayer and Karl Barth, *Späte Freundschaft in Briefen* (Zurich: TVZ Theologischer Verlag, 1977), esp. 17; see also Karl-Josef Kuschel, *The Poet as Mirror: Human Nature, God and Jesus in Twentieth-Century Literature* (London: SCM, 1999), 12–14.
23 Jürgen Habermas, *Theory of Communicative Action*, 2 vols (1981, English trans. Cambridge: Polity Press, 1984); for some responses, Helmut Peukert, *Science, Action and Fundamental Theology* (Cambridge, Mass.: MIT Press, 1984); Nicholas Adams, *Habermas and Theology* (Cambridge: Cambridge University Press, 2006).
24 Evident from the outset in the present canon since there are two versions of the creation narrative in Genesis 1–3.

36 Foundations

25 Recently republished in an annotated edition with a selection of essay commentaries; see Robert MacSwain, ed., *Scripture, Metaphysics, and Poetry: Austin Farrer's The Glass of Vision with Critical Commentary* (Farnham: Ashgate, 2013).
26 Immanuel Kant, *Critique of Pure Reason*, Preface to 2nd ed., B xxx.
27 For the manifesto of the new 'analytic theology' movement, see Oliver D. Crisp and Michael C. Rea, eds, *Analytic Theology: New Essays in the Philosophy of Theology* (Oxford: Oxford University Press, 2009); for some concerns, see my review in *Expository Times* 121.5 (February 2010): 254–255, titled, 'Is Clarity Always a Virtue?'.
28 An obvious modern philosophical example is Richard Swinburne, *Responsibility and Atonement* (Oxford: Clarendon Press, 1989). I myself have published three analyses of Anselm's argument in *Cur Deus homo*. To cite the two most recent, the formal character of his argument is explored at length in 'Anselm on Atonement', in *The Cambridge Companion to Anselm*, ed. Brian Davies and Brian Leftow (Cambridge: Cambridge University Press, 2004), 279–302, and his underlying preoccupation with questions of beauty is given most attention in 'Anselm, Knowledge and Beauty', in *The Oxford Handbook of the Epistemology of Theology*, ed. William J. Abraham and Frederick D. Aquino (Oxford: Oxford University Press, forthcoming).
29 *Mystery of Salvation* (London: Church House Publishing, 1995), 102–119. There eight different 'stories' are told.
30 For this argument pursued in more detail, see my 'Images of Atonement: Metaphor and the Dangers of Doctrine', in *God in a Single Vision*, ed. Brewer and MacSwain, 142–152.
31 For my defence of the social analogy, see *The Divine Trinity* (London: Duckworth; La Salle, Ill.: Open Court, 1985); for something closer to the personalist, see 'Trinity', in *A Companion to the Philosophy of Religion*, ed. Philip Quinn and Charles Taliafero (Oxford: Blackwell, 1997), 525–531.
32 See David Brown, 'The Trinity in Art', in *The Trinity: An Interdisciplinary Symposium on the Trinity*, ed. Stephen Davis, Daniel Kendall and Gerald O'Collins (Oxford: Oxford University Press, 1999), 329–356; this volume, 130–149.
33 Sarah Coakley, *God, Sexuality, and the Self: An Essay 'On the Trinity'* (Cambridge: Cambridge University Press, 2013), 190–265.
34 See, for example, her own summary, 260–261.
35 For the former, Titian's *The Trinity in Glory* in the Prado, Madrid; for the latter, Dürer's *Adoration of the Trinity* in the Kunsthistorisches Museum, Vienna.
36 Most famous is Masaccio's version in Santa Maria Novella in Florence. Other famous examples include those by El Greco and Ribera in the Prado in Madrid and a much more literal version by an anonymous Austrian artist in the National Gallery in London.
37 As in its repeated assertions, e.g. 'The Father is eternal, the Son eternal; and the Holy Ghost eternal. And yet they are not three eternals; but one eternal.'
38 There is a thirteenth-century image of three identical human figures at the pilgrimage site of Vallespietra in Italy. Three-headed single figures are more common, such as one from Cartmel Priory in Cumbria or another from Nazareth.
39 For the relevant quotation, see Brown, 'The Trinity in Art', 334, n. 17.
40 One from Florence by Andrea del Sarto survives from 1511.
41 This chapter was first given as a lecture in Oxford on 12 March 2015 as part of the Humane Philosophy Project, jointly sponsored by faculties at Oxford and Warsaw. I want to thank my hosts that evening, Ralph Weir and Mikolaj Slawkowksi-Rode, for the stimulating questions they and the audience raised. It draws in part on an earlier, more narrowly focused essay 'A Sacramental World: Why it Matters', in *The Oxford Handbook of Sacramental Theology*, ed. Boersma and Levering, those latter elements being used with permission.

3 Learning from Pagans

A Grounding in Jesus' Life

It is often the seeming accidentals of human life that have the most decisive impact upon what we do and say, and in that particular respect this essay is no different. I sat down to write it at the same time as I was due to preach a sermon on what is often regarded as one of the most problematic texts in the New Testament, Jesus' encounter with the Syrophoenician woman. The reader will no doubt recall the incident.[1] Jesus had ventured into the Gentile territory around the ancient seaports of Tyre and Sidon, home to one branch of the Phoenician race, the other now sadly depleted as a result of Rome's laying waste its major city at Carthage in modern Tunisia. A request to heal the woman's daughter is met with the comment from Jesus that 'it is not right to take the children's bread and throw it to the dogs', to which the woman responds: 'Yes, Lord; yet even the dogs under the table eat the children's crumbs.'

Commentators often try to lessen the severity of Jesus' words by describing them as ironic or even, since a diminutive is used, as affectionate: his talk is then really of 'little doggies'.[2] I for one just do not believe it. The longer version in Matthew emphasises how Jesus saw his role as being essentially to 'the lost sheep of Israel'. So the woman's reaction to his use of this common dismissive way of speaking about the Phoenicians must surely have brought Jesus up with a start, and made him think anew about the importance of the Gentiles in God's economy of salvation, kept as they were to a firmly subservient role in the Old Testament view of the last times.[3] Perhaps it is even the case that it is thanks to this exchange that Jesus came up eventually with the parable of the Good Samaritan, with the key role now assigned to someone of the mixed race that the Jews so despised. We shall of course never know for certain, but if the incident did play a crucial role in shaping Jesus' consciousness, such an explanation would provide a reason why the story was preserved despite its potential embarrassment for the later, largely Gentile Church.

Many Christians object to such a way of thinking about Jesus, making him partly dependent as it does for his developing consciousness on the insights of others. But is not that precisely what the glory of the incarnation is all about, a real entering into our humanity and so learning and growing in understanding in very similar ways to ourselves? Austin Farrer reminds us of how much Jesus must have owed to someone totally unknown to us, the local village rabbi at Nazareth, but of course there would have been many others. Rowan Williams puts it succinctly: Jesus *'learned* how to be human' and that meant learning within a specific context, including of course the parental home, and so from Mary and Joseph.[4]

All this may seem far from our theme of what Christians can learn from the arts, but it is not. Just as the temptation to see Jesus as a totally self-contained individual must be resisted if the incarnation is to be treated seriously, so, I believe, must a similar temptation about revelation in general. Readers familiar with my academic writings will know that I have argued this point at considerable length, particularly as this applies to the notion of developing tradition, which is what I take revelation to be.[5] Triggers can come from outside as much as from within, in encouraging new ways of thinking about God, and so providing a deeper understanding of his will and purposes for humanity. This is not the place to pursue such arguments. Instead, I now have a much more limited aim. A constant temptation among Christians when looking at art or music is to view their role, when legitimate, as at most illustrative, confirming or deepening faith but never challenging or subverting it. It is therefore hardly surprising that there is so much bad Christian art and music around, if even the more informed among us want to keep their influence in a safe pair of Christian hands, such as Rembrandt or Rouault in art, Bach or Bruckner in music. The more liberal-minded, in spreading the net more widely, may believe themselves immune from such criticism, but often the same fault is still there: art seen as merely illustrative of what is already believed on other grounds. I shall use two distinguished Oxbridge academics from opposite ends of the theological spectrum to indicate how pervasive the fault is. But in the main I want through the use of specific examples to encourage readers to reflect on the issue for themselves. Jesus, if I am right, learnt from a pagan; might not we also?

New Questions Posed by Art and Music

These days 'pagan' has become on Christian lips almost a pejorative term, equivalent to 'atheist'. That is not how I shall use the word. The Syrophoenician woman is herself likely to have been a worshipper of the local god, Eshmun. What I have in mind, therefore, is those who appear beyond the bounds of Christian orthodoxy but still engage with the question of God. Before proceeding to more controversial examples, I want to begin with two more straightforward challenges, one from the field of music and the other from the history of art.

My musical example raises questions about the inspiration of religious music and in particular whether it is possible to impose strict divisions between divine inspiration and sources in the wider culture. Although the German composer Hans Pfitzner (d. 1949) was nominally a Protestant, he seems to have moved in and out of faith throughout this life.[6] There is insufficient documentation to inform us whether his opera *Palestrina* of 1917 was written in one mood or its opposite. The theme, however, is clear. In the sixteenth century Palestrina saved polyphony for the Church despite considerable opposition from the Council of Trent, worried as it was by the fact that counterpoint in later medieval music no longer allowed the words of the mass to be clearly audible. The legend was that Palestrina's *Missa Papae Marcelli* did the trick. This is unlikely, if only because the pope to whom it was dedicated was dead within three weeks of taking office and Palestrina himself was forced to leave his job at the Sistine Chapel because he was married. But what concerns us here is how Pfitzner exploits that theme.

The decisive moment of inspiration comes at the end of the first act, when Palestrina first hears past composers urging him on, then angelic voices and finally the muse of his late wife.[7] As that brief outline may indicate, Pfitzner was in fact struggling between two competing conceptions of how Palestrina worked, whether his source of inspiration lay in God (the angels) or more simply in loyalty to his vocation as a composer (the more human voices). But does it matter in terms of what either Palestrina, or Pfitzner for that matter, has to say to us? We now know how incredibly complex a process of transmission lies behind the words of Scripture, and how hard it would be to claim one moment in that process as decisive. This is not to argue against divine inspiration, but it is to protest against focusing too narrowly as though only what lays claim to inspiration must be seen as part of God's providential guidance. Rather, what matters is the capacity, however this originates, of certain words or non-verbal forms to speak to us, and thus lead us into new ways of understanding our tradition as we attempt to absorb these new triggers to thought.

So Pfitzner's own views are ultimately less important than the challenge they came to embody: does external mediation really devalue divine address, and with it the related question of whether verbal comprehension need be an essential part of such address or not? At the decisive moment Pfitzner introduces a female angel singing in A major the opening line of Palestrina's original *Kyrie*, to which Pfitzner's composer responds by himself transposing key to echo its warm tones, thus abandoning his own earlier gloom (in C sharp minor). That mood of interchange is then carried right throughout the scene, with the Latin of the mass clearly audible against the German of the composer. It is a wonderfully lyrical and Romantic piece of writing, but of such a kind that for most of Pfitzner's listeners it will be the power of that musical interchange that will be seen, if anything does, to speak of God, not the words in themselves. So, despite Pfitzner's wrestling with the whole issue of an appropriate narrowing of religious focus, the irony is that he seems to draw us to a broader, more inclusive vision.

Words, though, do play an indispensable role in the story of the annunciation. Elsewhere in this volume is to be found a critique of Oxford theologian John Drury's treatment of several paintings of the annunciation in London's National Gallery.[8] He reads them as illustrative of universal human themes, whereas I want to pay attention to the specifics of historical context, and so to arguments about who should kneel to whom, and why Mary is presented in all three as reading. As that other essay indicates, the former raises major theological issues, but it is the latter on which I wish to focus here because it takes us beyond theology in the narrower sense and into wider issues of cultural dependence. Put Western and Eastern images of the annunciation alongside one another, and immediately some major contrasts are to be observed. Orthodox icons continue to this day to portray Mary at work spinning as she hears the angel's call. That was once also the Western image, but the typical later medieval and post-medieval form is quite different. Here Mary is reading. This may seem a matter of no great moment. Certainly, in terms of the origins of the image not much was at stake, for texts first appear with the words of Isaiah's prophecy on an accompanying banderol and so book or banderol was simply a way of making the appropriate allusion.[9]

But eventually the book appears on its own without accompanying justification, and that, I believe, is of considerable significance, for any remaining pretence of a historical record has now been abandoned. In effect, external cultural influence has been allowed to determine the shape of the image. The Virgin Mary was almost certainly illiterate and so the Orthodox convention is nearer to Mary's actual practice. Yet as representation it seems to me mere illustration and so rather dull, whereas in the later Middle Ages Western artists are in effect engaging in discussion of what contemporary women might legitimately do. Client and artist (whether devout or not) were arguing for women's access to literacy, initially through prayer books such as the newly popular Books of Hours but also in due course more widely. So we must not think that arguments over women's rights only began in modern times. Paintings of the Christian story, whether by devout artists or otherwise, were challenging Christians to think anew. The point is that Christians were being encouraged to think about appropriate roles for women through influences from beyond the text, whether these be explicitly religious in inspiration or not.

Learning from the Unorthodox

But there is no reason to remain in the distant past in our search for pertinent examples. The twentieth century is often described as a time of loss of faith, and in many ways that is true, but a surprising number of artists continued to engage actively with the Christian faith in their art. The natural tendency of Christians has been to focus on those who are explicit believers such as Norman Adams or Mark Cazalet, James Macmillan or John Tavener, but to do so exclusively would be merely to repeat the mistake against which I have been protesting. God does not just speak through the like-minded. So let me now take two pagan artists who challenge our understanding of the Christian faith in ways that lead, I believe, to its deepening and not to its destruction.

My first example comes from Jesus' infancy, Max Ernst's *The Infant Jesus Chastised by the Virgin Mary* (1926).[10] A highly controversial painting in its time (there were public protests in Cologne when it was first exhibited), it depicts the young child being spanked by his mother on his bare bottom as others look on. Where this painting still challenges Christian reflection is over the question of how full an incarnation we are actually prepared to believe in. For if Jesus fully entered into what it was to be an ordinary human being, growing up in one particular set of circumstances rather than another, would he not have been subject to the normal conventions of that culture, and so corporal punishment have been part of his life experience just as it would have been for every other boy in the ancient world? Such a conclusion is often resisted on the supposition that, had Jesus merited punishment, he could not possibly have been morally perfect. But this is to import into childhood judgments that are really only fully applicable to adult behaviour. Child psychologists inform us that children test the limits of their parents' tolerance not just as a way of irritating them but rather in order to discover boundaries in relation to which they will feel secure and self-contained. Jesus as a child would surely have been no different. So it is not so much that he sinned as that, like the rest of us, such testing of the boundaries was his way of discovering set limits, guides to what is right and what wrong.

Rather more, though, is at stake than what my remarks hitherto might seem to imply. For despite the flippancy of elements in this painting such as the lost halo on the ground or the three Surrealist witnesses in the background, Ernst is also telling us something about his own loss of faith. His artist father had employed him as a model to represent a young Jesus who was angelically perfect. No, indicates the adult Ernst, now no longer a believer: that is not the sort of saccharine God in whom I could ever believe. Not that this point had never been made before. A medieval roof boss in Nuremberg of the five-year-old Jesus being dragged to school or Simone Martini's depiction of the twelve-year-old sulking at his parents' reprimand might have been used to make the same observation.[11] It is a lesson that as yet has still not been fully absorbed by Christianity. The agnostic Ernst thus constitutes a continuing challenge to any notion of the infant Jesus as 'our childhood's pattern', 'mild' and 'obedient'.[12] Even Luke himself seems not immune from such criticism.

Consider now how a convinced atheist might help. That is how Francis Bacon understood himself, and yet he was obsessed with the crucifixion, which appears in one form or another in so many of his paintings.[13] Indeed, on his post-war relaunch he decided to destroy everything prior to his famous *Three Studies for Figures at the Base of a Crucifixion* of 1944. The agony he presents in so many such paintings is usually so unqualifiedly awful that his message is scarcely in doubt, that there cannot conceivably be any answer to the problem of suffering. If 'answer' is hardly the right word, Christians can scarcely countenance quite so negative a verdict. After all, John's Gospel repeatedly informs us that God's glory was to be seen even in so terrible an act as the crucifixion.[14] Yet even Bacon seems to yield at one point in a way that is both illuminating and challenging.

His erstwhile lover, George Dyer, committed suicide in a Paris hotel room in 1973, and Bacon portrayed the scene in one of his triptychs.[15] While the side panels depict Dyer first being sick into a basin and then dying on the toilet seat, the central image is of him as he enters the room, casting a shadow like a great bird of prey. It is what hangs above, though, that is of particular interest. It is a naked light bulb, suspended in a V shape from the exposed cord. Neither the hotel nor its clients were that impoverished, and so it seems to me correct to infer that for once Bacon is overcome by his love for Dyer to say something which did not come naturally to his cynical and promiscuous nature.[16] Obsessed at times by sado-masochistic desires, he also liked verbally humiliating, before his educated friends, the working-class boys whom he picked up. Yet, borrowing partly from Grünewald's Isenheim Altarpiece (for the angle of the cord) and partly from Picasso (for the light bulb) here he is declaring that his love will live on, and indeed he continued to paint Dyer even after his death. The naked light bulb and the angle of the cord thus alike hint at continuity, at hope, at love.

None of this can of course possibly turn Bacon into a Christian. The challenge is rather more subtle than that. These days, when Christians want to support gay relationships they often seek to model them as closely as possible on heterosexual ones, and so talk of the need for exclusive commitments. This is not the place to enter into the rights and wrongs of such questions. All I want to do is alert the reader to the way in which Bacon, struggling to express love, draws our attention to its presence even in highly flawed or promiscuous relationships. We all like to draw simple boundaries, but life is not quite like that. So even if the Church does change its rules, it will still not have answered all the questions of how it is to support those who struggle in imperfection to discover something of the reflection of divine love in their relationships with their fellow human beings.

In the case of Schubert's last song cycle *Winterreise* it is not the death of another that is being faced, but his own death. Schubert's early mass settings are so enjoyable and uplifting that we are often inclined to forget his unorthodoxy, his reluctance, for example, to include belief in the Church in his settings of the creed. Now here he is facing death from syphilis, as he sets to music a cycle of poems written by the contemporary Prussian poet Wilhelm Müller (d. 1827). Their nominal theme is an individual taking a walk, as he seeks to come to terms with rejection in love. Schubert, however, deepens their meaning, and makes the issue much more than just the typical Romantic exaggerated despair and longing for death. After quite a number of tempestuous and troubled songs, with the last three there seems a real attempt to face impending death. A song about courage in the absence of the gods leads to a mysterious vision of three suns,[17] with the final song then a meditation on a lonely hurdy-gurdy player working on the edge of town. Not once is there any reference whatsoever to the Christian God or to heaven, and yet, despite some who wish to speak of atheism, there is rather more than just the mere acceptance of the inevitable. It is more like an achieved, if somewhat bleak, serenity in the face of suffering and death. Of course, much will depend on performance and interpretation. The later Dietrich Fischer-Dieskau, for example, takes the last song more slowly than he did in earlier life, and so succeeds in stressing that acceptance.[18] Again, Ian Bostridge speaks of a 'religious aura' particularly in respect of the suns' song.[19] That would seem confirmed by the fact that Schubert was writing his last mass at about the same time, and it has a mystery and solemnity about it that the earlier ones lack.[20]

This is not to say that *Winterreise* is really Christianity in disguise. It is not. Where, though, it does address Christianity, it seems to me, is in our often too glib appeals to resurrection and life after death. Schubert seems to me to be saying that even where life is bleak and one feels thrown onto the edge of things like the hurdy-gurdy player, acceptance of one's destiny is important, perseverance whatever the future may bring. To look only to the marvellous coda to our lives in closer intimacy with God is to forget that this life too has had its value and its integrity, even if there is nothing beyond, and for that we should be accepting, even grateful.

'Secular' Contexts as Religious

John Drury would wish to see landscape painting as marking a similar narrowing of focus onto this world. He declares that such works 'exemplify the ... movement of Christian painting into the secular ... [L]ike the sacred bread in the Eucharist ... the myth has been consumed into the real, the other into the familiar.'[21] What one misses from his account is the way in which such art often continues to try to engage with God's interaction with the world at a deep level, and so substantial, if now more implicit, theological claims are still being made.

Take, for instance, as apparently conventional a painter as Constable. Prints of his works adorn many a modern household's walls, but few seem aware that he was a devout high churchman, many of whose canvases are a medium for reflection on divine presence in the world. Everyone knows and loves the familiar images of Salisbury Cathedral. I am sure the present Bishop of Salisbury[22] would never be as naïve as one of his predecessors (John Fisher) and object, as he did, to the presence of clouds in one of these, simply because they seemed to give too pessimistic a view of the Church.[23] We laugh, but unfortunately our level of reading of art, our desire simply for confirmation of what we already believe as Christians, can sometimes be just as bad. It may appear initially that Constable himself fell into precisely that fault in one of his later versions, where the building is set against a rainbow emerging after a storm.[24] Certainly Constable wanted to allude to the way in which the established Church seemed once again secure after all the threats made against it in the run-up to the great Reform Bill of 1832. But there is more than just symbolism here, a sort of one-to-one correspondence between Church and nature, with a piece of natural imagery only borrowed to speak of God's real sphere of action in the Church. What is going on is much more a question of parallelism, of us being invited to view the providential hand of God already operating in one sphere (nature) as confirmation of divine action in the other (the Church). In other words, Constable is actively challenging his fellow Christians of the time to think of God in a more immanent and involved way. If that was in some ways easier for him because in his day the biblical story of the origin of the rainbow was still being taken literally, the basic challenge is still there for us to think of Christ's Church as subject to such care, even when it appears to be going in a direction that we do not particularly like.

If Constable's conservatism only irritates, consider another, quite different example from later in the same century, where landscape art was to be used to issue a radical challenge, namely that Christianity was not immanentist enough. Vincent van Gogh had spent some of his youth as a missionary in the Belgian coal mines. Although he eventually lost his Christian faith, some of his late paintings leave us in no doubt that he was still wrestling with what might constitute a satisfactory account of God's relation to the world. Christianity he sees as too particularist and too transcendent. That is the implicit message behind his image of *The Sower*, where the sun forms a halo around the man as he works, or still more dramatically in his copying of Rembrandt's *Raising of Lazarus*, where this time the sun is actually made to replace Christ, showing the universal healer instead of what he has come to see as too narrowing and too constrictive a Christ.[25] As Christians we are bound to think van Gogh wrong in this estimate, but that does not mean that we should not listen and heed the warning in the dangers of too transcendent a God, a Christianity that despite the incarnation removes God too far from this world and ordinary people's lives; or of too particularist a Christ that neglects the world as a whole.

It was an issue with which another landscape artist from about the same time also wrestled. Van Gogh committed suicide in 1890, whereas Cézanne returned to the practice of the Catholic faith the following year.[26] Throughout the last years of his life he used a local mountain, Mont Sainte-Victoire, to work through what the relation between God and the world might be. In a few canvases the stress is very much on transcendence, with a sharp line drawn between the mountain and the surrounding terrain, but for the most part the colours and contours of the two interact and so evoke a lively sense of a God at one and the same time transcendent and immanent.[27] My point this time is quite a simple one. So far from landscape art being essentially secular, it too can be a locus for theological reflection, at times no less profound than what is expressed elsewhere by purely verbal means. Landscape art need not necessarily be just a mater of imitating or expressing nature. The artist can also be asking questions pertinent to theology, and for that to be so it is by no means essential that the artist should be a practising Christian. Van Gogh had lost his Christian faith, while Cézanne was clearly still struggling with his.

Coltrane's Love Supreme

My general theme is, I hope by now clear: art can of course illustrate faith but to insist that this is its only appropriate role is to belittle its achievements. Whether there are specific allusions to Christianity or not, the arts can at times offer a religious vision that we need to take seriously and engage with. Perhaps one last example of the sort of approach against which I am protesting will suffice, this time from the Cambridge theologian David F. Ford. He has many excellent things to say in his book *Self and Salvation*. Yet, although in its course there are quite a few artistic, poetic and musical allusions, none ever seems to rise above the level of the purely illustrative. It is almost as though the author already knows what he wants to say, and then looks round for confirmatory examples. The result is the very strange irony with which the book ends.[28] Ford quotes one of the poems of his friend Michael O'Siadhail, who uses jazz to illustrate his view of heaven. Ford's final words then take up the title of a jazz piece to which O'Siadhail had already alluded, 'A Love Supreme'. Ford seems to take the quotation as endorsing the christocentric emphasis that has run throughout the book. Indeed, he may even have had the cross subconsciously at the back of his mind. But herein lies a supreme irony, for the original jazz composition by John Coltrane was originally intended to pull in a quite different direction.

Coltrane had had a very difficult life, including drug addiction, and this piece was planned as his offering to the God who had preserved him through all life's traumas. But, despite his Christian upbringing, it was not of Christ that he was particularly thinking, but rather of a universal God operative everywhere.[29] Indeed, his first wife had converted to Islam, and he himself repeatedly declared that he thought all religions embodied essentially the same message, that of love. Significantly, in the poem that he wrote to accompany the piece, there is not one mention of Jesus Christ, though plenty of God and his care. Both his parents were children of ministers, and so it is quite likely that the title comes from an influential tract with a similar title by the Scottish minister Henry Drummond, who had insisted on the priority of love over faith.[30]

It is also such universalism that emerges from the music itself. Coltrane widened the scope of jazz by blending elements of African ritual with Indian and Arabian influences.[31] Here in the opening section 'Acknowledgement', an Eastern gong leads into a tenor saxophone fanfare that itself yields to the others in the quartet before Coltrane takes up the main three-note melody that is this section's primary tune. If that sounds boring, it is anything but, as it is subjected to numerous modulations, with frequent changes of key that produce an unsettling but challenging effect. The eventual utterance of the title words that correspond to the three-note melody is in effect unnecessary because through that very variation Coltrane has already informed us that 'God is everywhere – in every register, in every key.'[32] Indeed, in its only publicly performed version, at Antibes, the words were omitted.[33]

So I want to draw a rather different conclusion from that of Ford, that the deepening of our faith comes not only from within the resources of biblical revelation but also much more widely, from those of different religious belief and sometimes even from those of none. Certainly the glory of God was in the little child at Bethlehem but it was also in the Syrophoenician woman, pagan though she was. Art and music need to be viewed and heard and valued in their own right. The glory of God lies in a Love Supreme that speaks everywhere, sometimes confirming what we already believe but sometimes too challenging or even undermining what we suppose to be the case. Jesus learnt the value of pagan 'dogs'; so too can we.

Conclusion

In the course of the preceding discussion, my examples ranged from the first century to the twentieth. Even so, it might be objected that all came from those now 'safely' dead, in the sense that their voice is now no longer present to complain of how I have interpreted them. On the opposite side, though, this could be seen as wise caution, since judicious assessment usually comes easier with the passage of time. However, I would not like it to be thought either than I am contemptuous of contemporary artistic endeavours or that I believe God to be somehow now absent from the scene. Inevitably, with the decline in Christian belief, some pagan art is merely intended to provoke.[34] Nonetheless, I would suggest that the challenges continue, sometimes to ourselves as Christians to take a second look at Scripture and sometimes to the wider culture itself. So let me end with a few brief examples from contemporary British art: Tracey Emin on the horrors of abortion and Paula Rego on horrors resulting from its being banned;[35] Douglas Gordon on Christian misuse of the Hebrew Scriptures;[36] Marc Quinn's celebration of the disabled in the heart of London;[37] Chris Ofili on the potential for violence inherent in the story of the annunciation;[38] Paula Rego on the difference between spiritual and physical beauty;[39] environmental artists such as Andy Goldsworthy and Richard Long on the value of transient beauty, and so on.[40] Not one of the artists is a practising Christian, yet all have important things to say to the Church. This all seems to raise in acute form that lack of constructive dialogue.[41]

Notes

1 Mark 7:24–30; Matthew 15:21–28 (RSV).
2 Even as distinguished a New Testament scholar as Charles Cranfield insists that the reference is to pet dogs: *The Gospel According to St Mark* (Cambridge: Cambridge University Press, 1977 edn), 248.
3 For example, Isaiah 60:10–14.
4 Austin Farrer, *A Celebration of Faith* (London: Hodder, 1970), 89–90; Rowan Williams, 'The Seal of Orthodoxy: Mary and the Heart of Christian Doctrine', in *Say Yes to God*, ed. Martin Warner (London: Tufton, 1999), 15–29, esp. 19.
5 David Brown, *Tradition and Imagination: Revelation and Change* (Oxford: Oxford University Press, 1999); *Discipleship and Imagination: Christian Tradition and Truth* (Oxford: Oxford University Press, 2000).
6 Owen Toller, *Pfitzner's Palestrina: The 'Musical Legend' and its Background* (London: Toccata Press, 1997), 57, 81–86.
7 Act 1, scenes 5 and 6, especially the latter.
8 John Drury, *Painting the Word: Christian Pictures and their Meanings* (New Haven: Yale University Press, 1999), esp. 41–59; David Brown, 'The Annunciation as True Fiction', *Theology* 104 (2001), 123–130; reprinted as the first essay in Part III of this book, 105–112.
9 Isaiah 7:14.
10 Now in Museum Ludwig, Cologne; illustrated in *Max Ernst: A Retrospective*, ed. Werner Spies (Munich: Prestel, 1991), 301.
11 The roof boss is in the Frauenkirche; the Martini painting in the Walker Art Gallery in Liverpool. For further description and discussion of both items, see the essay on the annunciation that forms the first chapter of Part III of this volume.
12 The original words of Mrs Alexander's hymn, 'Once in royal David's city', now commonly changed as in *The New English Hymnal* of 1986.
13 For illustration and discussion, see Rina Arya, *Francis Bacon: Painting in a Godless World* (Farnham: Lund Humphries, 2012), esp. 58–83.
14 For example, John 12:23 and 28; 13:31–2.
15 The painting is in a private collection; illustrated in Michel Leiris, *Francis Bacon* (Barcelona: Ediciones Polígrafa, 1987), no. 84.
16 See further Daniel Farson, *The Gilded Gutter Life of Francis Bacon* (London: Random House, 1994).
17 Based on the phenomenon known as parhelia, when two phantom suns are seen either side of the real one.
18 Contrast the Deutsche Grammophon 1979 recording (Barenboim accompanying) with the EMI 1955 one (with Gerald Moore).
19 When interviewed in the BBC DVD version.
20 The Mass in E flat with its mysterious opening *Kyrie*, majestic *Gloria*, and dramatic symbolism in the *Credo*.
21 Drury, *Painting the Word*, 155, 147, quoted in that order.
22 The Bishop of Salisbury when this was written, in 2004, was David Stancliffe, and is now Nick Holtam.
23 John Walker, *John Constable* (London: Thames & Hudson, 1991), no. 26.
24 Formerly owned by Lord Ashton of Hyde, recently acquired by Tate Britain; Walker, no. 37.
25 Both paintings are in the van Gogh Museum in Amsterdam.
26 Pulitzer Prize-winning authors Steven Naifeh and Gregory White Smith have suggested that Van Gogh was in fact accidentally shot by a teenager with a malfunctioning gun in *Van Gogh: The Life* (New York: Random House, 2011), but the theory has not won general acceptance.

48 Foundations

27 In Maria Teresa Benedetti, *Cézanne* (New York: Crescent, 1995), contrast, for example, 256 with 258 and 260.
28 David Ford, *Self and Salvation* (Cambridge: Cambridge University Press, 1999), 280–281.
29 For the background to the album, Ashley Kahn, *A Love Supreme* (London: Granta Books, 2002). For first wife's views, 46, for his own e.g. xx.
30 Henry Drummond, *Love: The Supreme Gift* (1891).
31 Valarie Wilmer, *As Serious As Your Life: John Coltrane and Beyond* (London: Serpent's Tail, 1992 edn), 32, 36.
32 Kahn, *A Love Supreme*, 102, quoting Lewis Porter.
33 Interesting also in that improvisation meant that the piece as a whole was extended from 33 to 48 minutes.
34 Identifying such motives, though, is harder than one might think. Andres Serrano's *Piss Christ* (1987) actually came from a practising Roman Catholic, whilst Damien Hirst, though lapsed and a self-declared atheist, seems in some ways like Bacon, too obsessed with Christianity's symbols to succeed altogether in escaping from being an unwitting messenger. Indeed, his *St Bartholomew: Exquisite Pain* of 2006 is on long-term loan to the Church of St Bartholomew the Great in London, while in 2008 he produced a complete (and beautiful) series of butterfly paintings to illustrate the Psalms: subsequently reproduced as *The Complete Psalm Paintings* (London: Other Criteria, 2014).
35 For Emin, seen not just in depictions of her own abortions but also in a moving video engagement with her mother on the subject: *Tracey Emin 20 Years* (exhibition, 2008). For Rego's campaign against the laws in Portugal, her *Abortion Pastels* of 1998.
36 His installation used various reversals of Holbein the Younger's *Allegory of the Two Testaments* to challenge the Lutheran view of their relation upon which that painting had been based: *Superhumanatural* exhibition catalogue, 2006.
37 In his statue of his disabled (and pregnant) friend Alison Lapper for the vacant plinth in Trafalgar Square (2005).
38 Chris Ofili *Annunciation*, in *Devil's Pie* (New York: David Zwirner, 2007), introductory illustrations.
39 Her very ascetic portrayal of St Margaret of Scotland (in Durham Cathedral) evoked quite a number of protests, despite its likely historical accuracy. I had the privilege of meeting, and discussing the project with, the artist on a number of occasions. See my review in *Arts and Christianity* 37 (January 2004).
40 As in Goldsworthy's use of icicles or leaves, Long's of human tracks and even Robert Smithson's *Spiral Jetty*, which, despite its scale, is frequently submerged beneath the waters of Great Salt Lake, Utah.
41 Adapted from an essay originally published with the present title only as subtitle, the main one being 'The Glory of God Revealed in Art and Music', in *Celebrating Creation: Affirming Catholicism and the Revelation of God's Glory*, ed. Mark Chapman (London: Darton, Longman & Todd, 2004), 43–56.

Part II
The Power of Symbols

Introduction

Following on from the previous part, consideration might have been given to all the various key strategies employed to move reader or viewer from this material world to the world that is God's, including metaphor, analogy and so forth. Because of their frequent appearance, however, in non-religious discussion, many of these items are already given detailed consideration elsewhere, while this is less commonly so with symbol. Although it too finds a place in secular contexts, perhaps because of the primacy of its occurrence in the visual and in religious ritual, Christianity's predominantly verbal culture has tended to think it of lesser intellectual significance.[1] But this is far from being so, and so in Part II I would like to explore what exactly a symbol is and how it works.

In the first essay I attempt to clear away a number of misunderstandings that have inhibited appreciation of the full richness of the notion. In particular, conspicuous cases of the dogmatic defence of one particular meaning (most obviously in sacramental contexts) have led many to assume that its power derives precisely from such rigidity, whereas I shall argue exactly the reverse: what gives symbols their power is their multivalency. That is, it is precisely because they open viewer or reader to a plurality of possibilities that helps explain why they retain their irreducibility or non-substitutionability for some more prosaic alternative.

In the next essay consideration is then given to how one primary symbol might be seen to function in those controversial sacramental areas. The Eucharistic symbols of body and blood do not lend themselves easily to a brief discussion, and so the focus here falls instead on water and baptism. Through most of the history of the Church it has been taken as self-evident that the primary allusion for water in this context must be to its capacity to cleanse or purify. However, as strength of the commitment to the presence of original sin in children weakened, so in more recent times there has been a corresponding rise in the appeal to other meanings, not least among liturgical scholars, as they sought new ways of presenting the significance of baptism. Such discussions often appeal to the more forward direction of John's thinking, where baptism is presented as more like a commission for the future rather than any correction of the past.[2] Yet even such changing perspectives still tend to assume that the fault lies with Augustine and subsequent developments in theology, and that there is therefore little or nothing to be learnt from the use of water as symbol in the history of the Church. But I shall argue that the richness and multivalency of the symbol in fact survived in often strange and unexpected ways, and so could still provide an implicit corrective to the much narrower focus of the Church's official position.

The final essay then turns to another basic religious symbol, that of light, this time to note not only its own multivalency but also the way in which it can so easily transmogrify into its opposite, with darkness and not light now the principal symbol for the divine. While it could be argued that this has no more significance than the application of metaphors more generally where God can be at once hard like a rock and soft like a lamb, I want to suggest that rather more is at stake. First, it suggests an obvious point that we can never fully capture the essence of God in any particular linguistic concept, whether metaphorical or not. But, second and more importantly, it places a clear warning sign against any attempt to bind religious belief too tightly to one particular way of reading a text rather than another. The openness of symbols also entails the openness of the texts that employ them.

This is not at all to suggest that anything goes. Degrees of appropriateness in suggesting interpretations will still apply. My point rather is that words are not necessarily any more controlling than images. In the sixteenth century so worried were the Reformers by the openness of visual images that paintings were either banned from church or else the various symbols within them given labels so that viewers would not be misled.[3] But in that move, how symbols operate (whether it be in word or image) was equally misunderstood. Their power derives precisely from their capacity to open us to a variety of possibilities within which we may or may not then choose to situate ourselves. It is only a long tradition of directed reading from above that has led us to suppose biblical texts something quite different from paintings.

Notes

1 In this it seems clearly out of step with contemporary trends in culture more generally.
2 Not only does John link Christ's baptism directly to the crucifixion (1:29), he also connects the summoning of Jesus' disciples with that understanding (1:35–37).
3 A good example of such a trend can be found in the National Gallery in Edinburgh: Hans Holbein the Younger's *Allegory of the Old and New Testaments* (from the 1530s), in which every detail of the allegory is given an appropriate label (admittedly in Latin).

4 Understanding Symbol

Introduction

Our present use of words often deviates significantly from how those words were first deployed. So, for example, 'hierarchy' has now little or nothing to do with 'sacred rule', the literal meaning of the two Greek words from which the term was once derived. Care, therefore, needs always to be exercised when appeal is made to root or original meanings. However, with 'symbol' there does after all appear to be an element of continuity. The Greek verb from which the term originally came literally means to 'throw together', perhaps not especially illuminating in itself, but the noun *sumbolon* is more suggestive. It was used to indicate the other half of a broken piece of coin or pottery which functioned as a token whereby a guest or ally could reclaim the rights of friendship or hospitality when the two participants next met. As such, in the ancient world it suggested rather more than it would for us today, inasmuch as it not only indicated something shared but also such sharing even in a context of apparent difference. Thus, there was no need for such tokens where family or close friends were concerned. It was rather to cater for visits to strange cities or lands where one's own personal safety and overnight accommodation could not otherwise be guaranteed (an important consideration in a world in which inns were few and far between, and there was no formal police force).

Such a background helps explain why in early Christianity creeds were referred to as 'symbols', as indeed they still are in some modern European languages (e.g. German: *Symbolik*). They were seen as constituting marks of a common identity, a shared token of a common faith, even in situations where such individuals differed otherwise in race or rank. More concrete religious symbols could be interpreted in a similar way but it is important not to ignore that what is being 'thrown together' is not just different sorts of people but also two different kinds of thing: the divine and the human. Thus bread and wine, for example, are obviously intended not just to unite communicants but also those communicants with Christ and God. While secular symbols will lack this further dimension, they still help unite the disparate, as in appropriate use of a national flag, and can usually be associated, as in the Greek original, with some form of action rather than with a purely verbal expression.

That said, this is the understanding of symbol that has developed in discussions within religion and anthropology, whereas in logic and analytic philosophy more generally the tendency has been to give the term a much wider range, with it in effect sometimes simply equivalent to what is used to stand for something else. So, for instance, the American philosopher W. V. Quine opens one of his discussions of the topic by observing that 'a symbol, broadly speaking, is something that stands for something else', and then goes on to give as examples 'a fish for a man, an inscription for a man, a map for a province, a mercury level for a temperature'.[1] Designating through singular terms is then mentioned as its most common linguistic form, as with 'the author of *Waverley*' or 'Whittington's cat'. Such an account, probably influenced by discussion of symbol in mathematics, has clearly migrated a long way from the root meaning mentioned above. While the broader definition has undoubtedly proved useful in illuminating questions in the philosophy of language, its use here in the context of religion and art would unfortunately direct attention away from what are usually seen as some of the key issues. So it is no surprise to discover quite different definitions where these areas are the main focus. Here is one such example: 'a working definition for symbol would be a complex of gestures, sounds, images, and/or words that evoke, invite, and persuade participation in that to which they refer'.[2]

While this sounds promising as an account of what happens in religious symbolism, some may question whether it may be applied with equal effectiveness to artistic symbolism. Here, the legitimacy of the answer would seem very much to depend on how much symbolism is detected in art. Thus, if everything within the pictorial frame is also seen as symbol, then once again divergence is inevitable. But is it really appropriate to think of the average portrait or landscape painting in this way? Admittedly, truly great artists will seek to capture on canvas the essence of the person or the scene before them (what might be regarded as truly symbolic of them). Yet even so it could be argued that there is a more basic aim: representation, in enabling recognition of subjects, however differently they may appear in the painting. So in such cases it would seem that symbol is still very much subordinate to image, whereas it is clearly symbol that is involved when allusion is thereby made to something fundamentally different from itself. The distinguished art historian Sir Ernst Gombrich, while rejecting the view that artists plan to represent something external to themselves or internal to their minds, did nonetheless acknowledge that something recognisable was the artist's aim, though the form it took was determined not by the two possibilities just mentioned but rather by a shared communal tradition and existing artistic practices. Images, though thus culturally conditioned, were thus easily distinguishable from symbols. The symbol moved beyond images generated in this way into the visual equivalent of the verbal metaphor, sometimes explicable in the approach adopted to metaphor by Aristotle but more commonly requiring, especially within religious tradition, something more, what he called the Neoplatonic mystical approach under which 'they thought of the symbol as a mystery that could only be partly fathomed'.[3]

Why complete comprehension might be difficult, if not impossible, is an issue that I will discuss in due course but here it will suffice to note that symbol in art and its possible ramifications then becomes a matter of degree. The presentation of Jesus going about his ordinary life or even performing a miracle would be more of an image than a symbol, whereas God the Father as the Ancient of Days, or Christ as the Lamb would be primarily symbols, yet differing in their effectiveness both as communication and in the types of commitments generated. Thus it is surely no accident that the Reformation attacks on the first symbol resulted in its disappearance as much from Catholic churches as from Protestant, whereas it would be hard to see Christ as Lamb as dispensable given the numerous threads and connections that can be seen to run throughout Scripture and into the liturgy itself.[4]

In the modern world symbols have of course often been seen to rouse extraordinarily powerful and indeed destructive passions. Think, for instance, of the Vietnam War, and the way in which the burning of the American flag was used as a form of protest, creating outrage well beyond those who were strong advocates of the war. Again, more recently, desecration of the Qur'an and cartoons of Muhammad have generated far greater indignation, resulting sometimes in terrible reprisal atrocities.[5] In such reactions it is almost as though the contested symbol has come to be treated as the thing itself. Yet any particular Qur'an or symbolic representation of the prophet is hardly the eternal reality itself, unlike in the possible Christian parallels where, especially in the medieval period, desecration of the host was seen as actually an attack of the personhood of Christ himself, present in that host.[6] Thus, in theory at least, sacrament offers a layer beyond symbol in the promise of mediated divine presence or agency.

Even so, religious and secular practice alike have not always adhered to the difference, and so symbols have taken on in themselves a realism that it would be hard to defend on calm reflection. The reason of course is that they come to be embedded in a group's practices or ritual, and so are bound up with that group's sense of self-identity and self-respect. That is surely what explains the quite different American and British reactions to flag burning. Only Americans have grown up participating in rituals professing shared allegiance to the flag, in the schoolroom and elsewhere. Iconoclasm across the world's religions has no single explanation but one element would seem to be suspicion of such absolutising of symbols, where in effect the symbol has come to be seen as usurping the place of the reality itself. At any rate, that would help explain the periodic outbreaks of iconoclasm that have occurred not only within Christianity but also within and across all the world's major religions, as in early Buddhist attacks on Hinduism, Sikhs' condemnation of Indian culture or Muslims' of Christianity.[7] Symbols were seen as usurping a respect that was properly due only to God.

One common reforming strategy is to suggest that any potential such symbol should never be read as anything more than a sign, a mere pointer elsewhere rather than inherently valuable in itself. Such was the strategy tried at the Reformation. Both Luther and Calvin thought that the Lord's Supper could mediate the believer's relation to Christ, for Luther through Christ's miraculous presence in association with the bread and wine, and for Calvin by the believer being united through the work of the Holy Spirit with the exalted Christ in heaven. Where they differed from pre-Reformation thinking was in insisting that the symbols involved (i.e. bread and wine) acquired no new status. Particularly for Calvin the associated enacted rituals were to be seen as simply alternative sermons, as it were, an acted preaching of God's promises which were effected by other means, in the believer's heart.[8] No special reverence was, therefore, due to the bread and wine outside the immediate context of the service, and that is why any surplus bread and wine, though consecrated, could be taken home for domestic consumption.

Luther, however, did require a more reverential attitude, and this is also reflected in his more positive attitude to symbolism in the visual arts. A few centuries later it was also a position taken by the German Lutheran theologian Paul Tillich (d. 1965). He insisted that symbols differ fundamentally from signs. The latter are like traffic directions to towns that offer no sense of the town itself, whereas by contrast symbols do offer some sense of participation in the reality to which they point, while at the same time including some qualification that indicates that they are not that reality itself. In fact, 'religious symbols are double edged. They are directed toward the infinite which they symbolize *and* toward the finite through which they symbolize it. They force the infinite down to finitude and the finite up to infinity.'[9] So that is why this necessary way of thinking about God is able on the one hand to sacralise symbols such as 'father' or 'king' but on the other to call into question such a status and thus in turn even force the symbol's abandonment.

Whether such recognition of the capacity of symbols to fail is enough in itself to enable a distinction to be maintained between reverence (veneration) for symbols on the one hand and their actual worship on the other is a moot point. Calvinism has not itself been entirely exempt from such problems. Even in its contemporary worship it is not hard to detect some remote analogy between the solemn way in which the Bible is formally brought into church at the beginning of Presbyterian services and processions of the reserved sacrament in Catholic churches. But going further back in history, it would be difficult to contest the view that Calvinism has sometimes treated Scripture in a manner analogous to such reverence for the host or even indeed in some ways behaved like modern Islamic fundamentalism in its treatment of the text. In other words, it is not nearly as easy to escape the misuse of symbols as Calvin's theology implied. I want, therefore, to use the rest of this essay to explore how a more nuanced account of symbolism might succeed in contributing to the flourishing of religion and its associated rituals, as also to artistic endeavour, without falling foul of such traps.

Symbols: Natural and Otherwise

One basic question that one might ask is whether any religious symbols are 'natural' or not, that is, inevitably arising in virtue of the way the world is. Clearly, in many, perhaps most, cases this is not so. Whether one stands or kneels to pray, for instance, will depend on what meaning a particular culture attaches to such postures. Similarly, the Inuit rub noses as a form of welcome, whereas Anglo-Saxons shake hands. Yet the fact that God is seen as creator might be taken to imply that it is part of divine providence that the world should carry with it certain readings, and so become another book alongside the Bible as 'the book of nature' (an image as old as Augustine). To take symbols for divinity itself, not only do we find many of these crossing the religions but sometimes so deeply rooted that the word for the symbol and for the divine turn out be etymologically related. So, for example, the height of heaven as indicator of divine transcendence finds its echo in quite a number of languages (e.g. Sanskrit and Greek), where the word for 'god' was originally derived from that for 'heaven'. Again, increasingly it is being recognised that Jewish Temple symbolism borrowed symbols from nature that had detailed parallels in other cultures.[10] Émile Durkheim (d. 1917) and Claude Lévi-Strauss (d. 2009) sought to explain such phenomena in purely sociological terms, but some cultural anthropologists have offered a quite different perspective.

In marked contrast to sociological reductionism, for instance, Mircea Eliade (d. 1986), the Romanian historian of religion, insisted that the sacred is an irreducible and universal element in human experience that finds expression in myths and symbols that cross cultures. Deploying the term *hierophany* to describe the irruption of the sacred into the profane world through symbol, in his most influential work *Patterns in Comparative Religion* he notes both the celebration of spatial points of intersection such as cosmic mountains and trees, as well as temporal sacred festivals used to map macrocosm onto microcosm.[11] His strong stress on primordial time and place was perhaps unduly influenced by his early research in India as a young man. At all events, it is easier to follow him in noting common roots in the early developments of the various religions than it is to see how his insights might best be applied to the contemporary world. More pertinent to that latter context is the work of a cultural anthropologist like Arnold van Gennep (d.1957), who noted the virtual universality of initiation rites with their notion of liminality (the move over a threshold into a new form of existence) without distinction of time or place.

Van Gennep's work was developed by the Scot Victor Turner (d. 1983), whose research work focused on the Ndembu tribe in Zambia and in particular on the liminal effect of their rites of circumcision that marked a transition to early adulthood. Arguing that these conclusions could be generalised, later in his career he applied them to various aspect of Christianity, including pilgrimage and even as specific an event as the conduct of Thomas

Becket at the Council of Northampton.[12] An important element in his thinking was the way in which a multiplicity of associations for symbols can help provide a religious vision of unity to an apparently disparate world. Another famous British anthropologist, Mary Douglas (d. 2007), took a similar line, stressing the way in which symbols function as part of a larger social system, and derive their power in part from their ability to bear more than one meaning. Her position, however, inevitably complicates the question of how much the meaning of any particular symbol comes from the way the world is (nature) and how much from social construction (culture). Thus, in her work on *Natural Symbols*, she concedes their existence but insists that some will disappear under some forms of social structure, as with symbols of solidarity and hierarchy in a society of non-restricted codes of social rules.[13]

Yet one might argue that her preoccupation with social rules leads her to ignore some more basic forms of correspondence, as with Christianity's most basic symbols of water and blood, which occur in most religions and with similar connotations. Thus, although water can of course sometimes be destructive, refreshment and cleansing are surely its two most basic and readily accessible features, and as such are found in the rituals of all the major religions. Again, the virtual ubiquity of blood sacrifice raises acute questions of how Christianity's own distinctive theology should be set in the context of this wider background. Against such a background a contrast could be drawn with bread, where its staple character is far from ubiquitous, rice, for example, taking over that role in the Far East.

Given such variants, numerous contemporary theologians have raised the question of what has come to be known as inculturation, whether different social settings might legitimate alternative liturgical symbols.[14] The issue of rice as an alternative to bread has already been mentioned. But even where the symbolism connected with blood has proved ubiquitous, the appropriateness of always associating this with wine could be raised. Might, for example, the use of beer in some societies make more sense, that is, where beer is the more common drink? The change could be defended on the grounds that the symbol should primarily be focused on the element of sharing, as also on the capacity for the drink to suggest improvement in the quality of life through its flow. In support, one might note that white wine has in fact sometimes been used in some Calvinist churches to counter particular views of Eucharistic presence, while, ironically, even Roman Catholic canon law does not actually forbid white instead of red wine. Yet it could be argued that a considerable price would be paid, in any allusion to the colour of Christ's sacrificial blood thereby being lost. It would also sever the universality of the natural symbolism of blood to speak easily and obviously of both sacrifice and sharing.[15]

Yet, even if the existence of natural symbols can be defended, this does not entail that their significance will always remain the same. Change clearly sometimes happens where only the referent is something in nature and not the symbol itself. So, for example, in the Temple the menorah appears originally to have been intended as a cosmological symbol, representing the seven known planets,[16] whereas in medieval Judaism it came to represent the light of the Torah and the sciences which help support its study. But, equally, this can happen more directly with natural symbols themselves. Although the water of baptism has for most of Christian history been taken as symbolic of the washing away of sin, as the notion of original sin has declined in popularity, so liturgies have given a new stress to water as primarily life-giving (the refreshment element).[17]

Dispensability or Otherwise

In assessing the importance of symbols one question that is clearly of relevance is how far such symbols are dispensable, that is, translatable into other terms. Lucien Lévy-Bruhl (d. 1939) argued that they are part of 'a pre-logical mentality', and in this view he reflected a common Enlightenment assumption. In the early nineteenth century Hegel had attempted a major defence partly through widening the notion in a way that made all religious activity and thought symbolic, but it was a dubious compliment since he nonetheless insisted that primacy lay with the more abstract concepts of his own philosophy. Hamann (d. 1788) is therefore in some ways a more interesting rebel against the Enlightenment view. For him reality could not be adequately captured except through symbols, and in this he was followed by Herder (d. 1803), with his stress on poetry as the most adequate means of mapping our world. Similar claims were also canvassed by the Symbolist school of French poetry in the nineteenth century, among whom were numbered Paul Verlaine and Charles Baudelaire, both of whom were to make profound use both of Christian symbolism and, particularly in the latter case, of its inversion.

In the twentieth century one significant figure writing on symbols was the German philosopher Ernst Cassirer. It was while holding a chair at Hamburg in the 1920s that he wrote his *Philosophy of Symbolic Forms* in which he characterised human beings as essentially symbolic animals.[18] Whereas the rest of the animal creation, he suggested, manipulates the world that surrounds them entirely through direct sensory perception, in the case of humans this is frequently filtered through symbols, particularly in the case of religion and art. However, so far from intending such an analysis to demote information derived from such an indirect source, his argument was that, like natural science, the symbolic world could also aim for its own sense of objective validity through interpersonal agreement. It was an idea taken up by his most famous pupil, Susan Langer (d. 1985), who got to know him well while he was a refugee in the United States during the last years of his life (1941–1945). Rejecting traditional philosophical approaches that had used concepts like beauty and taste to account for aesthetic values, in her most famous work *Philosophy in a New Key* (1942) she draws a sharp distinction between discursive and presentational symbols.[19] While the former can be used to build up more complex ideas without ever returning to their original source, presentational symbols are, on her view, never intelligible apart from the specific contexts in which they are set, and which are, therefore, quite capable of accruing quite different meanings in new contexts. In a later work, *Feeling and Form* (1953), she argued that the non-discursive symbols of art, especially in music, encapsulate forms of intuitive knowledge that ordinary language is simply unable to communicate. Seen in general as the expression of moods and mental tensions that bear no relation to the artist's personal feelings, her analysis was carried to its logical extreme in the case of music, where what is abstracted is taken to be unadulterated expression of feeling without any reference to content. So 'art works' are held to 'contain feelings, but do not feel them', with the essence of art defined as 'the creation of forms symbolic of human feeling'.[20] An obvious criticism is that, although the intention is non-reductionist, in effect she does seem to reduce everything to an emotional content, which in her final work, *Mind: An Essay in Human Feeling* (3 vols, 1967–1982), comes close to a form of biological reductionism.

Ironically, at one level Langer's writings are not only entirely intelligible in terms of the philosophy of the time but also a laudable response, inasmuch as one can see her writings as an attempt to overcome the divide asserted by logical positivism, which claimed that the emotive, as distinct from the scientific and empirical, was cognitively valueless. But her mistake was surely to accept the positivists' own analysis, according to which art and religion are purely emotive.[21] In the end more helpful are the suggestions of the French philosopher Paul Ricoeur (d. 2005), who, like Eliade, also ended up teaching at the University of Chicago. In his writings there is not only much more stress on cognitive content but also on the transformative power of symbols. Interaction between their past history and present context results in new perceptions: 'an archaic symbol survives only through the revolutions of experience and language which submerge it ... [A] symbol is first of all a destroyer of a prior symbol'.[22] Expressed so starkly, such a declaration seems to ignore deeper continuities. Nonetheless, the essential rightness of his position is well illustrated by some of the examples he offers of such transformations, as with 'original sin' and 'father'.[23]

He too follows Cassirer and Langer in asserting that all thinking is to varying degrees symbolic. It cannot be denied that there are undoubted advantages to religion in such a contention, inasmuch as the common claim that God cannot be adequately captured in language could then be viewed merely as part of a much wider issue about the mapping of reality onto language more generally. But a price would surely be paid in drawing talk of God into an orbit where it might be thought that the deity did not properly belong. After all, it is surely something about the transcendence and profundity of God that prevents adequate translation and not simply a feature of language more generally. In addition, it would seem somewhat odd to claim that all language is symbolic, or as Ricoeur sometimes puts it, 'metaphorical', if only because the terminology of metaphor and symbol suggests a move from one defined area to another rather than a loosely floating terrain. Of course, much of language consists of dead metaphors (like 'terrain') but we surely call them 'dead' precisely because they no longer function as such.

Indeed, one might argue that the usefulness of symbol as a category of understanding has been seriously impaired over the centuries by too great a readiness to detect it everywhere. Examples from two ancient languages may suffice. Perhaps the strangest of Plato's dialogues is his early work *Cratylus*, in which hidden symbols are proposed as a pattern for explaining the origin of words. It is precisely to such a treatment that Zeus himself as chief god of the Greek pantheon is made subject,[24] all of which leaves one wondering what significance to attach to the revelation of the divine name in the Book of Exodus (3:13ff.). Aquinas saw in the passage the identity of God's essence and existence, whereas, more probably, the story was originally intended as a way of grounding belief in God's constancy and faithfulness ('I will be what I will be'). Yet, however illuminating such explanations are towards comprehending the nature and character of God, it is unlikely that either the earlier or the later account properly reflects any meaning actually inherent in what had become (or always was) a proper name.

In other words, there is a need for some restraint in identifying where symbolism is found. It is not that symbols are elusive because language in general is similarly placed. Rather, it is partly a matter of the topic to which they are applied and partly their capacity to range widely, and in the process acquire fresh meanings. It is to that latter aspect that I now turn.

Context and Multivalency

In reality, ease of translation may well be a less fundamental issue than how the workings of the symbol are best understood in relation to differing contexts. For Langer, the syntax and vocabulary of music was only ever seen as intelligible when viewed in relation to a piece as a whole. But, though important, it is not just one context that matters but how meaning may vary as the same symbol is set in each new relation. As Wittgenstein argued in his later philosophy, relying primarily on denotation or some one-to-one correspondence is usually a mistake; rather, words (and even more so, therefore, symbols) operate as part of wider frames, what he identified as a series of 'language games'.[25] Much the same might therefore be said about more concrete symbols, whether objects or actions. No religious symbol, it may be contended, is ever properly understood unless due note is taken of its ritual context. So, for instance, an observer comprehends little, if unable to explain why genuflection is made to bread in a church but not to a loaf at home even if a priest blesses it.

Such a contextual account would also help explain the capacity of symbols to operate successfully with multivalent meanings. It is not that the symbol is a muddled notion but that different aspects can be used to illuminate different features of what is nonetheless the same thing to which reference is ultimately being made. Recognising different contexts would then become integral to appreciating the variety of meanings that a single symbol can convey. Nor need an ability to appreciate such a range necessarily have anything to do with cultural advance. Instead, comparing actual practice, it becomes plausible to suggest that some earlier cultures were considerably more sophisticated on this matter than is our own.

In the history of Christianity perhaps the late Middle Ages and Renaissance are the most marked in contrast to our own times. For us the lion is a symbol of strength and courage, but in the Middle Ages to these attributes were added watchfulness,[26] the resurrection,[27] evil,[28] St Mark and by association the city of Venice. Again, there is plenty of evidence of the process operating in the opposite direction, that is, with a single referent attracting to itself multiple symbols, and readers or viewers apparently experiencing no difficulty in comprehension. An obvious case in point is patristic and medieval treatment of Mary in the Song of Songs and resultant applications in the various arts. So, for example, it is by no means uncommon to find within a single painting Mary as enclosed garden, burning bush, lily, fountain and tower.[29]

Undoubtedly, part of the reason lying behind the modern preference for a Madonna and Child by Henry Moore over a Renaissance painting on the same theme is the rejection of naturalism, but it also goes with resistance to a rich symbolic world – the ruined Classical arch, Christ toying with a goldfinch, genitals exposed, a lamb playing, the human figures forming a triangle, and so forth.[30] Rules of metaphor allow Christ to be both a rock and a lamb, but perhaps the metaphors are too quickly 'cashed', as though their only value lay in what they literally implied rather than allowing them to bring along with them a rich field of associated allusions that legitimate talk of complex symbols rather than simple metaphors. That simplicity is not necessarily a cultural advance seems well indicated by the history of Greece, inasmuch as Greek culture appears to have moved from being largely aniconic in its approach to deity to allowing a superfluity of symbolic representations in art, yet no one would deny that the later culture was the more advanced. Failure to appreciate the rich potential of such complexity may in part explain why a proper understanding of symbols has been for so long plagued by resistance to the possibility of even superficial contradictions or apparent overload in meaning.

However, perhaps the best way of assessing some of the points just made is to consider some specific cases of how religious symbols operate in practice, the topic of the next two essays.[31]

Notes

1 W. V. Quine, s.v. 'Symbol', in *The Oxford Companion to the Mind*, ed. Richard L. Gregory (Oxford: Oxford University Press, 1987), 763–765. 'Fish for man' alludes to the early Christian practice of using a fish to symbolise Christ because of its Greek letters spelling out 'Jesus Christ, Son of God and Saviour'.

2 Stephen Happel, s.v. 'Symbol', in *The New Dictionary of Sacramental Worship*, ed. Peter E. Fink (Dublin: Gill and Macmillan, 1990), 1237–1245, esp. 1238.
3 E. H. Gombrich, *Symbolic Images*, 3rd edn (Oxford: Phaidon, 1985), 13. For his fullest discussion, 123–195.
4 This may at first sight seem to be disproved by the fact that Eastern Orthodoxy successfully banned Christ as Lamb from its art, but it is to be noted that the verbal metaphor remains as firmly entrenched as in the West.
5 The year 2005 was an important one that witnessed both the desecration of the Qur'an by American military personnel at Guantánamo Bay, and the publication of various satirical cartoons of Muhammad in the Danish newspaper *Jylands-Posten*. Both elicited violent riots, a pattern that has been repeated on several occasions since.
6 Medieval legends of such conduct by Jews are all subsequent to the Fourth Lateran Council in 1215 that declared the doctrine of transubstantiation. Although most frequent in Germany, Paolo Uccello's painted series *The Miracle of the Profaned Host* at Urbino derived ultimately from a tale set in Paris.
7 For a recent British survey, see Tabitha Barber and Stacy Boldrick, eds, *Art under Attack: Histories of British Iconoclasm* (London: Tate, 2013), published on the occasion of the exhibition 'Art under Attack: Histories of British Iconoclasm' shown at Tate Britain, 2 October 2013–5 January 2014.
8 For a clear and helpful defence of such a position by a philosopher, see Nicholas Wolterstorff, 'Sacrament as Action, not Presence', in *Christ: The Sacramental World*, ed. David Brown and Ann Loades (London: SPCK, 1996), 103–122.
9 Paul Tillich, *Systematic Theology*, vol. 1 (London: James Nisbet, 1953), 264–277, esp. 266–267.
10 See Othmar Keel, *The Symbolism of the Biblical World* (New York: Seabury, 1978), where numerous visual illustrations are offered of parallels elsewhere in the Near East.
11 First published in French as *Traité d'histoire des religions* in 1949, then in English as *Patterns in Comparative Religion* (London: Sheed and Ward, 1958). *The Sacred and the Profane* (New York: Harcourt, 1959) appeared after his move to Chicago in 1956.
12 See the relevant chapter in Victor Turner, *Drama, Fields, and Metaphors: Symbolic Action in Human Society* (Ithaca, N.Y.: Cornell University Press, 1974).
13 Mary Douglas, *Natural Symbols*, 2nd edn (London: Penguin, 1973), 44ff., esp. 55.
14 For a general discussion of the issue, Anscar J. Chupungco, *Liturgical Inculturation* (Collegeville, Minn.: Liturgical Press, 1992).
15 Even today boyhood gang initiations sometimes take the form of symbolising a common identity through mixing blood from a cut finger.
16 Although no explanation is given in Scripture, this is one adopted by Philo (e.g. *Quis heres*, 221–224) and also by several of the Church fathers.
17 For a more extended defence of natural symbols, and in particular their possible role in revelation, see my 'God and Symbolic Action' (1990); republished in *Scripture, Metaphysics, and Poetry: Austin Farrer's* The Glass of Vision *with Critical Commentary*, ed. Robert MacSwain (Farnham: Ashgate, 2013), 133–148.
18 Ernst Cassirer, *Philosophy of Symbolic Forms*, 3 vols (New Haven: Yale University Press, 1953–1957). A fourth volume was published in 1996.
19 Susan Langer, *Philosophy in a New Key: A Study in the Symbolism of Reason, Rite and Art* (Cambridge, Mass.: Harvard University Press, 1942). It went on to sell more than half a million copies.
20 Susan Langer, *Feeling and Form* (New York: Scribner, 1953), 22, 40.

21 As in A. J. Ayer's popularisation of their ideas, in his *Language, Truth and Logic*, 2nd edn (London: Gollancz, 1946).
22 Paul Ricoeur, *The Conflict of Interpretations* (Evanston, Ill.: Northwestern University Press, 1974), 291.
23 Also discussed ibid.
24 At 396a we are told that the name hides the real meaning of 'Zeus', as the being through which everything gains life.
25 From first introduction to their variety and multiplicity, see Ludwig Wittgenstein, *Philosophical Investigations*, 2nd edn (Oxford: Blackwell, 1958), esp. sections 7–24.
26 Lions were thought to sleep with their eyes open.
27 Cubs were believed to be born dead until their father breathed on them.
28 Cf. Psalm 91:13: 'thou shalt tread upon the lion and the adder'.
29 While the enclosed garden (*hortus conclusus*) is the most common image, closely followed by the fountain, some artists do attempt to include them all, e. g. Juan de Juanes's *Immaculate Conception* (*c.* 1540).
30 Ruined Classical arches refer to the passing of the old order, and the baby Jesus playing with a goldfinch to his future wearing of a crown of thorns since goldfinches like thistles.
31 Some of the points in this essay were first made (much more briefly) in Adrian Hastings, ed., *Oxford Companion to Christian Thought*, s.v. 'Symbolism' (Oxford: Oxford University Press, 2000), 690–692.

5 Baptism and Water as Cosmological Symbol

Just as it is a natural inclination on our part to attribute one single meaning to any particular word (for why otherwise not invent another word?), so there is a parallel temptation with symbols. Nowhere is this perhaps more obvious than in the case of water. Judaism, Islam and Hinduism have all required washing before entry into places of worship, with physical cleansing no doubt intended to parallel the spiritual, and so likewise in Christianity the most common interpretation of baptism has been in the washing away of sins. This understanding was undoubtedly encouraged by the precedent set by John the Baptist in proclaiming baptism as offering remission of sin.[1] So, although Matthew did query whether such a notion could apply to what happened in the case of Christ,[2] even so, this was where the primary stress of much of the early Church's preaching seems also to have fallen[3]. Admittedly, John proposed a quite different emphasis, with a forward-looking aspect seen as primary,[4] while Paul's imagery appears to look in both directions.[5] So things might have developed quite differently.

One key development that ensured that they did not was Augustine's insistence on baptism's role in washing away not only actual sin but also the consequences of inherited or 'original' sin. It is often supposed that one major result of such a change of focus was the practice of infant baptism. So it is important to note here that Augustine's argument actually operated the other way round. Quite a number of early Christian texts had in fact spoken of the innocence and sinlessness of children, while, for whatever reason, their baptism was already quite common by the time of Augustine. So Augustine's argument was not that children needed to be baptised to escape sin, but that, since they were already being baptised, they must, therefore, actually be sinful.[6] Equally pertinent, though, in encouraging such a backward-looking emphasis were developments in the patristic period more generally under which the sacrament of penance came to be seen as the second part of a two-part rite for remission of sin, beginning with baptism.[7]

So, theologically, a pattern was set that continued until the liturgical reforms of the twentieth century.[8] Its baleful influence can be neatly illustrated from nineteenth-century British fiction. There is, for example, Charles Dickens's account of the baptism of 'Little Paul' in *Dombey and Son*: a

66   *The Power of Symbols*

quiet, private affair in a gloomy church with other events taking place at the same time.[9] But perhaps better known, and certainly more worrying, is Thomas Hardy's description of the baptism of Tess's child, Sorrow. She had pleaded with her father, Durbeyfield, to summon a priest but he refused. So, fearing that the child will otherwise go to hell, she performs the act herself over a washstand, with her siblings gathered round. Next day Sorrow dies, and, initially at least, the parson refuses the child burial.[10]

Yet that single meaning is by no means typical or even dominant when one takes into account the history of the symbol as a whole. Any deeper exploration of how that symbolic meaning functioned over the great sweep of history quickly reveals plural or multivalent uses, and this is true also of the ritual of baptism itself, whatever official teaching the Church had maintained in the interim. Indeed, what we shall discover is not only polyvalent meanings but also at times seemingly contradictory: both life and death, order and chaos, suffering and blessing. So far, however, from working to the symbol's disadvantage, in the past it proved one of its great strengths.

It is that diversity that I want to illustrate in what follows, with two fundamental objectives in view that build on the symbol's already noted richness. The first is to draw attention to the now largely forgotten cosmological significance once attributed to water that appears in both Testaments and which continued to resonate through much of Christian history. By 'cosmological' I have in mind the way in which images of water once entailed significance for the cosmos as a whole, and not just something narrowly local. The second is to note how it was largely cultural and artistic aspects that preserved that richness for baptism even as the Church narrowed its understanding to a mainly backward-looking emphasis.

In what follows, I would like to proceed by four stages. First, I explore the origins and use of the cosmological symbol of the fountain in relation to creation generally. Then, more narrowly I explore how water is used to give cosmic significance to Christ. Thereafter, third, I look specifically at how architectural and artistic practices helped preserve a wider understanding of baptism, even as social perceptions narrowed. Then, finally and more briefly, in a last section I suggest that, although recent liturgical revision has indeed opened up a wider range of imaginative possibilities, it is still the case that the work of artists can aid us in exploration of the full range of potential meanings for this symbol.

The Fountain that Restrains Cosmological Chaos

How far the symbol of the fountain is now largely forgotten can be nicely indicated by how few viewers of Hieronymus Bosch's famous painting *The Garden of Earthly Delights* (c. 1500) realise the significance of the fountains that appear in all three parts of the triptych, including the Garden of Eden.[11]

It will be helpful first to set such a notion against the wider backdrop of the role of water in creation myths. Although it would be possible to trace similar ideas in other earlier civilisations, it will suffice here to note the parallels with the Hebrew Scriptures in earlier Babylonian origin myths. According to these, the world had its beginnings in a battle between rival supernatural forces, with the ordered world only emerging once the sea monster Tiamat had been defeated. The term *tehom* or 'deep' in the opening chapter of Genesis (1:2) is in fact etymologically related to Tiamat. While in Genesis itself the opposing waters are brought under subjection simply by the divine word, elsewhere in the Hebrew Scriptures the more mythological language of the Babylonian original was retained: 'Thou didst divide the sea by thy strength; thou brakest the heads of the dragons in the waters', as one of the Psalms puts it.[12] Again, although the Bible itself does not provide any explanation of why there was an enormous laver or basin of water outside the Temple,[13] many scholars have connected its presence to the celebration of divine power over the primeval waters, and indeed for some the frequency of the theme in the Psalms points to an annual festival renewing that divine victory.

However, it is the three-decker character of the universe that most clearly introduces the relevance of fountain imagery. The idea was of a huge reservoir of water held in check by the land but also by the great vault of the heavens. Noah's flood is accordingly envisaged as involving not just the opening of windows in the heavens but also 'the fountains of the great deep' (Genesis 7:11). The consequence is of course great destruction, and it is that same destructive capacity that is alluded to in Jonah's description of how 'the depth closes me round about; the weeds were wrapped about my head' (2:5). Equally, it is also just such a literal understanding that is given a corresponding metaphorical force in Psalm 42: 'One deep calleth to another … all thy waves and thy billows are gone over me' (v. 7).

Yet these same waters are also seen as bringing blessing. So, not only are both types of water (in heaven and under the earth) urged to praise their Creator (Psalm 148:4 and 7), but even 'the deep' can be used as a symbol of blessing for father on son, as with Jacob's blessing of Joseph (Genesis 49:25). In understanding such an alternative positive significance, it is important not to think only of the benefits of agriculture. So plentiful was water deemed to be in the primal Garden of Eden that human irrigation proved unnecessary. However, the reason why this was so was explained by two significantly differing traditions depending on whether one followed the Hebrew text (on which the Authorised Version was based), or the Greek Septuagint (treated as authoritative, at least in this case, by Jerome's Latin Vulgate). Thus the Hebrew suggests (at Genesis 2:6) that it is a mist that keeps the land fertile, and it is this image that we find taken up two and half thousand years later by Tennyson. In one of his longer poems he talks of:

> a happy mist
> Like that which kept the heart of Eden green
> Before the useful trouble of the rain.[14]

But more influential in fact was the Septuagint imagery, where the same word is translated as 'fountain' – *fons* in Jerome's Vulgate.[15]

One obvious advantage in the Septuagint version is the way it enables an easy transition to the idea of such a fountain acting as the source of the single river that Genesis describes as eventually dividing into four, and thereby watering all of Eden (2:10–14). Such an idea was eventually taken up by the prophet Ezekiel as he envisaged a restored Temple with the four rivers now flowing from it, suggesting that for him the Temple was seen as at the very centre of the world's creation. Almost certainly the Septuagint is also the inspiration for the Book of Revelation's image of 'a pure river of the water of life' emerging from the throne of God and the Lamb (21:1) – the world's centre now, as it were, residing in a new fountain.

Christ as Water and Fountain of Life

That such symbolism was then used to help make sense of the significance of Christ for us can be established beyond doubt in respect of the later traditions of the Church. Whether it was also part of the intentions behind some of the imagery in John's Gospel can be contested, but here too there is a high probability, not least once we start to take account of how water symbolism is used elsewhere in that gospel. Thus, take the allusion to water and blood flowing from Christ's side.[16] Earlier references in the gospel to water and blood make it unlikely that it is simply a prosaic reference to what actually happened. And, if we are being encouraged to think symbolically, then surely it becomes a much more powerful thought if what pours forth is seen as more like a bountiful fountain than merely some small drops of liquid oozing from Christ's side. That at any rate is how the idea came to be understood throughout medieval literature and art. A good example from the written word comes from the medieval poem *The Pearl*.[17] But it is the same dual reference that one also finds in a famous painting like Van Eyck's *Adoration of the Lamb* in Ghent Cathedral. Although disputes remain about the primary purpose of the painting,[18] beyond doubt is the clear presence of the same double allusion as in *The Pearl*. Although the fact that the fountain and the altar with the Lamb on it are physically separate in this particular painting make modern viewers presuppose unrelated allusions, one to baptism and the other to the Eucharist, an earlier painting by the same artist leave us in no doubt about the real nature of the symbolism involved since there the fountain is filled by a stream flowing from directly under the Lamb that carries numerous Eucharistic wafers in its current.[19] The point is made even more forcibly by pictures of *The Mystic Bath* in which believers bathe in a fountain of water mixed with blood.[20]

In all such adaptations, one contrast with creation imagery is discernible. Whereas in the Septuagint it was a case of destructive waters held in check through a fountain that brings life and blessing, in the New Testament it is out of the actual destruction of a human life that such blessing now comes. Not surprisingly, the Hebrew Scriptures are then ransacked to produce appropriate parallels. One such is the treatment of Marah and Elim, two watering-holes in the wanderings of the Israelites in the desert. After crossing the Red Sea the Israelites stopped at a place where the waters proved bitter, and Moses threw a tree into the water to sweeten them. The result is that the place became known as Marah ('bitter'). Even as late as Tennyson the location is still being used as a symbol for unhappiness. He talks at one point of 'plunging into this bitter world again / these wells of Marah'.[21] But because the next place (Elim) to which the Israelites came had twelve pure wells, it was often seen as a symbol of the need to go through suffering (such as at Marah) to reach joy, and in fact it was on this basis, for example, that the Elim Pentecostal Church got its name.[22]

But can further evidence for such a way of thinking also be found elsewhere in John's Gospel? One possibility to consider is how we read that gospel's accounts of Jesus walking on water (and indeed the parallel passages in the Synoptics). Given the three-decker universe, it looks as if they were intended to imply rather more than just Jesus' power over the elements. For a contemporary there would also inevitably have come to mind mastery over the forces of chaos and evil. So the event once constituted a natural argument for divinity in a way that is much less obvious to us with our quite different understanding of how the universe is structured.

Peter, it is to be noted, fails to walk on the water, not because of any lack of trust in God but in Christ himself, and it is that pattern of exegesis that is followed in the most famous painting based on this theme, Konrad Witz's work of 1444, *The Miraculous Draught of Fishes*, on view in the Musée d'Art et d'Histoire, Geneva. For art historians the painting's importance lies in it being one of the earliest works to depict an actual recognisable country landscape (just outside Geneva), but its historical context is also significant. Geneva was at this time part of the Dukedom of Savoy and it is thought that it was commissioned by a former duke, Amadeus VIII, who had resigned in favour of his sons and retreated to a monastery. Europe had been divided since 1308 between competing popes. The solution proposed by the ecumenical council meeting at Basle was to ask Amadeus as a neutral figure to assume the papacy. This he did in 1439 as Felix V, but, when it became clear that the strategy was not working, he stepped down (in 1449). The contrast in the picture between Christ's majestic confidence and Peter's sinking into the waters is presumably intended to reflect Felix's own doubts and uncertainties about the awesome task he had assumed.[23] But the painting still also echoes that earlier tradition, of Christ as divine controller of the waters. There is not a trace of hesitation in his majestic tread upon the waters.

If any allusion to chaos imagery in the story of Christ walking on the Lake of Galilee is now largely hidden from us, so too is how much more widely fountain imagery in fact extends in the New Testament. For example, according to John's Gospel Christ portrays himself as 'living water'. It is a phrase that is often misunderstood. The implied contrast is not that Jesus is alive, whereas actual physical water is dead. Still less is he counterpoised with stagnant water. Rather, the point seems to be that 'living water' is guaranteed to be running, and so fresh and restorative. In a land like Palestine water was usually in short supply, and considerable reliance had, therefore, to be placed on springs, wells and cisterns.[24] The people's most common source in gathered rain water would not of course be 'active' or on the move. Jesus' promise of 'living water' to the Samaritan woman at the well (John 4:10) can thus be seen to mark a real contrast: Jesus as in effect the new fountain, captured, incidentally, with remarkable effectiveness in Stephen Broadbent's contemporary sculpture of the incident, *The Water of Life*, in the grounds of Chester Cathedral.[25]

Given such wide symbolic resonances, it should therefore come as no surprise that water is also linked elsewhere with Christ's summons to new creation. Because of the background knowledge required, this is usually not noted in respect of the same gospel's treatment of the feast of Tabernacles.[26] But in fact Jesus' earlier depiction of himself as living water fits perfectly with a major theme of this autumn feast: prayers for rain and the unusual rituals associated with such a plea. During the seven days of the feast, each day a priest would carry a golden pitcher down to the fountain of Gihon that supplied the pool of Siloam (the source of the Temple's water supply), and then bring it up filled with water to be poured out in front of the Temple's main altar.[27] It must have been an impressive ritual, but it was reinforced by the imagery of renewal that the prophet Zechariah also associated with this feast. A fountain, he promises, will open up to cleanse Jerusalem, and living waters flow out from the city as far as the Mediterranean on one side and the Dead Sea on the other.[28] It is worth observing at this point that, given how widespread such creation imagery was both in the Hebrew Scriptures and in Jewish liturgical practice and tradition, it is not impossible that Paul's imagery of dying with Christ in baptism and rising again (Romans 6:1–11; Colossians 2:12) is actually drawing on rather more than the metaphor of drowning and then being saved. It might also suggest going down into the waters of chaos and coming up again as living water, and so be much closer to John after all.

Architecture and Art Preserving Wider Resonances for Water and Baptism

Hitherto my examples of the application of such creation imagery beyond Scripture have been either literary or artistic. In both Christianity and Islam, however, there was an impact on architecture as well, in particular on gardens. The Qur'an in fact describes several times how Paradise is divided by four rivers that intersect in a basin of water that is their source.[29] It seems to me highly probable that it was such texts that directly generated the basic quadrant notion (*chahar bagh*) that was to characterise later Islamic gardens, though nowadays some scholars suggest a more indirect history, mediated through similarly structured Roman gardens and the Muslim practice of placing tombs in them.[30] Either way, certainly by four centuries after the death of Muhammad the theme of them as imitations of the paradise to come became increasingly common, not only in actual gardens but also in poetry. The net effect was to ensure that within Islam water ceased to be just a sign of purification. It also spoke firmly of the delights and joys to come for the faithful.

Although they were without the accompanying streams, monastic cloisters were often divided by four paths and similarly viewed as positive places for retreat, restoration and renewal, with the four quadrants seen as representing the earthly reality as it ought to be. Not that the symbolism of water was entirely ignored, since usually there was either a basin or fountain of water somewhere, and sometimes at the cloister's centre. This was especially so among the Cistercians.[31] In southern Europe the fountains were usually quite elaborate, with water cascading from a higher basin to a lower, and the whole thing roofed sometimes by means of projecting stonework from the cloister's edge.[32] Inevitably, given such a plentiful supply of water, the cloister also became associated with other functions. Ablutions took place here, together sometimes with associated symbolism. So, for instance, the Rule of Benedict specifies that the two monks finishing and beginning a week of kitchen duties were on the Saturday to wash the feet of all their fellow monks.[33] Later monastic writers applied both positive and negative metaphors to such cloisters. For Honorius Augustodunensis (d. 1157) 'the cloister represents paradise ... the fountain and tree of life designate Christ'; for Peter of Celle (d. 1183), as well as being a substitute for the cross and a torture rack, the cloister and its fountain is like being saved in the ark with Noah, surviving the belly of the whale with Jonah, being consecrated in the maternal womb like Jeremiah and awaiting the descent of the Spirit with the apostles.[34] Although this sounds like hopeless over-determination of the meaning of the image, the advantage was that it successfully captured every mood that monks might encounter in their daily perambulation, and so water in its negative aspects is brought to bear, no less than in its more positive.

Another image that came frequently to mind was that of the Virgin Mary. Pictorial representations of her as the *hortus conclusus* or 'enclosed garden' often include a fountain as part of the complex network of allusions that built upon imagery from the Song of Songs, not least because a fountain was mentioned in the key verse: 'A garden enclosed is my sister, my spouse; a spring shut up, a fountain sealed' (4.12). While the need to place Mary centrally in the pictorial frame usually militated against any clear representation of the four quadrants associated with a Paradise garden,[35] there would seem little doubt that monks and nuns would have made the connection nonetheless when walking their cloisters. Like the water bubbling up from the fountain in their midst, Mary could be seen as the source of their own Christian life in the child that comes tumbling forth from her womb.

The richness of allusion in the Song of Songs imagery, however, became more muddled – roughly from about the fourteenth to the seventeenth century – because of the increasing popularity of the idea that Mary was devoid of original sin, and so born 'immaculate', and the resultant need to find some corresponding pictorial representation. Although not formally made a dogma until 1854 and opposed by a number of distinguished theologians (among them Bernard, Bonaventure and Aquinas), the notion had been steadily growing in popularity over several centuries. Eventually the iconographic issue was resolved when the Spaniard Francesco Pacheco proposed Mary's identification with the Woman of the Apocalypse in Revelation 12, with twelve stars round her head and the moon at her feet.[36] But in the mean time confusion reigned, and so until the seventeenth century we find the imagery from the Song of Songs frequently usurped for this narrower purpose. A good example of the resultant confusion is the long-standing misidentification of a painting by El Greco in Toledo as the assumption, when in fact a fountain in a bottom corner clearly indicates the immaculate conception as the real topic.[37]

So, such cosmological imagery could at times be confusing as well as creative. Even so, that hardly undermines my main point, which is a richness to the past use of water symbolism which is now largely lost but which did succeed in preventing Christians of the past from reading its use in baptism too narrowly, even though the words of the liturgy were now largely directly to the elimination of original sin.

One indication that architecture and art continued to preserve wider symbolic resonances for water beyond mere cleansing is provided by the types of buildings produced for baptism and the art that came to be associated with them. Until the pressure for immediate baptism of the newly born child became too intense to resist any longer, separate baptisteries were in fact common, in which the sacrament was celebrated infrequently but with great splendour as large numbers were baptised together, usually on Easter Eve.[38] Even in the earliest-known surviving church from *c.* 240, at Dura Europos in Syria, there was a separate baptistery. What is especially surprising is the extraordinary range of imagery to be found in the room. Of the seven images, none are of Jesus' own baptism, though two do refer to water: the woman at the well in Samaria and Jesus and Peter walking on the water. In addition there was a canopy painted blue with accompanying stars. The natural inference to draw is surely that the event was presumed to be of cosmic significance, even if one of the other images (Adam and Eve with the serpent) did apply a more backward-looking allusion. Again, in the surviving mosaics at another early baptistery (Butrint in modern Albania) initiates were welcomed by the sight of peacocks surrounding a vase overflowing with vine tendrils, while in the distance they could see stags drinking at a fountain, the one image symbolising immortality through the Eucharist, the other refreshment and renewal through baptism.[39]

Slightly later in date are the two baptisteries at Ravenna, where images of Christ's own baptism are at last to be found. Placed in the cupola is a depiction of Christ immersed to his waist in diaphanous water, with John the Baptist above him on a rock. Ironically, thanks to an incorrect nineteenth-century restoration, the Orthodox baptistery is now less accurate than the Arian. In the former John already pours water over Jesus' head, whereas in the latter he merely rests his hand upon the head, presumably prior to the act of immersion. More relevant, though, to our overall theme is the inclusion in the Orthodox version of a personified River Jordan. Almost certainly an allusion to the liturgy of the Eastern Church, it speaks of the defeat of supernatural forces opposed to God in this baptism, as in these words from Compline: 'Of old the prince of this world was named king also of all that was in the waters; but by thy cleansing he is choked and destroyed, as Legion by the lake.'[40] Admittedly, the cosmological force of the imagery is greatly weakened by the decidedly unthreatening character of the god of the river. Nonetheless, the conservatism of Eastern Christendom has meant that even to this day such a figure, threatening or otherwise, is quite often included in icons of Christ's baptism and thus a reminder provided of this richer range of reference, even if it is now usually supplemented by trinitarian allusions such as three angels on one side and the heavenly light round the dove of the Holy Spirit forking into three.[41]

Of later baptisteries, undoubtedly those at Florence and Pisa are now the best known. The round shape of some early baptisteries seems to have been modelled on the common adoption of this shape for mausoleums in the ancient world. The intention was thus to imply that the water brought about a death to the old order, and it is this form that we in fact find at Pisa. More common, however, was the use of an octagonal shape, where a forward-looking allusion seems primary, given the traditional use of the eighth day to symbolise the beginning of new life. This was the form given to the Lateran Baptistery that Emperor Constantine founded in Rome, and which is the oldest baptistery still functioning. It is also the shape we find at Florence, which was probably first built in the following century but whose present form dates from the eleventh. It is a magnificent building with numerous renowned works of art, including on the outside Sansovino's sculpture of the baptism of Christ, Andrea Pisano's doors representing scenes from the life of John the Baptist and Ghiberti's so-called Paradise Doors.[42] Much of this imagery is not specifically related to baptism but to the Christian story more generally. However, it is worth noting that those more general themes are there because of the central place that baptism was seen to hold in the scheme of things. In earlier times baptism took place only a few times a year, and even then had to be performed either personally by the bishop or at the very least in his presence. So baptisteries were attached only to cathedrals, and when not in use were officially closed by use of the bishop's seal. Although the detailed form of the ceremony changed in numerous ways over the course of the centuries, it was not until the end of the nineteenth

74 *The Power of Symbols*

century that the diocese of Florence finally allowed baptism elsewhere than in its central baptistery.

The use of large amounts of water in such baptisteries helped to suggest a cosmological dimension which gradually faded in the parish churches of the West as sprinkling replaced immersion. Even to this day, baptism is by total immersion in the East, and so it was also in the West throughout the first millennium. Indeed, it is fascinating to reflect what a different history there might have been, had Western European translations not followed the Vulgate and so transliterated the Greek *baptizo* rather than translated it, for literally it entails total immersion. Similarly, *baptisterion* would have acquired some such term as meant elsewhere a bathing or swimming pool. Indeed, even to this day the Romance languages contain just such a reminder, in the term for the large fonts in baptisteries, which is *piscina* (literally, 'fish pond').

However, the wider range of symbolism was not entirely lost in the second millennium, as can be seen by considering some specific cases of the treatment of baptism in Western art. Among the most intriguing is Piero della Francesca's *Baptism of Christ* (c. 1460), now in the National Gallery in London. The picture is replete with a symbolism that suggests so much more than simply a backward-looking reference.[43] Christ himself stands on dry ground, the River Jordan having been driven back, just as had happened when an earlier figure of the same name had led the Israelites across the river into the Promised Land.[44] Healing plants also abound on the banks, while the three angels on the left are not there simply to reinforce the usual trinitarian reference, but also to help allude to one of the other two liturgical celebrations of Christ's Epiphany or 'manifestation' as God. In this case, the way one angel rests his arm on his neighbour's shoulder recalls medieval betrothal ceremonies, and thus indirectly the wedding at Cana, while in the background three figures (the wise men) can be seen journeying across the picture frame. Then the nut tree under which Christ stands alludes not only to the cross (hard on the outside but with soft fruit within) but also helped to engage locals, since the painting was originally commissioned for Spoleto in the Valle del Nuce or 'Nut Valley'. So, all in all there are more pointers to the future than there are to the necessity of removing sin. The latter idea is of course present in the allusion to the cross, but precisely because Christ was sinless the pressure was to look elsewhere for the main point.

In the seventeenth century perhaps the finest depiction of Christ's baptism is to be found as part of Nicholas Poussin's two series on the Seven Sacraments. Somewhat surprisingly, there are relatively few detailed discussions,[45] in particular of the quite different approach he adopts between the two compositions. A consistent feature of both series is Poussin's desire to draw us back into the historical reality of the world at the time of Christ, and make incidents come alive for us in that way. In some of the other paintings this is much more obvious, as with the *Eucharist*, where the scene is of a Last Supper in which the typical dining pattern of the ancient world is employed, with reclining couches and one side left free for access by the servants. In the case of the two *Baptisms*, however, the differences are perhaps more pronounced than the recurring similarities.[46] Whereas in the earlier work Jesus is standing to the side to receive baptism, in the later painting not only does he kneel but also he is placed at the painting's centre. While undoubtedly this helps in ease of reading the canvas, as do the hands of the spectators on the right conspicuously pointing to the sky, to indicate the source of the unseen voice from heaven, the theme of old life renewed and transformed has been considerably weakened. Since the old man at the centre of the earlier work is scarcely able to stand without the young boy's support, inevitably a symbolic role is suggested. In the later painting, however, it is now a young adult who kneels alongside him, and in a less obviously supporting role. So viewers are far more likely to think of young and old alike called to baptism, rather than of any underlying notion of the transformational change that seems so crucial to the earlier canvas's interpretation. Yet, even though the high aesthetic quality of both paintings can scarcely be doubted, there is none of the richness of symbolic allusion that Piero provided. Even physical frailty as a symbol for sin seems questionable, which is perhaps why it is omitted in the later version of the painting.

Where Poussin was innovative was in his use of a pointing bystander to indicate the Father's unseen voice, instead of the usual convention of both Father and Spirit being represented by images. Presumably, it represents Poussin's attempt, as in other ways, to return to the sources but in this he had few followers. It is an instance that well illustrates how Bible, liturgical practice and representational image do not always march closely hand in hand. Ready adoption of such an assumption can all too easily lead astray, as in the common presumption that the reason why Christ was no longer portrayed immersed in water was simply because of changes in post-biblical baptismal practice. In fact, the two changes do not seem to have proceeded at the same pace. More likely in explaining artistic practice is an issue that Matthew's Gospel had already raised, namely whether Christ needed baptism in any case.[47] In other words, might his baptism not have been just representative? If so, the notional bowing of the head and gentle sprinkling of water would exactly catch the presumed meaning.

While almost all the best-known paintings of baptism are of Christ's own, this is not of course to deny the existence of many portraying individual Christians being baptised, both adult and infant.[48] However, most provide few hints of wider meaning, except in one aspect now largely forgotten, and that is through the status of godparents. With the determination of the number of sacraments at seven, inevitably some baptismal paintings were commissioned as part of this theme. In England only very few representations survive, with about fifty on baptismal fonts, all bar two in East Anglia.[49] It has been suggested that their prominence is indicative of counter-moves against Lollard distrust of sacraments.[50] By contrast on the continent the aim was usually educational, and the most common pattern a large central painting of the Eucharist with the other six portrayed in surrounding panels.

76   *The Power of Symbols*

Perhaps the most famous is one painted by Rogier van der Weyden for the Bishop of Tournai in the mid-fifteenth century. Its central panel has Christ on the Cross with the four Marys and John beneath, all placed within a light and spacious Gothic church in which a priest can be seen in the distance celebrating mass.[51] The two smaller side panels are then allocated three sacraments each, with on the left baptism, confirmation and confession in that order. A modern viewer, seeing the way in which the priest is deliberately set to one side, is likely to suspect that the aim is simply to complement the godparents, who are now in full view. But rather more than the flattery of specific individuals is in play, as their positioning actually represents the legal importance of godparents at this time. The issue is perhaps seen even more clearly in another Seven Sacraments series from three centuries later. Although the painter (Giuseppe Maria Crespi) has the priest using a large spoon to pour water over the child, it is the godmother's firm hand on the child's back that the viewer first notices, as she pushes it forward over the basin.[52] There is none of the cradling in the priest's arms that was to become the fashion later. Yet to talk of legalities is to put matters altogether too weakly. In effect, thanks to baptism the child was being moved to a new community of social influences (represented by the godparents) that would radically shape its future. Gradually over the centuries the language of co-parents, with correlative rights and responsibilities, had emerged, with much expected of godparents both spiritually and socially. Indeed, so seriously was the parallel treated that from the code of Justinian (530) onwards prohibited areas of sexual contact came to be modelled on those applying to the natural parents.

Thus in short, so far from focusing exclusively on the washing away of sin, art and architecture encouraged a much wider range of reference than was true of modern baptismal practice until relatively recently, when churches once more sought to reduce the number of references to original sin and widen the range of reference elsewhere.[53]

The Contemporary Situation

Thanks to the various liturgical movements of the twentieth century public baptism has once again become the norm. In modern churches much thought was given to the symbolism of fonts, while ministers working in older buildings sought to enhance the significance of the sacrament with additional imagery, such as anointing and presentation of candles.[54] However, it cannot be claimed that the Church has succeeded in fully recovering the richness of past allusions. Of course, in some respects at least, that would be an impossibility in any case. Thus we can scarcely return to a three-decker universe, or to the meaning that fountains would once have conjured in believers' minds. Nonetheless, it comes as a surprise that sometimes contemporary artists have recaptured that past richness better than liturgical scholars, or the Church more generally.

So, for example, although Anthony Gormley has now lost all trace of the Catholicism of his youth, his sculpture of 1986 in Winchester Cathedral crypt of a man deep in water (*Sound II*) possesses just such a nice ambiguity about it. At the most basic level it leads one to think of the potential of this part of the building to flood, and so of the individual to drown, but also because the figure is contemplating some of the water which he holds in his hands, further meanings are thus implied, and viewers of the sculpture invited to think well beyond its setting. It was on the same ambiguity that Bill Viola (who is more sympathetic to religion) played in Durham Cathedral in the same year, in his video installation *The Messenger*. The image of the naked man diving down and coming up again hints not only at the narrow sense of Paul's meaning in Romans 6, of drowning and of being brought back to life, but also at the wider cosmological metaphor that I suggested was also implied, of the waters of chaos being replaced by the water that gives new life.

I want to end, though, with the work of the Russian film director Andrei Tarkovsky. It is his use of water that most nearly approaches the earlier tradition. Water is in fact a significant symbol in quite a number of his films. To take a simpler case to begin with, in *Ivan's Childhood* (1962) the boy hero is faced with a brooding lake as the test for his manhood and resolve. It is a medium through which he has already successfully passed, unlike his mother and sister, both of whom have been murdered by the German occupying forces. But, even as he dreams of how in the past he played with his sister by the sea, he knows that he must once more cross the lake to an uncertain future and indeed, as it turns out, to his own eventual torture and death.

However, somewhat surprisingly, it is in a science fiction film, *Solaris* (1972), that Tarkovsky experiments most with water as symbol. The story begins for the central character in his lakeside home but progresses quickly to the alien ocean exercising its destructive capacity on the crew of a spaceship, its 'neutrons' manipulating their minds and their memories. Through this process the scientist concerned eventually comes to some kind of understanding of himself and of his proper place in the world. This is represented in the film's conclusion, back at his home. The seething currents of the ocean are replaced by at first gentle water but then by rain that falls even inside the house, all culminating in reconciliation of father and son. It is hard not to make such a description sound either absurd or trite, but anyone who watches the three-hour epic from beginning to end cannot but be impressed by the way in which apparently mysterious contradictory meanings for water as threat and as healing resolve in the film's conclusion.[55]

Conclusion

Some historians of the Church's worship may well take exception to the general thrust of this essay, and argue that the wider implications of baptism

78 *The Power of Symbols*

have always been present in the Church's liturgical practice. If so, even they would need to concede that they have been somewhat muted, and that it is only really with the reforms of the twentieth century that they have returned to prominence. My point in any case is not that these elements ever entirely disappeared from practice but that they were preserved more effectively elsewhere, in the symbols of art, architecture and poetry, and that even today a gifted film director or video artist can sometimes make the point more powerfully than much of the rather pedestrian language on which the Church still relies.[56]

Notes

1 For example, Mark 1:4; Acts 13:24.
2 Matthew 3:13–15.
3 For example, Acts 2:38; 10:43.
4 For example, John 3:1–6.
5 For example, Romans 6:3–4.
6 For children as sinless, e.g. Hermas, *Similitudes*, 9:29.1–3; Athenagoras, *On the Resurrection*, 14 (though possibly not by Athenagoras). For infant baptism in the third century, Origen, *Commentary on Romans*, 5:9; Cyprian, *Epistle*, 58. Although he opposes the practice, Tertullian at the beginning of that same century is already acknowledging its existence: *On Baptism*, 18. In view of Jesus' positive comments on children, Augustine was willing to concede that they would only suffer 'the mildest condemnation' (*De peccatorum meritis*, 1.16.21). Even so, he insists that they can only be saved through baptism (1.18.23).
7 So e.g. Tertullian describes later confession of sin as 'a second penance': *De Paenitentia*, 4.
8 Inevitably, the history is more complicated than I suggest in the main text. What concerns me there is general tendencies rather than details. But for those details, some pulling against the predominant trend, see e.g. Edward Yarnold, *The Awe-Inspiring Rites of Initiation* (Slough: St Paul Publications, 1971); Maxwell E. Johnson, ed., *Living Water, Sealing Spirit* (Collegeville, Minn.: Liturgical Press, 1995); J. D. C. Fisher, *Christian Initiation: Baptism in the Medieval West* (London: SPCK, 1965); Hughes Oliphant Old, *The Shaping of the Reformed Baptismal Rite in the Sixteenth Century* (Grand Rapids, Mich.: Eerdmans, 1992).
9 Ch. 5. Much of the relevant section is reprinted in David Brown and David Fuller, *Signs of Grace: Sacraments in Poetry and Prose* (London: Continuum, 2000), 26–27.
10 Thomas Hardy, *Tess of the d'Urbervilles* (1892), ch. 14.
11 For detailed illustrations, Wilhelm Fraenger, *Bosch* (Amsterdam: G + B Arts International, 1999), 64–107.
12 Psalm 74:13 (AV). The theme continues in the following verse; cf. also Psalm 89:9–10.
13 Exodus 30:18; 1 Kings 7:23ff.
14 'Geraint and Enid', 768–770 (Part of *Idylls of the King*).
15 'There went up a mist from the earth, and watered the whole face of the ground' (AV); '*fons ascendebat e terra, irrigans universam superficiem terrae*' (Vulgate).
16 John 19:34.
17 Line 649; cf. 1055–1056; with John 19:34 as the ultimate point of reference.
18 For some art critics the primary aim of the painting was to reinforce clerical authority. See, for example, Craig Harbison, *Jan Van Eyck: The Play of Realism*

(London: Reaktion, 1991), esp. 193–197, where Olivier de Langhe is postulated as theological adviser. The use of the papal tiara for God the Father might seem to support this view. Others, though, assign a more creative role to the artist himself, including the influence of new forms of lay piety. See Otto Pächt, *Van Eyck and the Founders of Early Netherlandish Painting* (London: Harvey Miller, 1999), 119–170.
19 Only a copy now survives in the Prado: ibid., 133. For the purposes of simplicity, I assume a single artist though it is often argued that both brothers were involved.
20 As e.g. in the painting of that name by the fifteenth-century artist Jean Bellegambe of Douai.
21 From his play *Becket*.
22 Contrast Exodus 15:23 and 15:27. Elim was founded in 1915 by the Welshman, George Jeffreys.
23 There is a good general discussion in R.-M. and R. Hagen, *What Great Paintings Say* (Cologne: Taschen, 1997), III: 12–17.
24 Of course a well is not quite the same thing as a fountain but they are related, the fountain's waters drawing from the earth as from a well.
25 There may also be a further point. The promise of running water is also the promise of an end to the usually female but back-breaking task of drawing water from deep wells. Notice the woman's implied delight about no longer needing to come to the well: 4:15.
26 John 7:2, 37–38.
27 For an account of the feast, Raymond Brown, *The Gospel According to John* (New York: Anchor Bible, 1966), I: 326–327.
28 Zechariah 9–14, esp. 13:1 and 14:8.
29 For the four rivers e.g. Qur'an 47:15; for a fountain, 15:45.
30 D. Fairchild Ruggles, *Islamic Gardens and Landscapes* (Philadelphia: University of Pennsylvania Press, 2008). For Roman influence, 40–41; for placing of tombs in such gardens, 103–116.
31 For reasons of cold in northern Europe long basins or troughs were usually substituted, and placed somewhere on the wall of the cloister gallery.
32 Terryl N. Kinder, *Cistercian Europe: Architecture of Contemplation* (Grand Rapids, Mich.: Eerdmans, 2002), 137–138; for some illustrations (from Poblet, Zwettl and Maulbronn), plate 6, xii–xvi.
33 *Rule of St Benedict* 35:7–9; clearly based on John 13.
34 The images from Honorius' *Gemma animae* and Peter's *De disciplina claustrali* are discussed in Daniel Faure and Veronique Rouchon Mouilleron, *Cloisters of Europe: Gardens of Prayer* (New York: Viking, 2001), 28.
35 A possible exception is the Master of the St Lucy Legend's *Virgin of the Rose Garden* (now in the Detroit Institute of Arts). The waters of Bruges in the background may be intended to suggest Mary's four companions similarly dividing the garden into quadrants. I am grateful to Chris Brewer for this observation.
36 In his *Art of Painting* of 1649.
37 Illustrated in David Davies *et al.*, *El Greco* (New Haven: Yale University Press, 2003), 201.
38 Christmas and Pentecost were subsequently added.
39 Cf. Psalm 42:1. Dating from the early sixth century, the site was discovered in 1928.
40 For this and many other relevant liturgical allusions, John Baggley, *Festival Icons for the Christian Year* (London: Mowbray, 2000) 48–57, esp. 53.
41 For two versions of the fork, Konrad Onasch and Annemarie Schnieper, *Icons: The Fascination and the Reality* (New York: Riverside, 1995), 67 and

80 *The Power of Symbols*

      107. The second not only includes the god of the river Jordan but St Thecla being saved from drowning by a bear.
42 Sansovino's original is in fact in the Cathedral Museum.
43 For an illustration and discussion of some of these details, Marilyn Aronberg Lavin, *Piero della Francesca* (London: Thames & Hudson, 1992), 62–66.
44 'Jesus' is the Greek equivalent of the Hebrew name, 'Joshua'.
45 See in particular Tony Green, *Nicholas Poussin Paints the Seven Sacraments Twice* (Watchet: Paravail, 2000), esp. 42–48, 78–93, 244–261. The second series is the only one which remains a unity in a single place (at the National Gallery in Edinburgh).
46 To view the two paintings side by side, ibid., illustrations 16 and 17.
47 Matthew 3:13–15.
48 The adult baptisms are usually conversions in the early history of the Church.
49 The eighth side is devoted either to Christ's baptism or to his crucifixion.
50 Ann Eljenholm Nichols, *Seeable Signs: The Iconography of the Seven Sacraments 1350–1544* (Woodbridge: Boydell, 1994), esp. 90–128.
51 The painting is now in Antwerp's Fine Art Museum. The bishop in question (Jean Chevrot, bishop from 1436 to 1460), can be seen administering confirmation.
52 Dating from 1712, the series is now in Dresden. For an illustration, Andreas Henning and Scott Schaeffer, eds, *Captured Emotions: Baroque Painting in Bologna* (Los Angeles: Paul Getty Museum, 2008), no. 32.
53 Modern Roman Catholic liturgy now only has one solitary reference to original sin.
54 The symbolism of fonts is explored in Regina Kuehn, *A Place for Baptism* (Chicago: Liturgy Training Publications, 1992). For two examples of effective symbolism in fonts old and new, 18 and 62. A particularly impressive example is the font designed by William Pye that was installed in Salisbury Cathedral in 2008.
55 Terence Mallick's more recent 2011 film *The Tree of Life* also uses images of water to suggest connections of cosmological significance.
56 I am grateful to Professor David Knight, Professor of the History and Philosophy of Science at Durham University, for asking me to contribute to a series of public lectures which he organised on the general theme of water in 2010, and which led to this hitherto unpublished essay.

6 'The darkness and the light are both alike to thee'
Finding God in Limited Light and in Darkness

'Light of Light, very God of very God' is what Christians affirm in their recitation of the Nicene Creed week by week. From such an assertion it is but an easy step to suppose that the divine should always be identified with unqualified light. But, as I hope to demonstrate in this essay, symbols are seldom that simple. Not that I want to deny that within the biblical tradition and subsequently 'light' is almost always used to symbolise divine integrity, truth and goodness, with 'darkness' then applied to all that is evil and opposed to God.[1] Occasionally, however, some different patterns emerge, and it is these that I want to explore in this essay. Symbols naturally encourage exploration more readily than literal language through opening up unexpected possibilities, as when apparently contradictory images are permitted with God described, for example, as both rock and water, or as both shepherd and lamb. Similarly then here, as we shall see, God has been associated not just with brilliant or clear light but also with dim light, a cloudy sky, shadow and even pitch darkness. Nor is it the case that, even where light alone is employed, the meaning is always the same. For example, light is not always used to suggest clarity, but sometimes its dazzle is portrayed as having similar effects to darkness itself.

In exploring some of these transformations I shall begin with two examples from the biblical world. Thereafter, I shall take a rather different pair from the world of art and architecture, before concluding with consideration of a number of contrasting approaches to light in the modern, scientific world.

The Biblical World: Darkness and Divine Mystery

Here I want to offer two case studies; first, at greater length, the identification of God with darkness, and then much more briefly, a similar identification with cloud and shadow. In both cases subsequent exegesis modified the original meaning in illuminating ways, but not so as to exclude altogether continuing relevance for the original meaning. Admittedly, in respect of the first, it would be possible to argue on the basis of the psalm from which my title is drawn (139:12) that no more is meant in the Old Testament passages that equate God with darkness than that God's presence is to be found everywhere, even in the darkness; so darkness then becomes as day. But that rather more than this seems indicated soon becomes apparent once note is taken of how darkness may even have been the primal image for God. Divine mystery will then be the primary connotation.

Thus even in the creation story God's presence in the world antedates creation of light: 'darkness was on the face of the deep; and the spirit of God moved upon the face of the waters' (Genesis 1:4). Although in its present context the verse is relatively late (according to source criticism, part of P's creation narrative), its assumption of an antecedent chaos rather than *creatio ex nihilo* argues for adaptation from earlier material. Certainly, in an indisputably early passage (Genesis 15) that describes God's inaugural covenant with his chosen people the strange ritual of the 'cutting' of the covenant takes place only when the sun had gone down (v. 17).[2] Although the smoking fire pot and flaming torch that are described as passing between the various animal sacrifices are no doubt intended to indicate divine endorsement of the covenant, even so they do so in a context of darkness and mystery rather than unqualified light.

Turn now to a better-known divine appearance, on Mount Sinai, and a similar complexity is to be observed. Because of Paul's various allusions to the incident (2 Corinthians 3:7; 4:6), Christians are likely to think first of how the skin of Moses' face shone when he came down from the holy mountain (Exodus 34:30), and the greater glory that now shines on the face of Christ. But in its immediate context we are told how, in order to encounter God, Moses had to enter a descending cloud (34:5) that at the earlier giving of the Decalogue had been described as 'thick darkness' (20:21), accompanied by 'thunderings and lightnings' (20:18).[3] Nor are we left in any doubt as to the point in this context: 'when the people saw it, they trembled, and stood afar off'. Darkness is thus once again being used to evoke the divine, and with it an accompanying sense of awe and mystery.

Equally, the application of light and darkness to the Temple is not quite as straightforward as may initially appear. Certainly there are plenty of passages, especially in the Psalms, that speak of the presence of a divine glory in ways that make it natural to interpret such glory in terms of the splendour of light (e.g. 26:8; 63:2), while others allow of no other alternative. Ezekiel, for example, tells us that the earth 'shines' with such glory (43:2). Yet in the two key passages describing the dedication of the Temple under Solomon, that same 'glory' is interpreted as 'deep darkness': 'When the priests came out of the holy place, a cloud filled the house of the Lord, so that the priests could not stand to minister because of the cloud; for the glory of the Lord filled the house of the Lord. Then Solomon said, The Lord has set the sun in the heavens, and has said that he would dwell in thick darkness' (1 Kings 8:10–12).[4] One way of reconciling these two views is to look to the more literal meaning of the Hebrew word for 'glory' (*kabod*), with its notion of a 'weight' or what overwhelms, for light or darkness might thus have very similar effects.

Both brilliant light and impenetrable darkness might 'weigh' or 'press down' on the human observer in similar ways, creating awe and fear.

But, that said, it is still worth pursuing further the question of why darkness might nonetheless have once been the preferred image, to represent the divine. It may have had something to do with the features that differentiated the Temple from other such structures in the ancient world. Admittedly, in most respects it was remarkably similar. As with temples in the ancient world more generally, animal sacrifice and other forms of worship took place out of doors, while the building itself remained reserved as a dwelling place for the deity. So the Temple at Jerusalem was by no means unique in this respect. Where the difference lay was in the absence of any symbolic representation of the deity, with no statue of YHWH to compare with that of Athena on the Acropolis, or of Zeus at Olympia. Instead, in the Holy of Holies the place between the sculpted Cherubim and above the Ark of the Covenant remained vacant. Not that these were the only forms of decoration, but it was all shrouded in darkness, since the building as a whole lacked any proper windows, while this, the smaller and more sacred part, was separated by a curtain from the main source of light in the building, the seven-branched candlestick known as the menorah. Even here, the seven lights seem scarcely adequate for so large a building, and so suggest a marked contrast from, for example, Olympia, where various means were employed to augment visibility and luminosity.[5]

The nineteenth-century New Testament scholar and Bishop of Durham B. F. Westcott, in an appendix to one of his commentaries, wrestles with the question of why such differences should have existed. In what is a fascinating essay he argues that the darkness in the Holy of Holies must play a key role in any adequate Christian approach to art. Commenting on the apparent violation of the second commandment in the Temple's contents, he observes that the ancient Israelite

> learnt from the records of the Old Testament that it was the Divine will that in the unapproachable darkness of the Holy of Holies the costliest works of Art should render service before the revealed presence of the Lord. No human eye could rightfully ever again trace the lineaments of those cherubims [sic] and palm trees and open flowers when they were once placed in the oracle, but it was enough to know that they were there. In no other way could the Truth be more eloquently or solemnly enforced that the end of Art is to witness to the inner life of Nature and to minister to God. ... Philosophers and poets have dwelt upon the veiled statue at Sais; there is an open secret in the sacred gloom of the Holy of Holies more sublime and inspiring.[6]

In short, for Westcott the Temple strikes a body blow to the notion of art as imitation. It is not there to copy, but to point beyond itself to the underlying spiritual character of the visible world and its eventual transfiguration under

God. The merely partial veiling of a deity like Neit at the Egyptian temple of Sais was thus a poor hint of what the Temple expressed more profoundly in its far deeper veil of darkness.[7]

As a matter of fact, it is doubtful whether Westcott's analysis can be sustained. Artistic representation was after all found elsewhere in the Temple, and not just in this dark place. Taking their cue from later Jewish writers, many commentators now find in the art of the Temple deliberate cosmological allusions, with the menorah, for example, intended to represent the then seven known planets and the laver or basin of water outside the Temple the waters held back at creation.[8] If so, the emphasis might be more on the mystery already inherent in creation rather than a mysterious transcendence or future transfiguration. However, either way, the art, like the darkness, was not intended to explain but rather to enhance a sense of mystery. Just as the laver and menorah point beyond themselves, so does the darkness: a God present in the Holy of Holies yet not penetrated or contained.

The image is thus the very opposite of the Prologue to St John's Gospel, where the positions of light and darkness are reversed, with darkness unable to penetrate or contain the Light (1:5). Later in his Prologue (at v. 14) John uses temple imagery to describe Christ 'tabernacling' among us. So it could be that he is deliberately inverting Old Testament imagery here, in order to suggest the different character of the divine presence that is now in our midst. The Logos is here to bring clarity and intelligibility to our lives rather than mystery. Certainly, that is how Light functions throughout the rest of John's Gospel.

But divine mystery of course continued to be a key element within Christian theological understanding of the divine. So it is not surprising that mystical theology in particular wrestled with the exegesis of such passages, and in particular with the question of whether the heart of the divine presence could best be described as light or darkness.[9] One patristic tradition deriving from Origen and followed by Gregory of Nazianzus, had it triumphed, might well have resulted in exclusive use of light imagery and unqualified optimism about the possibilities of transcending human limitations in a joyful union. But in the end it was Gregory of Nyssa's account of Moses' two experiences on Mount Sinai that was the more influential.[10] Light, he maintains, is succeeded by darkness because darkness reveals the more fundamental reality:

> When, therefore, Moses grew in knowledge, he declared that he had seen God in the darkness, that is, that he had then come to know that what is divine is beyond all knowledge and comprehension, for the text says, *Moses approached the dark cloud where God was*. What God? He who *made darkness his hiding place*, as David says, who also was initiated into the mysteries in the same inner sanctuary.[11]

In other words, what is sought is envisaged as an experience that 'transcends all knowledge, being separated on all sides by incomprehensibility, as by a kind of darkness'.[12]

The result was a tension transmitted to all subsequent writers, with some attempting reconciliation between the images of light and darkness, and others not. Denys the Areopagite is the most noted reconciler. Although he follows Gregory of Nyssa in accepting that all ends in a 'truly mysterious darkness of unknowing', he gives the expression a much more positive and intimate aspect than Gregory had seemed prepared to allow.[13] So the final result is one in which the individual concerned 'belongs completely to him who is beyond everything ... united by a completely unknowing inactivity of all knowledge, and knows beyond the mind by knowing nothing'. While such language verges on the incoherent, what Dionysius seems to want to affirm is that the union is an affective and ecstatic one, but inexplicable in words. As he promises elsewhere, 'shedding all and freed from all, you will be uplifted to the ray of the divine shadow which is above everything that is'.[14] Indeed, that talk of 'a ray from a shadow' is even more prominent in the words with which his *Mystical Theology* begins, where darkness is almost in effect equated with light: 'the mysteries of God's Word lie ... in the brilliant darkness of a hidden silence. Amid the deepest shadow they pour overwhelming light on what is most manifest.' Dazzling light can of course have the same effect as deep darkness in preventing vision. Paul's experience on the Damascus Road is a case in point.[15] But I think that probably rather more is implied here. Verbalised, intellectual knowledge has been denied, but not the warmth of personal intuitive insight that cannot be so expressed. So the brilliant ray lifts up the believer into the divine presence, but not in a way communicable to others.

By no means all, however, followed Denys. A more negative strain (that was probably also the position of Gregory of Nyssa) continued into the Western medieval tradition, and can be found in the German Meister Eckhart and the English mystical treatise *The Cloud of Unknowing*.[16] Some modern exegetes see in such writers a denial of even the possibility of any human experience of God.[17] In my view that is to go too far. Nonetheless, the experience is clearly quite different from later talk of 'the dark night of the soul', as in St John of the Cross. This alludes to the penultimate stage of encounter before the deepest affective relationship is formed. The term is intended to describe how, as the soul draws closer to God, it becomes ever more aware of its own unworthiness, and so of the yawning gap that exists between divinity and humanity, unable to be crossed without divine aid. Nonetheless, divine love can draw our wills and emotions across that great abyss.[18]

The second biblical image that I want to consider here (but more briefly) is that of 'cloud' and 'shadow', and again with respect both to possible original meanings and subsequent applications in later exegesis. The people of Israel were accompanied in their wanderings through the wilderness by a pillar of fire at night and by cloud during the day. While some passages suggest that the cloud also partakes of light and so reflects the glory of the Lord (e.g. Exodus 16:10), others assume the more mundane purpose of simply guiding the people on their way (e.g. 13:21). Given the usual cloudless desert sky, the latter is perhaps the earlier explanation, though eventually it was the theme of divine glory that came to predominate, and it is in this sense that the cloud of divine glory is said to fill the Temple (e.g. 1 Kings 8:10–11; 2 Chronicles 5:13–14). Even so, other passages do seem to pull in a rather different direction.

In Canaanite mythology Baal is frequently described as 'rider on the clouds', and it may well be a borrowing of such imagery that leads to clouds being treated in the Bible as God's chariot for war and judgment: 'Behold, the Lord is riding on a swift cloud … and the idols of Egypt will tremble at his presence, and the heart of the Egyptians will melt within them' (Isaiah 19:1). In similar vein Nahum tells us that 'the clouds are the dust of his feet' (1:3), while a variant reading in one of the psalms (adopted by the AV) equates such conduct with the desert itself: 'cast up a highway for him that rideth through the deserts' (68:4). Ultimately of course that same imagery enters Christianity through Daniel's 'night' vision of the 'one like unto a son of man' coming 'on the clouds of heaven' (6:13). While all such images are externally directed (it is others whom the cloud separates from God), in Lamentations a similar fate befalls Israel itself: 'How the Lord in his anger has set the daughter of Zion under a cloud! He has cast down from heaven to earth the splendour of Israel' (2:1). So clouds in this sense are clearly indicative of divine judgment, and have little, if anything, to do with the imagery of light with which they have been elsewhere associated. Instead, they represent the dark and threatening side of God.

In most subsequent Christian exegesis it was the negative side of cloud imagery that was to take precedence, in which cloud is directly equated with darkness. But there are some exceptions. One of the most intriguing, not least because it is pursued right through his writings, is in the work of the blind nineteenth-century Scottish preacher and poet, George Matheson. Commenting, for example, on Isaiah 32:3 (God described as 'the shadow of a great rock in a weary land'), Matheson observes:

> There are times in which man needs nothing so much as a withdrawal of light. There are times in which the only chance for a human soul is in the pulling down of the window blinds. We pray 'Enlighten our eyes!' but often we can only get our inner eye enlightened by having the outer eye shaded … God puts the multitude all out, and locks the door. He closes the shutters of the casement. He interrupts the music in the street; he forbids the dancing in the hall. He says, 'Your nerves are weary with excitement; in this desert place you shall rest awhile.'[19]

In other words, instead of reading the non-light and negative references to cloud in purely negative terms, Matheson insists on positive results emerging from such negativity.

There is not the space here to explore what may be termed Matheson's shadow theology. Undoubtedly, through such reflections he was enabled to perceive his own blindness in a more positive light as conferring advantages not necessarily so easily secured by the sighted. Indeed, Job 12:22 with its talk of light emerging from the shadows is taken as indicative for a general stance on life: 'How couldst thou learn, if the natural life never failed thee? How could faith begin, if sight were perfect? How could trust exist if there were no darkness? ... Out of thy deepest darkness God says, "Let there be light."'[20] Although he never expresses matters quite so explicitly in his writings, clearly for Matheson cloud and shade have become more than just surrogates for light, but in themselves the very best mediators of the divine presence.

In the World of Art and Architecture: God in Limited Light

Here once again I want to consider two examples, this time both indicative of a more complex understanding of the metaphor of light, with God not necessarily found in light at its most intense or strongest. One concerns how Gothic architecture's rationale in light is found not to be quite so straightforward as is commonly supposed; the other, the way in which Christ at his weakest comes to be regarded as the greatest focus of light.

Conventionally, the beginnings of Gothic architecture are traced to the work of Abbot Suger in building his new abbey church of St-Denis just outside Paris. Arguments continue about the extent of the influence of the writings of Pseudo-Denys on him.[21] In part Suger may have been influenced by the confused identification that was sometimes made with the French missionary saint of the same name to whom the monastery was dedicated. Certainly, Denys had written a great encomium on light as an image of the archetypal Good that is God.[22] In true Platonic fashion, material things, including lights, are seen to mirror their intellectual counterparts, and so to point ultimately to God himself: 'So, then, forms, even those drawn from the lowliest matter, can be used not unfittingly, with regard to heavenly beings. Matter, after all, owes its subsistence to absolute beauty and keeps, throughout its earthly ranks, some echo of intelligible beauty. Using matter, one may be lifted up to the immaterial archetypes.'[23] Suger in similar vein talks of how the loveliness of many-coloured stones in the church's altar can lead us from the material to the immaterial, and of how the shining gilded bronze reliefs on its doors are such that they 'should brighten the minds (of those who enter) so that they may travel, through the true lights, to the true Light where Christ is the true Door'.[24]

So far, such comments might suggest Gothic formulated on quite a simple notion of lightness in contrast to the earlier Romanesque: lightness in materials and light streaming into the church, all intended to draw our contemplation heavenwards. But anyone who has been to that most famous of Gothic cathedrals, Chartres, knows that its magnificent stained glass often renders it quite a dark building, and day and hour need to be quite carefully chosen, if their rich glow is to be fully experienced, still more their details read. Denys had already warned that dissimilarity in the material might be potentially less misleading than similarity, with God as 'corner-stone' or even 'worm' as more suitable than 'sun' or 'golden or gleaming men'.[25] So perhaps the splendour of the glass appearing only occasionally and even then coming multi-hued and with multiple images could be seen as guarding precisely against any such simple and misleading identifications.

But there is a deeper paradox to be observed. In the nineteenth century, Ruskin, like Pugin, believed Gothic to be the quintessential Christian style and, again like Pugin, defended it in terms of the care with which it promoted lightness of overall impression in stone and glass alike. Nonetheless, he rejected any view that supposed such principles simply equivalent to the maximising of light. Thus no one's outrage could have been greater than his when he learnt that it had been the decision of the canons of Amiens Cathedral in the eighteenth century that had led to the removal of much of the cathedral's medieval stained glass, apparently all justified in terms of the production of a stronger, clearer light. Lightness of form and of perception, he insisted, were by no means the same thing as brilliant daylight. If the latter is permitted, then it will deliver its own message rather than allowing the building to speak in its own right.

Somewhat surprisingly, Ruskin finds a twentieth-century ally in Paul Tillich. In an intriguing passage Tillich initially expresses himself in favour of clear glass, partly because 'the rational element in religion' is thereby stressed and partly because 'the idea is, or should be, to draw nature into the sphere of the Holy Presence'. However, he goes on to admit that the opposite in fact often happens: 'the members of the congregation are drawn away from concentration on the Holy Presence to the outside world'. His solution, therefore, is to accept stained glass. Although he draws attention to the way in which it 'effectively shields the congregation from the outside distractions' and can be seen to conform to the principles of Protestant art 'because it is an architectural element, even though technically not a necessary one', his real reason for endorsement seems to have been because it sheds 'a deeper and more mystical illumination upon the interior of the church'.[26]

Given Tillich's somewhat reluctant Protestant concessions to stained glass, it is therefore salutary to note who first coined the phrase 'a dim religious light'. It was in fact another convinced Protestant, John Milton in his ode to Melancholy, *Il Penseroso*. There he talks of 'the high embowed Roof'

> And storied Windows richly dight,
> Casting a dimm religious light
> Which, when combined with music,
> Dissolve me into extasies,
> And bring all Heav'n before mine eyes.[27]

The poem was probably written during Milton's undergraduate days at Cambridge or, if not then, shortly thereafter. So, almost certainly, his sentiments here reflect that great Gothic building at the heart of Cambridge, King's College Chapel.[28] As such, they contrast markedly with his later extensive use of light, as in its invocation at the beginning of Book 3 of *Paradise Lost*.[29] Indeed, Milton's use of light imagery is so extensive that he has been credited with being decisive in moving English poetic use away from 'good' and 'true' and towards 'bright' and 'light' as the dominant terms for moral goodness.[30]

Yet already in the same century the phrase 'the light of reason' was beginning to be used independently of reference to God, and by the following century such usage had become the norm. Even a Christian poet such as Alexander Pope could speak of reason as 'the God within the mind'.[31] Significantly, William Cowper finds it necessary to remind his readers of the source of unbelievers' wisdom:

> Their fortitude and wisdom were a flame
> Celestial, though they knew not whence it came.
> Deriv'd from the same source of light and grace
> That guides the Christian in his swifter race.[32]

It is such developments that help explain modern contrasts between 'the light of reason' and 'the darkness of superstition'. But even so the numinous character of 'a dim religious light' continues to have appeal. Turn on almost any television programme that has a religious context, and churches will be lit, not with just one or two but many candles, intended to be suggestive, I suspect, of just such an evocative atmosphere. So, while the paradox in Gothic appeal to light now passes most people by, the notion of God found not in brilliant light but in a Gothic suggestive haze continues to resonate in modern secular culture.

The second paradoxical application of light I want to consider here is the placing of the greatest light where it would have been perhaps least expected, at Christ's birth in a stable. Considering Christian art in the abstract and without reference to its history, there are many places where the use of light by artists might have been anticipated, most obviously perhaps in depictions of the creation but also surely in momentous happenings such as the resurrection. As it was, the halo became ubiquitous. Yet the most remarkable use of light finally occurs where it might have been least expected, in the fourteenth century, when for the first time in painting we find the infant Christ emanating rays of light from his own person: divinity at its apparently most vulnerable now seen as at its most radiant. The person responsible for this new development was not in fact an artist but a saint, St Bridget or, more accurately, Birgitta of Sweden, who had a vision of the nativity in 1372 while in the Holy Land. Joseph was seen as an old man, solicitous for his wife but deferential. So he places a lighted candle on the wall of the cave, and then goes outside. Mary then gives birth, painlessly and instantly while kneeling in prayer. Here is how Birgitta describes the scene:

> While she was thus in prayer, I saw the one lying in her womb then move; and then and there, in a moment and the twinkling of an eye, she gave birth to a Son, from whom there went out such great and ineffable light and splendour that the sun could not be compared to it. Nor did that candle that the old man had put in place give light at all, because that divine splendour totally annihilated the material splendour of the candle.[33]

The Child trembling from the cold is then taken up into his mother's arms, but not before she had saluted the infant God: 'Welcome my God, my Lord and my Son.'

Thereafter, the theme was quickly taken up and disseminated by artists. Perhaps the finest and most familiar painting of this kind in Britain, hanging as it does in the National Gallery in London, is by the fifteenth-century Dutch artist, Geerten tot Sint Jans.[34] But examples are so numerous for the next few hundred years subsequent to Birgitta's death (in 1373) that regular visitors to galleries have almost come to anticipate and expect just such a depiction, whoever the artist happens to be. There are no haloes in Geerten's painting. It thus anticipates trends in later painting more generally, where internal light is used to identify divinity, eventually, as in Caravaggio, presented in such naturalistic terms that the source of the light is not always immediately obvious to the viewer. A reversal then occurs in Caravaggio's disciple, Rembrandt. Instead of light, it is now darkness that is used to suggest divinity. Ruskin saw such darkness as artificial and dishonest, but, more likely, it was Rembrandt's own distinctive way of opening up the viewer to a larger dimension of the divine: the vulnerability of darkness now disclosing the majesty of divinity.

Rembrandt's approach is altogether too large an issue to pursue further here. Suffice it to say that both my examples illustrate how Christian artistic tradition has refused to place God and light in any simplistic relationship with each other. Just as God had been found in dim religious light set against apparently weightless, soaring Gothic architecture, so now here the luminous brilliance of divinity is discovered in the fragility of childhood or in meditative and often elderly figures emerging from deep darkness, as in Rembrandt.

In Relation to Modern Science: Artificial Light Substituting for, or Suggestive of, God

Attempts to relate religion and theories of light are by no means new. It will be helpful to provide some of the pre-modern background before exploring the use of modern scientific approaches to light either to undermine or else enhance a religious perspective.

In pre-scientific Europe at least two forms of connection were postulated. First, the possibility of perception was presumed to presuppose an underlying 'sympathy' or connection between the viewer and the object perceived.[35] As early as Empedocles it had been suggested that each object gives off effluences from its spores which, when they come in contact with similar content in the percipient, produce the relevant sensation.[36] Although Plato and Aristotle developed more subtle versions, the basic nature of the relationship between subject and object remained unchanged, and it is such ideas that passed into Christianity, with the Creator now guaranteeing those underlying connections.[37] The way the subject is envisaged as transformed by the object meant of course that vision was seen as having a moral dimension, and so this is sometimes postulated as an element in disputes about images in church.[38]

Then a second factor was the new role Augustine gave to divine aid.[39] Plato had described how 'truth flashes upon the soul, like a flame kindled by a leaping spark'.[40] For him it had been a metaphor to explicate the relation of his theory of forms to the sensible world. Augustine, by placing those same forms in the mind of God himself, now ensured that all intellectual understanding required divine aid. That is to say, just as sensible awareness was believed to require the light of sun, so now all intellectual understanding was taken to need divine illumination through participation in awareness of the seminal forms out of which God had created the world. Although Aquinas's revived Aristotelianism weakened this approach, it was really only with Descartes that such ideas were wholly abandoned, with his claim that in effect the capacity to illuminate lay in the objects themselves, in the ability they gave us to form clear and distinct ideas of their nature.[41]

So, as we turn to examine religion interacting with the modern theory and use of light, we must not think of such interaction as something wholly new. What is new is the range of positions taken. To reflect that range, my examples will include hostility, reconciliation and something in between. The accuracy of the science is in some ways less interesting than what is done with it.

My first case study is the use of light to express hostility to religion. A group of Italian artists that includes Giacomo Balla, Umberto Boccioni, Carlo Carrà and Gino Severini signed in 1910 what they labelled their Futurist Manifesto. It had as its aim the liberation of Italy from the oppressive weight of its past, and the endorsement of everything scientific and modern, in particular machinery, speed and violence. While their language lacked caution, it is as well to remember that such ideas were being expressed without awareness of the horrors to come in the First World War, and to many of their contemporaries they appeared new and exciting. Instead of the Impressionist instant or the rather dull colours of Italian Divisionism, one found, for example, the simultaneous representation of the successive movements of a horse in a race, all within a single frame. Everything from dogs to dancers is subjected to similar treatment, usually in strong and rich colours.

Although Boccioni admired the religious paintings of the Divisionist Gaetano Previati, all the group were united in an anti-religious stance, with Christianity seen as part of the past that had to be rejected.[42] It is perhaps in Giacomo Balla's *Street Lamp* (1909) that this inherently anti-religious thrust of the movement is made most obvious.[43] The painting is a celebration of the technical achievements of artificial light, in which its diffraction into coloured rays is treated as like an explosion of light from its own sun. Meanwhile, the moon as part of the created order is set in the top right of the painting in such a way as to suggest by way of contrast its purely passive and insignificant character.

It is intriguing to see that such a stance continues in the world's only museum dedicated exclusively to the use of light in works of art, situated as it is in Italy. Founded by Targetti of Milan, one of the world's major manufacturers of lights (lamps, architectural lighting and so on) towards the end of last century, it is housed in the Villa Sfacciatta, a fifteenth-century villa near the Certosa monastery in Florence. Although the director, Amnon Barzel, is well aware of religious symbolism involving light, he is adamant that light can no longer function in this way. As he observes in the introduction to the official guide, 'light as the expression and symbol of the divine ... could now be substituted by real electrical light elements based on technical, scientific and manufacturing achievements'.[44] That is then how he reads all the various exhibits he introduces, with even the American artist James Turrell, well known for his more spiritual use of light, represented by a strictly secular work.[45] W. T. Sullivan's title for his 1968 photograph of the world as viewed from a space satellite is therefore seen as the natural and appropriate culmination of such ideas. 'The Light of the World' is no longer Christ but what we ourselves produce with the concentrations of yellow glow in the United States and western Europe.[46]

At the other end of the spectrum, it is interesting to find Christians drawing apparently diametrically opposed conclusions from the same scientific research. For the painter Salvador Dalí the work of scientists was seen to bring the physical world closer to a religious perspective because the physical was coming to be viewed as less material, more ethereal, like the spiritual world. That at any rate was the intended message of a number of his paintings such as *Celestial Coronation*, *Madonna in Particles* and *Nuclear Head of an Angel*.[47]

The American novelist and poet John Updike read matters rather differently. In 'Seven Stanzas at Easter', a poem that pleads for a traditional account of the Empty Tomb which rejects metaphor and analogy (seen as 'side stepping transcendence'), Planck's quanta are deployed to give even the observing angel a distinctive kind of materiality. Presumably, this is Updike's own distinctive way of insisting that the angel has become part of our own material world since 'Planck's quanta' are photons, measurable units of real light and not just a spiritual vision. Yet there remains a paradoxical element to the description since photons as pure energy are, strictly speaking, without mass, unless perhaps Updike wants us to think of their gravitational pull. However intended, what is obvious is that Updike's use of physics lies at the opposite pole to Dalí's expectation of the dissolution of matter.

Yet in some ways it is more tentative uses of light imagery that are more appealing, simply because they allow readers or viewers to explore the questions for themselves. That is perhaps why I am particularly fascinated by the work of the American artist Dan Flavin (1933–1996). What makes his light installations of particular interest here is the way in which art critics and the general public have often found in his work a strong spiritual dimension, despite his own insistence that none existed. Brought up in a devout Roman Catholic home where he was encouraged to serve daily at mass and to enter a seminary to train for the priesthood, to which his father had aspired, Flavin rebelled in early adulthood, and his first art works were pastiches of Catholicism.[48] He then went on to develop the Minimalist art with which his name is associated. When asked, he always insisted that his works bore no more meaning that what appeared on the surface, the standard set at the time by the then dominant art critic of the day, Clement Greenberg. But there are a number of reasons for supposing that at least some of his installations mean rather more.

First, his mentor was Barnett Newman, who had likewise used abstract art to explore religious themes. Newman himself said of Flavin and his work that he was

> a man with a personal vision, and that personal vision … stretches the imagination. He is not … a man intoxicated with a love of science, or the light itself, as are some of the light sculptors, who are bringing together science and art… He has taken the light bulb which is a thing and turned it into an innate material, as if it were paint, or canvas … and he has turned this thing, this material, into something personal, in order to make a statement that goes beyond the material as formal material.[49]

Second, there is the material he used and the way he used it. His favourite medium was florescent light, which, unlike tungsten lamps, produces light not in the wire itself but in a reflective glow from phosphorus or similar materials placed along the inner tube, the colour depending on the type of phosphorus used.[50] These colours inevitably opened up possibilities of further meaning, as did the unconventional angles at which the tubes were hung. A third factor is his Catholic background. James Joyce, another lapsed Catholic, developed Aquinas's theory of beauty to speak of 'epiphanies' out of ordinary things, and I do not think it too farfetched to envisage Flavin doing the same thing.[51] When prepared to give titles to specific installations, Flavin honours significant figures in his own life; so why not sometimes something that would transcend his materials in an even more fundamental way, namely God himself? One of his last installations was specifically designed for a church, while several others allude to artists who did avow a spiritual purpose, among them Brancusi, Mondrian and Newman himself.[52] If I am right, then once again there is an element of subversion with which to end my survey: a manufactured light whose meaning cannot be contained despite its author's best intentions. If so, intriguingly, the relevant examples work in exactly the opposite way from how the Divisionists envisaged their task in their religious paintings: through strong and powerful light, not in gentle translucence; in other words, more like the Futurists, who had intended exactly the opposite meaning.

Conclusion

What I hope my survey illustrates is the danger of latching onto one single meaning for key Christian symbols for God. As I have shown, God's presence has been associated at various times with brilliant light, clear light, dim light, a cloudy sky and pitch darkness. None of this is to deny that the predominant use is to be found in applications I have chosen not to discuss, where light is in uncomplicated ways identified with goodness and truth and darkness with all that is evil and opposed to God. These other instances do, however, subvert any claim to absolutes in the more common usage. There are at least four reasons why it is important that such a conclusion should be acknowledged. The first is linguistic. Only close attention to context will determine what sort of meaning is appropriate. It is not something that can be imposed in advance. Second, the avoidance of such impositions is essential if Christian experience of the divine is not to be unnecessarily limited. Suppose, for instance, that Tillich's equation of a Protestant perspective with clear light were accepted. Anything like the encounter of the High Priest with God in the darkness of the Holy of Holies would then come to be seen as a matter of pagan influence rather than something that could offer real insight into another facet of God. Third, there is the doctrinal point. Again and again, Christianity has been plagued by single theories imposed on multiple metaphors. To take up once more the example considered in the preceding essay, Augustine directed the Western Church into an absolute equation of water with cleansing, and so baptism became essentially about the remission and washing away of original sin. But, as we noted, water has in fact quite a number of other resonances in Scripture, not least, especially in John, that of being refreshing and life-giving, attention to which might have moved the Church in quite a different direction. So similarly here, dazzling light and deep darkness balance the clarity of truth and goodness suggested by clear light. In other words, they subvert any absolute claims by imposing an element of mystery and wonderment. Again, strong light could so easily make us identify divine presence with power, but 'dim religious light' hints that this is not always so, as does Birgitta's vision of the Saviour at his most glowing when he is also at his weakest and most

Finding God in Limited Light and Darkness 95

vulnerable. Finally, the Church has nothing to fear from human inventiveness. It is not always essential to look back to analogies with the sun. Even the ordinary fluorescent lamp can evoke a sense of the transcendent, and the agnostic help us in such perceptions of the divine.

In a final reminder to the reader of the complexity of light as symbol and the resultant need always to engage with specific contexts of use, let me end with the poet Dante's most famous application of the symbol. His *Divine Comedy* ends with a clear perception of the Light Eternal as Trinity and limned with our own image. Yet a few cantos earlier he had already subverted any simple application of that image with his vision of the divine unity as a light so intense that it sears his eyes and forces him to close them in wonder.[53] In the modern world symbols are often used unreflectively, but that is not what gives them lasting power. It is the way in which, as with light and darkness, we are ever called to think anew about God as we hear divinity so variously described.[54]

Notes

1 For example, with Christ as 'Light of the world' (John 8:12; 9:5), and the heavenly Jerusalem a city with 'no need of sun or moon to shine in it, for the glory of God is its light, and its lamp is the Lamb' (Revelation 21:23).
2 'Probably one of the oldest narratives in the tradition about the patriarchs': Gerhard von Rad, *Genesis: A Commentary* (London: SCM, 1972), 189.
3 Parallel imagery is used in Deuteronomy 4:11 and 5:23.
4 Paralleled in 2 Chronicles 5:13–6:1, apart from the omission of any reference to the sun.
5 The huge image (13 metres high) was reflected in a pool of oil at its base which also prevented the ivory covering from drying out. Pausanias informs us that there was a spiral staircase to an upper gallery for closer viewing of the face. For an imaginative reconstruction, Judith Swaddling, *The Ancient Olympic Games*, 2nd edn (London: British Museum, 1999), 18.
6 B. F. Westcott, 'The Relation of Christianity to Art', in *The Epistles of St John* (London: Macmillan, 1883), 319–360, esp. 323.
7 Neit came to be identified with Athena/Minerva, and so was used as a model for divine 'Wisdom'.
8 For the menorah representing the sun, moon and five planets, Philo, *Quis heres*, 221–224. For later understandings of the Temple more generally, C. T. R. Hayward, ed., *The Jewish Temple: A Non-biblical Sourcebook* (London: Routledge, 1996).
9 For two excellent overall surveys, see the chapters by Kallistos Ware and John Behr in *Light from Light: Scientists and Theologians in Dialogue*, ed. Gerald O'Collins and Mary Ann Meyers (Grand Rapids, Mich.: Eerdmans, 2012), 131–159 and 183–194.
10 A contrast was drawn between the darkness of Exodus 20:21 and God's earlier appearance to Moses as fire (19:18).
11 The passages in italics are quotations from Exodus 20:21 and Psalm 17:12 (Septuagint).
12 Gregory's *Life of Moses*, Book II, 164, 163; translated in *The Classics of Western Spirituality* series (New York: Paulist Press, 1978), 95.
13 This and the next quotation are drawn from *Mystical Theology*, 1.3, 1001A in *Pseudo-Dionysius: The Complete Works*, Classics of Western Spirituality

96 *The Power of Symbols*

(London: SPCK, 1987), 137. For a similar positive interpretation, Andrew Louth, *The Origins of the Christian Mystical Tradition: From Plato to Denys* (Oxford: Clarendon Press, 1981), 159–178, esp. 174–176.
14 For this and the subsequent quotations, *Mystical Theology*, 1.1, 997A–1000A (135).
15 Acts 9:3–4; 22:6; 26:13–14. Not dissimilar effects are suggested by the evangelists' accounts of the transfiguration. Although only Matthew has the disciples fall on their faces (17:6), both he and Luke describe a dazzling effect: Matthew17:2; Luke 9:29.
16 Philo was probably a key influence on Gregory. See Philo's discussion in *De Posteritate Caini*, 4.12–5.16.
17 For example, Denys Turner, *The Darkness of God: Negativity in Christian Mysticism* (Cambridge: Cambridge University Press, 1995).
18 For a helpful exposition, Rowan Williams, *The Wound of Knowledge: Christian Spirituality from the New Testament to St John of the Cross* (London: Darton, Longman & Todd, 1979), 173–175.
19 For this and other examples in Matheson, see I. C. Bradley, ed., *O Love that wilt not let me go: Meditations, Prayers and Poems by George Matheson* (London: Collins, 1990), 49–59, esp. 54–55.
20 Ibid., 50.
21 For a strong statement of the case in favour of such influence, see Otto von Simpson, *The Gothic Cathedral: Origins of Gothic Architecture and the Medieval Concept of Order*, 3rd edn (Princeton: Princeton University Press, 1988), 103–141.
22 *Divine Names*, 4, 697C–701B (74–76).
23 *The Celestial Hierarchy*, 2, 144B–C (151–152).
24 *De administratione*, xxiii (63–64); xxvii (47–48) in Erwin Panofsky, ed., *Abbot Suger and the Abbey Church of St-Denis and its Art Treasures*, 2nd edn (Princeton: Princeton University Press, 1979).
25 *Celestial Hierarchy*, 2 (esp. 148, 152). God is referred to as a worm in Psalm 22:6, if it is read christologically.
26 'Contemporary Protestant Architecture', in Paul Tillich, *On Art and Architecture* (New York: Crossroad, 1989), 214–220, esp. 218–19.
27 *Il Penseroso*, lines 155–166, esp. 159–160 and 165–166. Quoted from Helen Darbishire, ed., *Poetical Works of John Milton* (London: Oxford University Press, 1958), 428.
28 Though his old college of Christ's may also have played its part.
29 *Paradise Lost*, 3, 1–6; Darbishire, ed., *Poetical Works*, 53.
30 Josephine Miles, 'From Good to Bright: A Note in Poetic History', *Publications of the Modern Language Association of America* 60 (1945), 766–774; cf. also Merritt Y. Hughes, 'Milton and the Symbol of Light', in *Ten Perspectives on Milton* (New Haven: Yale University Press, 1965), 63–103.
31 *Essay on Man*, Epistle II, 204; quoted from Herbert Davis, ed., *Pope: Poetical Works* (London: Oxford University Press, 1966), 256.
32 From his long poem on 'Truth', lines 531–534.
33 *Book of Revelations*, VII, 20, 6; quoted from M. T. Harris, ed., *Birgitta of Sweden: Life and Selected Revelations* (New York: Paulist Press, 1990), 203.
34 The unusual name indicates that he lived with the Knights of St John at Haarlem. He is thought to have died, aged twenty-eight, sometime between 1485 and 1495.
35 Such sympathy or influence was part of course of a much larger pattern that included the influence of the stars. For a sympathetic treatment of its use within Christianity, see C. S. Lewis, *The Discarded Image* (Cambridge: Cambridge University Press, 1964), 92–121.
36 Empedocles, fragment 3, 9–13 and 89.

37 For Plato's version, *Philebus* 33D–34A; *Timaeus* 64A–D; for Aristotle's, *De anima*, II, 412, 417A–418A, 423B–424A.
38 For example, Christopher Joby, 'The Extent to Which the Rise in the Worship of Images in the Late Middle Ages Was Influenced by Contemporary Theories of Vision', *Scottish Journal of Theology* 60 (2007), 36–44.
39 For more detail on Augustine's views, see Robert Dodaro's chapter in O'Collins and Meyers, eds, *Light from Light*.
40 *Seventh Letter*, 341C: cf. 344B.
41 For Aquinas, although the *lumen intellectuale* was no longer thought of as requiring divine aid, it did still participate in the *lumen divinum* that was ubiquitous.
42 For religious themes in Divisionism, see Vivienne Greene, 'Divisionism's Symbolic Ascent', in *Radical Light: Italy's Divisionist Painters 1891–1910*, ed. S. Fraquelli et al. (London: National Gallery, 2008), 47–59. Mystic, gentle colours were preferred.
43 Illustrated in Amnon Barzel, *Light Art: Targetti Light Art Collection* (Milan: Skira, 2005), 8.
44 Ibid., 17.
45 Ibid., 38–43.
46 Illustrated ibid., 25. The title is almost certainly intended as a deliberate contrast to William Holman Hunt's famous nineteenth-century painting of the same name, versions of which are to be found both in Keble College Chapel, Oxford and in St Paul's Cathedral, London.
47 Illustrated in Robert Descharmes and Gilles Néret, eds, *Dalí* (Cologne: Taschen, 1997), 444–445, 458–459.
48 For Flavin himself on his Catholic upbringing, Michael Govan and Tiffany Bell, *Dan Flavin: A Retrospective* (New Haven: Yale University Press, 2004), 189–190; for an example of pastiche, *East New York Shrine*, 28.
49 From the transcript of a talk given by him at the opening of a Flavin exhibition on 12 September 1969: National Gallery of Canada (Ottawa) archives, Flavin Exhibition files.
50 For this point, Govan and Bell, *Dan Flavin*, 59.
51 James Joyce, *Stephen Hero* (New York: New Directions, 1955), 213.
52 For the church example executed in the last year of his life, Govan and Bell, *Dan Flavin*, 104–105. For allusions to the artists mentioned, 35, 69, 84.
53 *Paradiso*, XXXIII, 124–185; XXVIII, 16–19.
54 This essay has been adapted from one first published in O'Collins and Meyers, eds, *Light from Light*. The material is reproduced here with kind permission of the publishers.

Part III
Artists as Theologians

Introduction

In Part I I sought to undermine some of the most common objections to assigning a role to the arts in the exposition and development of Christian theology. Here, however, I want to go further, and provide some more specific examples of how visual artists in particular might contribute to debates about the nature and content of Christian doctrine. Unfortunately, it is still overwhelmingly the case that their role is seen as merely illustrative, of what, if correct, can be discovered in any case more effectively through careful reflective reading of the Scriptures. Nor is the work of professional historians of art necessarily of much help. Although some signs of change are evident, many still continue to confine their attention to formal aspects of the work rather than content as such. All three essays that follow challenge such views by exploring the potential contribution of artists across the centuries to three areas of Christian doctrine: the annunciation, the ascension, and the Trinity. However, given that very specific areas are thereby addressed, it will perhaps be helpful to preface their reading with some more general remarks on what I was attempting to achieve. In particular, two general points need to be made.

First, there is perhaps a natural temptation to suppose that artists are mere amateurs in theology compared to preachers and professional theologians, and indeed even the evangelists themselves. So anything distinctive that comes from them must of necessity be inferior to what can be gained elsewhere. Certainly in many, perhaps in the majority of cases, neither their knowledge nor their piety may have been especially profound. Even so, there were at least three factors that helped pull in the other direction. In the first place, there was the knowledge that their patrons (mostly clergy) had, and which would have fed into the precise form the commission took. Occasionally such detailed input is known but more often than not we simply do not know where the balance of ideas lay. So perhaps one should talk of the art as theology rather than artists themselves functioning as theologians. But against this two other points need to be taken into account. Unlike with so much modern art, historically artists worked within traditions of representation; so, even if not especially knowledgeable themselves, there was a wealth of expertise on which to draw. It is thus no accident that a story can be told of developing patterns of representation with only the occasional artist radically departing from established precedents.[1] But, finally, there is the fact that any artist, however ignorant, when faced with such a commission would be concerned to engage the viewer, and so would never simply reproduce but reflect on how to achieve such a result.

As a matter of fact, of course, many artists were learned in their own right. Thus, quite a number were monks or friars,[2] while, to give a lay example, there is plenty of written evidence to suggest Michelangelo's engagement with both traditional and Counter-Reformation concerns.[3] Again, while knowledge and piety can undoubtedly combine to produce great works of art,[4] it would be a mistake to suppose that both are a *sine qua non*. Caravaggio's violent and licentious behaviour is an obvious case in point. Although books and films have been produced to 'out' him as a gay icon,[5] the reality of his life was almost certainly more complex. But in any case more important to observe is that he was nonetheless capable of producing great Christian art that successfully communicated some of the major concerns of Counter-Reformation piety.[6] Thus in a similar way to Gesualdo in music,[7] his art can be seen to transcend the nature of his life or perhaps, put more controversially, his own imperfections may actually have helped generate in him deeper reflections on the significance of the gospel than might otherwise have been the case. Without in any way suggesting that bad conduct justified the result, in a similar way it is surely too simplistic to deny the positive virtues of parish clergy who have significantly fallen short in some respect, just as Paul Tillich's whole theological system is hardly called into question by later revelations of his unrestrained promiscuity.[8]

The second general point I want to make concerns how the contribution of artists should be assessed. Christianity's primarily verbal culture inevitably puts a high premium on verbal assessment which can easily lead to the presumption that art should be assessed no differently from the written observations of evangelists, preachers and theologians. In effect, a simple translation exercise is then embarked upon, with what is allegedly 'said' by the paintings or sculpture judged in precisely the same ways as what is said more directly through words elsewhere. It cannot be emphasised too strongly that this is entirely the wrong approach. Painting, like music, needs first to be evaluated in its own right. As this point is frequently misconstrued, let me offer a couple of rather different examples. First, to state the obvious, a biblical narrative may well choose to leave open some aspect of an event over which necessarily the artist will have to take a decision if there is to be a picture at all. So, for example, as the first essay that follows illustrates, the artist has to choose how Mary and the angel relate to one another: that is, decide on a matter on which the Bible gives no guidance, and so indicate who shows deference to whom. Again, the visual may well have to choose between two different sets of rules, both of which have been accepted in verbal discussion but which it is hard, if not impossible, to accommodate, within the visual. Thus, in the essay on the Trinity I observe how frequently any representation of the procession of the persons had to yield if the equality of the persons was to be made a visual reality.

It is only once these different kinds of constraint are given due acknowledgement that a proper comparative assessment can be made of what has been said through the different media of word and vision. Even then, a hostile reader may well propose that the visual should nonetheless always yield to the verbal since revelation was after all given exclusively through the verbal. But this would seem wrong on at least two grounds. First, as I have indicated elsewhere in this volume, biblical revelation was not in fact exclusively verbal. Much of the narrative is itself focused around visions,[9] while its descriptive language moves back and forth between metaphor and image, that is, between verbal and visual images. But, second, to suppose that from such a mixture only verbal deductions may be properly drawn would be to give priority to one way of thinking that itself could be seen to be more prone to error in this area than the visual. Throughout the centuries there has been a temptation to treat the verbal over-literally, thereby ignoring the imagistic character of biblical language, whereas at least with art there can be no doubt at all that we are in the world of image and metaphor, and so appropriate caution is required. That may sound as though I am advocating that in the light of the work of artists always less should be claimed rather than more, but that is not at all my point. As my essay on the annunciation notes, art can raise profound questions about the believer's relation to Mary, while, if artists' portrayals of the Trinity do suggest caution in the advocacy of particular models or ordering of the persons, at the same time they also indicate a great variety of ways in which the doctrine might be made to 'come alive' for the ordinary believer.

Notes

1 In all three articles such a story is told.
2 Famous illuminated manuscripts such as the Book of Kells or Lindisfarne Gospels derive from such hands. Fra Angelico (d. 1455) and Fra Bartolommeo (d. 1517) were both Dominicans, Filippo Lippi (d. 1469) a Carmelite, Hugo van der Goes (d. 1472) an Augustinian, Andrea Pozzo (d. 1709) a Jesuit and Albert Chmielowski (d. 1916), the founder of the Albertine order.
3 See further Robert J. Clements, *Michelangelo's Theory of Art* (New York: Gramercy, 1961); Alexander Nagel, *Michelangelo and the Reform of Art* (Cambridge: Cambridge University Press, 2000).
4 Fra Angelico was beatified by John Paul II in 1982, while rumour has it that Pope Francis will soon beatify or canonise the Barcelona architect Antonio Gaudì.
5 As with Peter Robb, *M* (London: Bloomsbury, 1999), and Derek Jarman's film *Caravaggio* (1986).
6 Well brought out in books such as Helen Langdon, *Caravaggio* (London: Chatto & Windus, 1998) and Andrew Graham-Dixon, *Caravaggio: A Life Sacred and Profane* (Harmondsworth: Penguin, 2011).
7 Carlo Gesualdo (d. 1613) mutilated and murdered his wife and her lover, as well as composing some incredibly beautiful sacred music.

8 First made public after his death in the volume by his widow, Hannah *From Time to Time* (New York: Stein and Day, 1973).
9 One need only think of the experiences of Moses, Elijah and some of the prophets in the Old Testament, or the role of vision in the life of Jesus, Paul and the author of Revelation in the New.

7 The Annunciation as True Fiction

No one could deny that the gospel narratives are exceedingly sparse in their description of events. In the case of Mark this may well have been deliberate, as it adds to the urgency of his appeal, with one event rapidly following another. But even with the other gospels it is more a framework that is proposed rather than something that can immediately be given a determinate visual picture. Although such filling out provided rich opportunities for conventional Christian art, it could be argued that, in religious terms, it is merely of very secondary importance since it constitutes no part of the original narrative. By contrast, I shall argue that such 'fullness' can sometimes provide a more profound analysis or description than the historical original.

In short, I want to use the story of the annunciation to indicate how fact and fiction are not always wholly opposed; symbolic fiction can sometimes convey historical truth no less effectively than the bare factual record. To help focus the issue, let me begin by setting the reader something of a challenge, and ask him or her to envisage the scene in their mind's eye. Does the angel kneel before Mary, or Mary before the angel, or do both stand? Many, perhaps most, may be inclined simply to dismiss the question out of hand as irrelevant, partly because Luke's narrative offers no guidance either way, but in the main because doubts about the historicity of the narrative seem to make the question irrelevant in any case. It is that curt dismissal of story as somehow inevitably inferior to literal truth that I want to challenge by considering why artists in their depictions went now in one direction, now in another, on this issue of how the angel and Mary should be portrayed in their interaction with one another. But in the process I also want to suggest that the gap between artist and evangelist is not as great as may initially appear, with one (the artist) apparently concerned with purely fictional elaboration, and the other (the evangelist) with simple factual truth.

Certainly, this issue of symbolic truth is one that modern Christianity desperately needs to face, given how intricately interwoven are symbol and event, fact and fiction, in its inheritance from its past. Although it is a view now held by a minority of scholars, even the dating of the feast of the Annunciation to 25 March may have had its origins in just such a way.[1] That is to say, so far from putting the feast exactly ninth months earlier than

Christmas, it may have been the date of the annunciation that was first fixed, in the desire of the Church to have Jesus' conception happen on precisely the same day as he was believed to have died. Not only can such symbolic considerations, with life matching death, be shown to have influenced contemporary Jewish understandings of the lives of the patriarchs, but also the general form of the argument was once a common pattern in the ancient world. One might think, for instance, of the way in which the second book of Chronicles deduces that Mount Moriah must be identical with Mount Zion, since so important a sacrifice as that of Isaac could not possibly have taken place elsewhere than on the Temple mount, or again, how Golgotha (the place of the skull) is quickly transformed from any old cemetery into the very one in which Adam was buried, with the new man thus emerging at the very place where the old ceased.[2]

To modern minds such inferences from symbol to fact often seem merely perverse, but in my view they deserve sympathetic treatment, not least because such symbolic worlds do sometimes open up alternative ways of reflecting and accessing truth. How this might happen in visual adaptations of Luke's narrative of the angel's encounter with Mary I shall come to in a moment, but first I want to stress what I am *not* attempting to do, but where it might be thought the general direction of my argument is tending: that symbol can at least offer some general truths about the human condition. While not denying this, my aim rather is to alert the reader to the way in which what is admitted to be fiction can nonetheless sometimes communicate truth about specific historical individuals, in this case Mary.

To see the difference, let me pay two courtesy calls on cathedral deans, the first John Drury at Christ Church in Oxford.[3] In a recent book he has explored the significance of religious paintings in the possession of the National Gallery in London. His commentary is full of valuable and helpful insights, and undoubtedly will do much to make such works more accessible, particularly to an increasingly secular public. Nonetheless, it contains what for me are two surprises. First, despite his interest in symbolism the author shows little interest in the alterations the painters make to the biblical narrative, and that seems confirmed by the volume's title, *Painting the Word*, as though there were some direct one-to-one correspondence.[4] Then, second, the symbolic value he derives from the gospels is overwhelmingly of the generic kind I have just indicated, applicable indeed not only to Christians in general but equally of value to the population at large, and in this his treatment of the annunciation is no exception. 'The clean heart', he suggests, 'is ready for the creative spirit' in a way that can 'enlighten us in hundreds of similar experiences of encounter and exchange' where virgin eyes become 'receptive and active'.[5] In a moment I shall use the same annunciation paintings on which he focuses to draw a quite different conclusion, to argue for the legitimacy of going beyond the general and into the particular, but first a visit north, to my own former cathedral city of Durham.[6]

A couple of years ago, when the dean was absent, I got up into the pulpit and proceeded as sub-dean to offer an apology on his behalf, explaining at some length what he was doing that weekend, because, as I said to the congregation, I was sure they would wish to know and indeed could take some satisfaction in the range of activities upon which John Arnold was then engaged.[7] At the end of four or five choice paragraphs in this vein, I then announced that not a word of what I had just said was literally true. There was a quite audible intake of breath from those present before I asked them to reflect why they had believed me. In part, I suggested, this was because they had come to know me in general as a trustworthy person, but there was also, I felt, a more interesting reason: that I had invented precisely the sort of actions and responses that had made Durham so fond of its then dean, and indeed, so successful was I in this that a group came up to me afterwards and suggested that what I said would have made an excellent obituary for him!

Very, very occasionally one finds modern professional historians engaging in a similar ruse, as in Simon Schama's book *Dead Certainties*,[8] but my point is of course intended to refer to the more distant past, and the way in which the gospels were written, that occasionally invented incidents were resorted to, in order to convey Christ's underlying significance. Just as I attempted to cram into a single weekend the splendid contributions of John Arnold to his cathedral and to the life of the Church as whole, so the evangelists sometimes found symbolic fiction an easier way of identifying Jesus' value for us today. Through building on what they already knew of him, they elaborated and perhaps sometimes even invented incidents in order to bring out the significance they knew he now had in the light of his resurrection. That, it seems clear to me, is precisely what has happened with Luke's annunciation narrative. The sentiments Mary expresses in her Magnificat well illustrate the point. They marvellously anticipate how Christ's story will end in the resurrection, but make little sense on the lips of an as yet powerless young girl. Luke, like the master storyteller he is, right at the beginning of his narrative is setting his readers in an appropriate frame of mind for learning who Jesus was and his relevance to us. Equally, then, in respect of the exchange with the angel Gabriel, Luke's focus seems really to be on the message conveyed, the astonishing birth to come, rather than on either angel or recipient, and against such a backdrop even Mary's hesitation looks more like a dramatic device intended to underline the stupendous nature of what will happen, rather than convey anything to us about Mary as such.

But, as we all know, later tradition did come to show interest in Mary in her own right, and that is fully reflected in the artistic tradition. We can therefore quite properly ask whether their form of the symbol or fiction might be able to tell us something significant about this particular woman. Of the three National Gallery paintings which so fascinate John Drury, the earliest was once part of Duccio's famous and complex *Maestà*, an altarpiece with numerous scenes, first installed in the cathedral at Siena in 1311, while the other two were intended to function on their own: Filippo Lippi's version from the fifteenth century and Poussin's from the seventeenth. In Duccio's case both Mary and the angel stand, while with the latter two the angel is either already kneeling or in the process of doing so. Such contrasts can all too easily be misread. Thus Duccio may leave this angel standing, but his companion angel is forced to kneel in the parallel scene, originally located above and depicting an annunciation of Mary's forthcoming death.[9] Again, if in this annunciation Lippi's angel kneels, and in others the sense of adoration is heightened by Mary being made to stand as Gabriel does obeisance, yet, as if by way of corrective, at the end of Mary's life we find her on her knees for her coronation, a depiction markedly different from the more conventional pattern where she sits while her son stands.[10]

Such variations could of course be due to nothing more than the predilections of patrons, or wider dissemination of the popular late thirteenth-century Franciscan devotional text, *The Meditations*, which has the angel kneel, but some note also needs, I think, to be taken of the artists' wider theological awareness. Filippo Lippi, for example, was himself a Carmelite friar.[11] Given the fact that the medieval Church thought of Mary as sinless throughout her life, one might have thought that the angel kneeling was the only appropriate response, but her assumed humility pulled in the opposite direction, as did the thought that as yet, though sinless, she still lacked any close identification with her Son or the depth of character that went with it. Duccio thus chooses to indicate the still potential character of her significance by having both stand, but even with Lippi, where the angel always kneels, it would be a mistake, I think, to suppose that he necessarily views matters differently. Unlike Duccio, he had only a single incident with which to convey Mary's significance, and so he wants us to kneel with the angel, knowing the heavenly role she now has. If you like, he resorts to the same sort of anticipatory technique as Luke's Magnificat.

But there is also another more controversial reason that lies behind the decision to make the angel kneel, and, ironically, it is here that we encounter the strange paradox that the same reasons that make us doubt the historicity of the event also pull towards stronger endorsement of some historical truth after all lying beneath the symbolic or fictional kneeling. What is at stake is recognition that not only must Mary depend on divine grace throughout her life – so powerfully indicated by Filippo Lippi in his paintings of her coronation, with her still kneeling – but also, equally, God chooses to depend on her. In other words, her consent became integral to the entire process, and so the angel must kneel. It is something of which St Bernard makes much in his sermons on the annunciation, and it is a theme which was widely disseminated through Jacobo Voragine's quotations of these sermons in his *Golden Legend* of 1265. Even God's angel had to wait for her voluntary assent, and it was a union of wills through love, not force.[12]

Now, initially, it might seem that such a perspective loses its force once we move to the pattern of development accepted by most modern biblical scholars, with even Jesus himself only gradually becoming aware of his own mission and destiny, still more obviously so with his disciples or mother. But, on the contrary, might that not argue for a greater dependence on his mother and her role? We are aware from Mark and John of various heated exchanges between Jesus and his mother and brothers as Jesus attempted to forge his own distinctive identity, yet also from Luke, and by inference from John, that those disagreements were eventually resolved, and that by the time of Pentecost Mary had become a faithful disciple, joined also by another of her sons, James, as leader of the incipient Jerusalem Church.[13] There is thus no shortage of evidence to suggest that it was partly through family interaction that the human Jesus worked towards his own unique self-understanding.

All this might seem quite obvious. Yet to speak of the incarnation as involving not only our dependence on God but God's dependence on us can still rouse surprisingly strong passions, as is well illustrated by recent debates in the Church of England's General Synod, over the precise wording of the relevant clause of the creed.[14] Nor is it only Protestant hackles that can be raised. Integral to the theology of Pope John Paul II's favourite theologian, Hans Urs von Balthasar, is what he called his 'Marian principle' that Mary's life was one of passive obedience and so that is why the Church must remain essentially feminine.[15] But, if we accept that the shape of Christ's teaching and even the form which he used to express his understanding of the nature of his unique relationship with his Father are heavily dependent on a specific historical context, why should matters be any different when it comes to the particular individuals most likely to have had a decisive influence on his character and education? There is an extraordinary passage in the nineteenth-century Jesuit Gerard Manley Hopkins, in which it becomes clear that he envisages Jesus' earthly body totally unaffected by the normal complaints to which Jews of the time were subject as part of a typical subsistence economy.[16] Yet I suspect a similar docetism today among many of my fellow Christians in attitudes to Mary. There is great reluctance to concede the obvious and acknowledge that in a real and full incarnation God's plan had to operate through those in Jesus' immediate environment, and that must mean giving greater recognition not only to the fact that Jesus was a Jew living in a particular and definite cultural milieu but also that he was a Jew brought up by a specific set of Jewish parents.

Though an unintended consequence of their art, it seems to have been artists who first brought to Christian awareness that wider sense of dependence. In all three of the National Gallery 'Annunciations' Mary carries a book. At one level of course it was merely a useful device for recording the words of the two actors in the drama or else Isaiah's prophecy that it would happen, but we must not suppose the book was always there, or that when it first arrived, it was without further impact. Our earliest representations of the incident have in fact Mary drawing water from a well. That yields to her being busy spinning. Then words on a banderol finally merge into a book, but the book requires a purpose, and so Mary is presented as either meditating on its contents or else praying through it, and in other contexts sometimes teaching her Son to read. If I may put it like this, Mary the mere domestic has become Mary the reflective individual, someone capable of helping to shape her Son's consciousness. Given attitudes in first-century Palestine, it is of course unlikely that someone like her from the lower social orders could read. Even so, that does not mean that this image or symbol cannot therefore contain any truth, for, as we all know from modern societies where women are kept hidden, their influence on their children can still be immense, and in this case of course given the absence of any further mention of him it looks as though Joseph must have disappeared from the scene before Jesus embarked on his adult ministry. Indeed, even if we were to confine Mary's role to pregnancy alone, we all know how much children may be affected by interaction with their mother even before they are born.

But, rather than argue further in this vein, let me use another, more recent painting to focus the issue. In 1926 so shocked were some of the citizens of Cologne by Max Ernst's painting *Jesus Chastised by the Virgin Mary* that they succeeded in securing its removal from public exhibition. To the protesters it seemed certain that Jesus could never have incurred so severe a parental reprimand, far less that Mary should have countenanced such a conflict with her Son. But is this not exactly what one would have expected of a child growing up in the culture of the time? Children learn by testing boundaries, and in the past corporal punishment played an integral role in defining those boundaries, and so in giving the child the security of knowing where it stood. Nor, it should be added, are these reflections hopelessly modern, or peculiar to our own age. For, had the people of Cologne looked further south, they would have found a medieval roof boss in the Frauenkirche at Nuremberg that depicts a very similar scene.[17] There Jesus is portrayed as the typical reluctant schoolboy on the way to his first day at school, with satchel in one hand, and the other firmly gripped by his mother, who, significantly, carries some taws in case he should prove recalcitrant. Meantime, an angel hovers above, hands clasped in prayer, hoping that such punishment turns out to be unnecessary.

Contemporary Christians often worry when theologians tell them that parts of the biblical narrative are unlikely to be historically true. Of course, if the doubts are based on dogmatic disbelief in the possibility of miracle or incarnation, they have every reason for concern. But, if it is simply a matter of recognition that a story has been told to bring out more fully the ultimate significance of what has happened, their anxieties are, I believe, misplaced. The historical has of course to bear some relation to the narrowly factual, but that emphatically does not mean that the fictional or symbolical is for ever precluded from illuminating that history. The evangelists set a clear precedent for artists in their free use of symbolic invention. Theologians and artists who then followed that precedent in inventing a kneeling angel had the right intuition: God in submitting himself to an incarnation not

The Annunciation as True Fiction 111

only makes us as human beings dependent on him but also, equally, him dependent on us; God's representative (the angel Gabriel) now kneels before representative humanity. The feast of the Annunciation thus celebrates not only God's entry into our world but also that his entry was as a vulnerable child, dependent like us on others and not least upon his mother, Mary.[18]

Notes

1 For a discussion of the arguments for and against this view and the alternative, that the date of Christmas was determined by the desire to combat pagan celebrations of *Sol Invictus*, Susan K. Roll, *Towards the Origins of Christmas* (Kampen, The Netherlands: Kok Pharos, 1995), 35–164, esp. 90–91, 150.
2 Hence the explanation for the presence of a single skull at the foot of so many paintings of the crucifixion; for the identification of Mount Moriah with the Temple mount, 2 Chronicles 3:1.
3 John Drury (b. 1936) was Dean of Christ Church from 1991 to 2003.
4 Though the author tells me the choice of title was the publisher's and not his.
5 John Drury, *Painting the Word: Christian Pictures and their Meanings* (New Haven: Yale University Press, 1999), 43–59, esp. 47, 53, 54. What follows in my text is not intended to deny the value of this type of analysis, only to insist that the symbol can also point to important, *particular* truths.
6 As Van Mildert Professor of Divinity at Durham University I was also a residentiary canon of the cathedral.
7 John Arnold (b. 1933) was Dean of Durham from 1989 to 2002. He was successively vice-president (1986–1992) and then president (1992–1997) of the Conference of European Churches, a post that necessitated frequent absences abroad.
8 Simon Schama, *Dead Certainties: Unwarranted Speculations* (New York: Knopf, 1991), particularly its 'Afterword'.
9 In 1771 Duccio's *Maestà* was dismantled, and many of its constituent parts distributed elsewhere. For an illustration of the London piece and its companion piece, still in Siena, and also for the structure of the *Maestà* as a whole, Diana Norman, 'A Noble Panel: Duccio's *Maestà*', in *Siena, Florence and Padua: Art, Society and Religion 1280–1400*, ed. Diana Norman (New Haven: Yale University Press, 1995), 55–81, esp. 64.
10 For illustrations of Lippi's two coronations, both of which take the same format, known respectively as the *Maringhi Coronation* and the *Marsuppini Coronation*, Jeffrey Ruda, *Filippo Lippi: Life and Work* (London: Phaidon, 1993), 140, 149–150 (plates 77 and 82–83). Of the large number of 'Annunciations' illustrated in that work, all have the angel kneeling, and the majority Mary standing rather than sitting.
11 The *Meditations* speaks of the angel 'kneeling reverently before his Lady with pleasing and joyful countenance and fulfilling his embassy faithfully': so Isa Ragusa and Rosalie B. Green, eds, *Meditations on the Life of Christ: An Illustrated Manuscript of the Fourteenth Century* (Princeton: Princeton University Press, 1961), 18–19. For a careful study of the influence on Lippi of his membership of the Carmelite order, Megan Holmes, *Fra Filippo Lippi: The Carmelite Painter* (New Haven: Yale University Press, 1999).
12 How common a theme this is in Bernard is well illustrated in the *Sources chrétiennes* collection of his sermons, *À la louange de la vierge mère* (Paris: Éditions du Cerf, 1993), e.g. Homily 3.4, 178–180, or 4.8, 226. In the latter case, Bernard even conjures up an image of the whole world awaiting Mary's free

response: 'This whole world, prostrate on its knees, awaits ... O Mistress, give the reply that the earth and everyone above and beneath longs for' (my translation). For his influence on Voragine, *The Golden Legend* (Princeton: Princeton University Press, 1993), I: 196–202, esp. 200.
13 For the conflicts, Mark 3:31–35, 6:1–6 and John 7:5; for their resolution, Acts 1:14. John 19:26–27, even if not historical as inference from the Synoptics' 'from afar off' seems to imply, can still be read as supporting Luke's view that Mary was still alive at this point, or in other words that it was not incongruous to place her in this situation.
14 The Prayer Book has 'was incarnate by the Holy Ghost of the Virgin Mary'. The International Commission's recommendation that 'of' be used in respect of both was strongly opposed, with various alternatives being canvassed before 'from the Holy Spirit and the Virgin Mary' was eventually accepted. It is hard not to suppose that Marian suspicions played some underlying role, since even in Scripture unlike partners are sometimes conjoined, e.g. Acts 15:28.
15 I discuss Balthasar's use of this alleged feminine principle in *Discipleship and Imagination: Christian Tradition and Truth* (Oxford: Oxford University Press, 2000), 274–278.
16 Sermon of 23 November 1879; e.g. in *Gerard Manley Hopkins: A Selection of his Poetry and Prose*, ed. W. H. Gardner (Harmondsworth: Penguin, 1953), 137–139. Teeth, for example, could not but be affected by the grit that remained in the grinding of meal for bread.
17 For illustration and discussion see Bridget Heal, *The Cult of the Virgin Mary in Early Modern Germany: Protestant and Catholic Piety, 1500–1648* (Cambridge: Cambridge University Press, 2007), 70.
18 Adapted from a University Sermon at Oxford (given for Lady Day, 2000), this chapter was first published in *Theology* 104 (2001), 123–130. It is reprinted here with permission in a slightly revised form.

8 Why the Ascension Matters

In this essay I want to examine the doctrine of the ascension and the way it has been appropriated across Christian history, particularly through the visual arts but also to a limited degree in some other media, including poetry, music and more literary sermons. My objective in doing so is not to decry more conventional doctrinal treatments but rather to consider what happens when attempts to engage an audience are more directly in play. Inevitably, questions of significance and relevance become more important, as strategies are devised to ensure, on the part of viewer, reader or listener, continuing interest in the doctrine. There may be some interesting lessons for the Church and theology, as perhaps of all the doctrines concerned with Christ's life this is the one that is most often treated as marginal to the whole story. To the typical conservative it appears as merely transitional, a marker for the end of Christ's earthly life and promissory of the gift of the Spirit to come; to the more radically minded resurrection and ascension are in any case to be seen as one, and so Luke's two accounts viewed as merely rather wooden ways of saying that the appearances had now come to an end.[1] Neither group thus accords the notion much weight in its own right. But, precisely because the concern of the artist is for continuing engagement, there will be a creative pull in the other direction, to find things worth saying. In other words, significance secured by doctrinal enlargement will be their aim in its own right.

Admittedly, it must be conceded that the artistic image of the ascension that is most familiar these days – with Christ's feet peeking beneath a cloud – scarcely at first sight appears any more promising. Yet I want to suggest that a more extensive examination of the range of imagery employed compels a rather different estimate. To see why, I propose considering in turn two major types of focus, first Christ's exchange with Mary Magdalene in the garden and then the departure as such. The latter in particular will enable us to draw on poetry and music as well as art. The advantage of the former is that it reminds us that the biblical material is in any case far wider than the two familiar references in Luke-Acts. So part of my intention will be to highlight the way in which artists draw on that wider material, as well as note some of the tensions in moving from one medium to another (from the literary to the visual). In both cases I shall contend that precisely because the artistic tradition is concerned to engage, there is much more emphasis on the potential relevance of the doctrine to the viewer, listener or reader, and so as much concern with the impact on us as on Christ. This means there is a desire to speak of a body transfigured that opens up the possibility of our own transfiguration.

Mary Magdalene's Encounter and Transformation

'Touch me not; for I am not yet ascended to my Father' (John 20:17). So common are representations of this theme in art, of Mary Magdalene being repelled by Christ, that it has generated its own specific name (from the Vulgate), *Noli me tangere*. That very familiarity, though, can all too easily hide from us the startling oddness of what is being said. A more easily explicable comment would surely have been for Christ to enjoin just such a touch precisely because it was the last opportunity Mary Magdalene would have had before Christ entered a different sort of reality. Little wonder then that textual emendations are sometimes proposed to ease the strain, with, for example, Mary told instead 'not to fear' because Christ had not yet entered into his more august, supernatural state.[2] However, on the whole commentators both ancient and modern have preferred to keep with the rebuke, 'do not keep holding on': Christ's destiny is calling him elsewhere. In patristic exegesis both Chrysostom and Augustine postulate insufficient reverence on Mary's part for Christ's new, more august existence.[3] Chrysostom adds that Christ tried to express this as gently as possible, and that is why his meaning is not as clear as it might be. Among modern commentators Barrett's view may be taken as representative: she is wrongly 'trying to recapture the past'.[4] Something, though, still seems to be lacking in such explanations, as the grammar surely speaks of promise as well as of threat: the 'for' entails a connection, and so appears to imply touch once more or something greater once Christ's new identity is established. If I may draw a rather trivial parallel, think of a child rebuked, 'Don't touch the chocolates; the guests have still to arrive.' Certainly, part of the point is deprivation in the immediate moment, but there is normally also an implicit promise as well: being allowed to share with the guests when they finally arrive.

It is intriguing, therefore, to observe that painters have generally insisted upon just such a promise also for Mary in that rebuke, and so an ascension that impinges on her life no less than on Christ's. Take, for example, Giotto's work from the early fourteenth century at the Scrovegni Chapel in Padua.[5] On the bottom left-hand side of the fresco five soldiers lie asleep, while two large angels sit behind on the closed sarcophagus tomb – closed, perhaps to emphasise the supernatural character of Christ's emergence. Behind is a barren landscape that slopes down towards the right of the painting, where Christ is walking out of the fresco carrying a banner in his left hand that declares him *Victor Mortis* ('victor over death'). He looks back towards a kneeling Mary, his right hand indicating a stay for her hands already stretching towards him. Their eyes, however, meet tenderly, and in between them blossoms the only green shrubbery visible in the entire painting. If the predominant white and gold of Christ and the two angels contrasts markedly with the more substantial colours for the soldiers and for Mary, she not only shares a golden halo with the heavenly figures but the deep red of her cloak is also taken up in both the tomb and the patterning of the angel's wings (only one pair is visible). All this suggests to me a deliberate attempt on the part of Giotto to hint that the stay is temporary and a closer relationship in the offing, one that will blossom into the eternal life that the angels already have. One might contrast that work with Fra Angelico's of the same incident a century later in one of the cells of San Marco in Florence, where no hints of such a future resolution seem offered.[6] Here the garden setting is taken literally, and a palisade encloses a green lawn richly carpeted with flowers with tall cypresses and palms in the background. On the left is a large rock tomb with a door entrance, the encounter with Mary and Christ being placed centre-stage. Although Christ has a mattock over his shoulder and their eyes do meet, the overall impression is of an encounter between two different orders of reality without resolution, for Mary's head is set against the backdrop of the tomb, while Christ's feet seem scarcely to touch the ground, as though he were virtually already elsewhere.[7]

While Fra Angelico may be more consonant with exegesis of the passage both ancient and modern, it is Giotto who better captures, for whatever reason, the tensions implicit between the two halves of the verse. Yet he does so, not because of meditation on the meaning of the text as such but rather because of the way in which by his time the legend of Mary Magdalene had developed. Ever since Pope Gregory the Great had equated Mary Magdalene with the sinner who had anointed Jesus and with Mary of Bethany, the composite figure had become the most popular saint in Western Christendom after the Virgin Mary.[8] This development allowed both men and women to locate themselves within the story of Jesus, and so see themselves as not only sinners like Mary but also, again like her, part of a continuing and deepening relationship with Christ that now offered still greater possibilities of intimacy. Anselm's prayer puts the point well: 'Most blessed lady, I the most wicked of men do not touch once more upon your sins as a taunt or reproach but seek to grasp the boundless mercy by which they were blotted out... For it is not difficult for you to obtain whatever you wish from so loving and so kind a Lord, who is your friend living and reigning.'[9] Indeed, it is a pattern that has continued up to our own day, as in the familiar song attributed to her by Tim Rice in Andrew Lloyd Webber's musical *Jesus Christ Superstar*, 'I don't know how to love him'. She has 'had so many men before' but she is 'really changed' and so does not know how to respond: 'Should I bring him down: should I scream or shout?' Indeed, she confesses: 'I never thought I'd come to this; what's it all about?' If the uncertainties are typically modern, the general strategy is not: a character in the story is being used to negotiate one's own personal attitude to Jesus, and so not only his change of status but also one's own. Bodily sin is thus a metaphor for a much wider issue, a transformation or transfiguration of one's present identity. As we shall see, Giotto is by no means alone in applying his art in this way.

Correggio's version from the 1520s, now in the Prado in Madrid, is intriguing for a number of reasons, not least because almost certainly it was commissioned for a private patron rather than for a church.[10] This may be one reason why the vegetation behind the encounter is done in such detail (scarcely a garden but luxuriant with various kinds of trees and bushes), for the painting could be better lit than was ever likely to be the case in a church. The absence of a halo or any sign of Christ's wounds should not, however, be confused with secularisation, as though a private patron necessarily brought a lessening of religious focus. Rather, what we have is the typical Renaissance interest in using the human to mediate the divine. The gardener's implements are cast aside, inconspicuously in the bottom right-hand corner, and the primary focus in now in the intensity of the gaze between Mary Magdalene and Christ. Her loose hair and yellow patterned dress suggest the prostitute of the composite figure to which I have already alluded. The kneeling figure stretches her head to gaze longingly and hopefully at the young figure of Christ who returns her gaze but points heavenwards. An oak behind gives an age, solidity and height that his own youthful form lacks, reinforced by the symbolic heavenly blue of the robe he is wearing. It is the sort of painting which, the more one looks at, the more one is drawn by its power into its underlying religious message. Mary's right hand steadying herself at the bottom left in fact creates a strong diagonal that forces one's own eyes through hers into Christ's, and beyond into his upward-pointing left hand and the tree rising above. Christ, we are being told, is able to draw Mary despite her sin into his own heavenly direction, a perspective that puts in the past his own wounds (they are not shown) and thus Mary's also.

Roughly contemporary and with similar symbolism for the tree is Titian's version, one of the best-known paintings in the National Gallery in London.[11] A youthful work (Titian was to live another sixty years), it is nonetheless highly creative.[12] Gone is any reference to the tomb itself, and the scene is set in idyllic rolling countryside with a large farmstead in the background and sheep grazing nearby. Intriguingly, X-rays have revealed that Titian's first thought was to portray Christ in the traditional manner with him walking away from Mary Magdalene and wearing a gardener's sun-hat. In the final version, however, Christ turns fully round to face her, and only a subdued reference to her mistaken identity of him survives (a hoe in Christ's left hand). Instead, Mary is allowed (on bended knees) to reach even as far as the white grave-clothes with which Jesus has vested himself. The eyes of the pair are entirely for each other, and there is no contrary gesture from Christ, apart from a gentle pulling of the shroud slightly closer to himself. It is only gradually that viewers discover a deeper dimension to what is being portrayed, as their eyes are drawn along the curve of Mary's bent body and up through the tree between them and so heavenwards. In short, given the composite identification of Mary mentioned above and her popularity in the Venice of the time, all sinners are in effect being told that, like Mary, they too can through their penitence before Christ win through and advance heavenwards.

Other examples with a similar emphasis might be mentioned, but perhaps more interesting, by way of contrast, is Rembrandt's approach a century later. Not only does he choose a different moment in the encounter from the norm but also a quite different focus.[13] The impact on Mary as our representative so noticeable in earlier paintings is now replaced by a focus on Christ himself as divine. Although dressed as a gardener, light seems to emanate from him, and in turn prevent shadow from falling on Mary, who is looking up towards him. It is a transcendent light which one of the two angels sitting on the tomb also shares. In the latter case the intention may be to underline the supernatural way in which Christ has broken out of the tomb, since, as with Giotto's version, the angels sit firmly on the lid. With Christ, though, the motive is more profound, to transform Mary's look from the alarm suggested in her hands (caught in mid-motion with the anointing cloth still in her grasp) to the reverential awe of recognition now indicated in her face. Unobserving, the other two female visitors to the tomb are already travelling down the path back to Jerusalem, visible in the distance with its cathedral-like temple (identifiable as such, if only because of the two pillars of Jachin and Boaz in front).[14] Yet, although it is a powerful picture, one cannot help feeling that nonetheless something has been lost, in omitting the direct engagement of the viewer. Mary's experience is now unique, a divine epiphany, and so no longer comparable to our own.

The work dates from 1638, and so from relatively early in Rembrandt's career (he was thirty-two). A couple of decades earlier, Bishop Lancelot Andrewes preached three powerful Easter Day sermons on the theme of the ascension.[15] Like Rembrandt he too stressed the divinity but in a way that insists on the continuing relevance of Christ's humanity to our own. He is convinced that the ascension is more important than the resurrection: 'better lie still in our graves, better never rise, than rise and rising not to ascend'.[16] Picking up the theme of Christ as gardener, he speaks of him as the one 'who made such a herb grow out of the ground this day as the like was never seen before, a dead body to shoot forth alive out of the grave... By virtue of this morning's act, he will garden our bodies too, turn all our graves into garden plots.'[17] But for that to happen we must follow the example of Mary and learn the due reverence that can pull us heavenwards. For Andrewes Mary discovered the right kind of reverence subsequently when she caught at his feet, as described in Matthew.[18] But, if that supposition differs from the pictorial representations which already show her kneeling in this incident, Andrewes insists on a still greater sense of intimacy after Christ has departed, in his Eucharistic presence. Modern commentators tend to dismiss the possibility that this is what was intended (in particular by the 'for'), but on the other side three observations may be made. The first is that the importance of touch is stressed generally in John. Second, metaphorical as well as literal uses occur elsewhere in Scripture, and so it is not as though to accept the implication requires a crudely literalistic reading of what is meant by 'touch'.[19] Finally, in John 6 Christ as our Eucharistic food is actually explicitly linked with the ascension.[20] So, however one reads that earlier passage, John 20 could be referring back to the new type of intimacy which it suggests – Christ once more present but in a new way.

If Eucharistic presence is not an aspect taken up in modern art, it is nonetheless surprising how strong the other continuities remain. As an initial example, consider a painting from one of the founders of the Nabi movement, Maurice Denis (1870–1943), himself much interested in religious art.[21] It shares the decorative emphasis associated with that movement.[22] Christ seems almost to dance heavenward. Although he looks back, neither Mary nor another accompanying woman looks at him. Instead, their heads are bowed in prayer, each engrossed in their own flowering plot whose richness echoes the larger formalised garden in the background. In the centre of Mary's plot a tree blossoms. It looks as though, despite the painting's Latin title *Noli me tangere* (recorded within the picture itself), the artist intended to capture a moment subsequent to Christ's rebuke. Mary now, like us, relies on faith alone. She is at the foot of the steps that take Christ to heaven and knows that with prayerful attention to her own allotted sphere she too can progress that way in due course.

Among twentieth-century representations in Britain, three in particular seem worth singling out. As one enters Ely Cathedral, the exchange between the two is presented by two skeletal metal figures sculpted by David Wynne, Mary recoiling a little as Jesus points heavenwards with both hands upraised. It offers a simple but effective message, as one enters the church, of Christ's summons to a different order of living and reality. In the Methodist Art Collection is Roy de Maistre's 1958 work.[23] Here a massive Christ overwhelms a diminutive Magdalene kneeling at his feet. While any doubt about Christ's divinity is silenced not only by the scale of his person but also by his yellow halo and the light emanating from his person, it is hard to detect any clear impact on Mary, for her face is turned away from us and towards Christ. In a sense that could be an improvement since it allows an unmediated response from us to this august figure, but the disadvantage is that all cues for an appropriate response must now come from the figure of Christ himself. Perhaps that is why de Maistre added the letters for 'love' on Christ's cloak, to help guide our response. In the early 1960s Walter Hussey commissioned from Graham Sutherland a version of the scene for the Magdalen Chapel in Chichester Cathedral. Although the various exhibitions organised in 2003 to celebrate the centenary of Sutherland's birth seem to have done little to revive his declining reputation compared with that of his erstwhile friend Francis Bacon, he remains a significant artist.[24] Best known of course for his work in Coventry Cathedral, the two versions that he did for Chichester are nonetheless also impressive.[25] In both Mary is portrayed kneeling at the foot of an open metal staircase (apparently borrowed from the garden wall of Sutherland's French home), up which Christ is advancing, his outstretched left arm pointing the way. The cathedral version, which has Christ wearing a gardener's hat, is to my mind too cluttered, but, whichever version is preferred, the introduction of the staircase was an inspired thought, since it reminds us of John's first use of ascension imagery, with Christ himself the staircase upon which angels descend and ascend.[26] A strong claim is thus made for the indispensability of his mediatorial role.

Intriguingly, in that last painting it is an assertion addressed once more to Mary in her role as sinner, for her tightly hugging dress is apparently evocative of the type of clothes once to be seen on 1950s prostitutes in London's Bond Street. It looks as though despite the animadversions of biblical scholars the old equation lives on, and not just in art. Twentieth-century poets as varied as Boris Pasternack and David Constantine make the same sort of appeal, and one can understand why. Mary is there for sinners like us, to assure us that Christ's upward pointing is not simply a destiny reserved for himself but also applies to our own flawed condition. It is the nature of that transformation that the artistic tradition tries to address, not always very successfully, in the other major type of representation to which I now turn.

Humanity's Ascent as Part of the Ascension Event

The most familiar depiction of the ascent itself has now become the common butt of jokes, used to parody art at its most naïve and literal. As we shall see, by no means all attempts are of this kind, but before examining the more adventurous it will be worth considering a few of the type under suspicion, to see what exactly has gone wrong. One of the great masterpieces of English Romanesque art is the so-called Cloisters Cross, now owned by the Metropolitan Museum in New York. On the cross's front there is a depiction in ivory of the ascension with all of Christ's body above the waist already disappeared within the clouds.[27] The Virgin Mary and three disciples look on close by, while the heads of four more are immediately beneath his feet.[28] The strangeness of the literalism lies not so much in itself as in its juxtaposition with the exact opposite: the four heads are just above a tiny, triangular pinnacle of rock used to represent the mountain on which the scene is set. Literalism and symbolism are thus placed in uneasy tension. Apparently, this form of representation was itself an English invention.[29] On the continent Christ was depicted either departing on a cloud or else being pulled by the Father's hand into the heavens. English preachers, however, apparently worried about the potential implication that the Son might be thought to need help, and so insisted on him piercing the clouds by his own efforts.

The aim was thus a laudable one, of emphasising Christ's full divinity. The sadness was that it made the incident seem quaint or ridiculous rather than itself awe-inspiring. To restore mystery and majesty, there was a need to move in one or other of two opposing directions: either to depict the scene after the disappearance or else to elaborate and enhance the disappearing feet. The potential of the former is well illustrated by a carving from eleventh-century Cologne. The sadness of the Virgin Mary and the disciples as they look heavenwards leave us in no doubt to which event allusion is being made. Even so, there is too much of a sense of absence for the depiction to be entirely satisfactory, whereas an 1170 Psalter illustration points to what can be achieved by turning in the opposite direction. Angels attend to Christ's feet while he himself disappears into no ordinary cloud but a multi-coloured penumbra of concentric circles that suggest the perfection of a divinity that is all-embracing in its power.[30] Unfortunately, few artists experimented with those more elaborate forms, and so feet sticking out from a cloud continue to proliferate over the subsequent centuries. Normally, a crowd of disciples is to be found as onlookers, but occasionally the Virgin Mary is there on her own, contemplating what has happened to her Son. The intention is not to exalt Mary but rather to use her as a medium (like Mary Magdalene in the other incident) to negotiate a relation for the believer with her Son.[31] Sadly, it was the simple English version that was also eventually to become the norm on the continent, as in a painting by Schongauer (d. 1491), now a sad contrast in its location at Colmar to the brilliance of Grünewald's Isenheim Altarpiece located nearby in the same museum.

Schongauer may equally be used to illustrate more pedestrian representations of the resurrection in which Christ stands victorious on his open tomb. The problem is not the truth of the claim but that it seems to say almost too little – a great mystery has become a laboured fact. It was a conclusion to which artists also came in the sixteenth and seventeenth centuries. In their attempts to rectify the problem and thus give adequate expression to the mystery and majesty of the resurrection, however, any clear division between resurrection and ascension seemed to dissolve. To set the issue in context, we need first to retrace our steps and observe the earlier alternative iconography for the ascension in continental Europe. Giotto's work in the Scrovegni Chapel may be used by way of illustration.[32] Everything is focused on Christ sailing heavenwards on a cloud, his hands upraised. The disciples below are in two groups separated by two angels pointing heavenwards. There are, however, two further groups in the heavens themselves, also with arms upraised. Two centuries later, Perugino, Raphael's teacher, attempted a similar strategy, with angels playing instruments in the heavens as Christ ascends.[33] Nonetheless, Giotto's simpler gesture seems the more successful, not least because he mixes saints and angels and gives the impression of the saints having been carried into the heavens through the adoption of a similar gesture to Christ's: faithful trust pulling them through.

In 1475, however, Giovanni Bellini set Christ's resurrection similarly in the sky amidst clouds, with the soldiers looking on astonished from below.[34] Although the idea did not immediately catch on, certainly from the time of the Council of Trent onwards it was to become quite a common form of depiction, and one can see why.[35] For the majesty of the event was no longer now in doubt. A century later, El Greco's version (now in the Prado in Madrid) is one of the great triumphs of art.[36] Christ is visibly rising in triumph, even pulling most of the semi-naked soldiers with him. One exception leans on his elbow, his flippant indifference accentuated by the helmet he wears, adorned as it is by coloured feathers. The other major exception, however, exercises a quite different role, his whole body thrown back towards us as he rejects Christ and attempts a counter-thrust to the general direction of the picture. The play and counter-play of forces cannot help but involve us in the action, and call from us some sort of response or decision.[37]

Such depictions become especially interesting where direct comparison is possible between how the artist has conceived resurrection and ascension. This is so with Tintoretto's work for the Scuola Grande of San Rocco in Venice, work done in the late 1570s. In his *Resurrection* Christ has almost become a bird as he flies out of the tomb which four large angels have forced open, his pink shroud billowing in the wind like the wings of a great bird.[38] The pink may well be intended to recall the distant pink figure of God the Father in his own magnificent depiction of Jacob's Ladder elsewhere in the room.[39] There, however, the Father is a tiny figure in the infinite distance, whereas here Christ dominates the picture. There is drama in abundance, but the two women on the left have yet to arrive on the scene, while we are denied sight of the faces of those already there. It is almost as though Tintoretto wants us to focus on the miracle itself, whereas in his *Ascension* human interplay is undoubtedly part of his aim.[40] Awe is the predominant response as angels accompany Christ rising in the clouds, olive and palm branches in their hands. The great surprise, though, is the reversal of reality. It is now this world that appears insubstantial compared with the reality to which Christ is returning.[41]

Rembrandt also has a *Resurrection* and *Ascension* only three years apart (1639 and 1636), both now at the Alte Pinakothek in Munich.[42] The former also has a dramatic, flying figure, but it is an angel rather than Christ, emblazoned in a heavenly shaft of light. Apparently, it was a late decision on Rembrandt's part to include Christ himself. Unfortunately, this was clearly a mistake since he remains a weak figure only just emerging from the tomb and from death. The *Ascension* by contrast is a marvellous evocation of Christ inviting us into participation in his own exaltation. Little cherubs clutch at his cloud as he ascends in a blaze of light emanating from the dove of the Holy Spirit far above. The disciples, however, are not so much awestruck as caught up in wonder and rapture and the desire to share, eyes and hands alike exhibiting a fervid intensity. It has been suggested that in this work 'Rembrandt went as far as he dared toward Catholic apostasy', in attempting a likeness of God.[43] But the point is not that Christ has become or is becoming divine, but rather that his humanity is now exalted to a new and heavenly state. Indeed, as if to underline the fact, Rembrandt gives Christ a rather chunky set of legs.

In the twentieth century the range of experimentation has been quite broad. If angels accompanying Christ in heaven continue to be used to try to give a greater sense of majesty to the ascension,[44] equally resurrection scenes sometimes borrow imagery that would seem to be more appropriate to the ascension. So, for example, André Kamba Luesa from Zaire adopts a majesty figure of Christ dancing as symbolic of the resurrection, with rocks rent apart and diminutive human figures on either side sharing in his joy.[45] That same image of the dancer is also used by the Indonesian artist Bagong Kussudiardja explicitly for the ascension, with a young Christ dancing his way heavenwards as a graceful swan accompanies him in the background.[46] Even where there can be no doubt that the allusion is to the resurrection, dance can still sometimes be implicit. Paul Granlund has a magnificent sculpture that depicts Christ at the moment he splits apart the tomb.[47] But it is not just strength that is depicted, for in the process he seems almost like a bird ready to take elegant flight.

But of all modern ascensions it is Salvador Dalí's of 1958 that is the most distinctive, the most original.[48] The sea-line of his beloved Port Lligat is just visible at the bottom, but the painting is dominated by an ascending Christ viewed from below as tunnel-like he enters what looks like a great hollow globe or cone stretching ever upwards, at the top of which perches a welcoming dove, its presence accentuated by a larger feminine form above.[49] The yellow cone pierces dramatic, red, fissured clouds in the background, but perhaps the most interesting feature is Christ's feet. For they are in no sense idealised. They have the same dirt and roughness that is to be found in the hands of Christ in Dalí's Glasgow painting *The Christ of St John of the Cross*. It looks as though, like Rembrandt, he wanted to stress the continuing corporeality of Christ even in his exalted state.

This complex history does pose a number of difficult questions. The inappropriateness of literal representations, whether of ascension or of resurrection, can almost go without saying. The resultant merging of the two is, however, not without its problems. Biblical scholars, even some of a more conservative mould, often do speak in similar terms, with resurrection experiences sometimes seen as what the already ascended Christ offered to his disciples.[50] But, however the chronology is tackled, the experience and content of the two doctrines do seem significantly different. The resurrection speaks of triumph over death as Christ continues to be available to his disciples in an intimate, if not always immediately recognisable, manner; the ascension about his location elsewhere. To make his resurrection already a shooting off elsewhere, however figurative, is surely to allude to something else, and is scarcely endorsed by Scripture, which significantly offers no description of the actual event in any of the gospels. Admittedly, the description of the ascension is itself also minimal. Yet it does speak essentially of glory in a way that the resurrection appearances, at least as we now have them, do not. God the Son is once more with his Father, but so too is his exalted humanity, a humanity that is stressed by the angelic witnesses declaring that he will return in like manner. It is that joint reality that both Rembrandt and Dalí were attempting to express in combining glory and more obvious signs of an earthly humanity. In this they succeeded where many another artist failed. They also thereby underlined how profoundly significant the words of the angels in Luke's account really were: it is the human 'Jesus' who is being taken up into heaven and who will return again.[51]

Poets and composers too have struggled to find adequate imagery to capture that sense of a continuing but transfigured humanity. Easier is the more basic assertion of its continuing relevance to us, as in these lines of John Donne's:

> Nor does hee by ascending, show alone,
> But first hee, and hee first enters the way.
> O strong Ramme, which hast batter'd heaven for mee,
> Mild Lambe, which with thy blood, hast mark'd the path;
> Bright Torch, which shin'st, that I the way may see.[52]

His near-contemporary, Henry Vaughan, has several poems on the theme, but perhaps the most intriguing from a theological perspective is the one which toys with what the ascension's new human reality might be like. The first and last verses of his 'Ascension-Hymn' plays with two types of transformation:

> Dust and clay
> Man's ancient wear!
> Here you must stay,
> But I elsewhere;
> Souls sojourn here, but may not rest;
> Who will ascent, must be undressed.

If these lines sound as though Vaughan wishes to speak only of an ascent of the soul, the final verse indicates that here we are dealing with metaphor ('undressed' is 'the old Man'), and that in fact he envisages the whole of what Christ or we are entering in this new reality, that is, body no less than soul:

> He alone
> And none else can
> Bring bone to bone
> And rebuild man,
> And by his all subduing might
> Make clay ascend more quick than light.[53]

Modern poets such as John Updike or Denise Levertov often assume a very physical resurrection, but when it comes to the ascension their judgment can be more uncertain.[54] Denise Levertov, for instance, asks:

> Can Ascension
> not have been
> arduous, almost,
> as the return
> from Sheol, and
>   back through the tomb
>   into breath?
> Matter reanimate
> now must relinquish
> itself, its
> human cells,
> molecules, five
> senses, linear
> vision endured
> as Man.

At one level her questions look exactly right. Whatever heaven is like, it is not contiguous with our space and time, and so Christ's human reality there cannot be the same as it was here. But in this verse it looks almost as though she is questioning whether that new reality is human at all. Yet, like Vaughan, she too ends on a different note, speaking of the 'last self-enjoined task of Incarnation' being that:

> He again
> Mothering his birth:
> Torture and bliss.

There is a new human reality mothered into birth, a body hugely different from what he had on earth but nonetheless one that continues his incarnational identity into that new context.[55]

   Both art and poetry are thus, with varying degrees of success, struggling to give adequate expression to the doctrine. Christ's divinity has to be asserted, but so too does his transformed humanity, and both pictures and words have difficulty in finding the right images or metaphors for such a transformation. It might be thought that music would fare better, since progression in music inevitably speaks of movement and so of change. Perhaps the most commonly sung ascension anthem these days is Gerald Finzi's 'God is gone up', his setting of Edward Taylor's poem based on Psalm 47. It is a fine piece of music, but the stress is all on acknowledgement of Christ's divinity. We need, therefore, to go further back in time if a more balanced emphasis is sought. Anonymous 4, a now internationally known group of four female singers based in New York, in 2000 reconstructed and sung a mass setting for ascension, as they believe it might have sounded in AD 1000.[56] Appropriate tropes have been added to the ordinary throughout.[57] The introit takes the form of a dialogue and specifically addresses the question, *quem creditis super astra ascendisse?* ('whom do you believe to have ascended beyond the stars?'), stressing in response both humanity and divinity, a theme that is repeated at the offertory when Christ is described as 'carrying into heaven the wounds of his life-giving cross as his emblem'. If the Alleluia before the gospel picks the biblical image of 'captivity led captive',[58] at the troped communion we are told 'the body which we now receive on earth already sits at the right hand of the Father in heaven'. Jumping to the eighteenth century, we can listen to a setting of the events, admired by both Mozart and Beethoven, C. P. E. Bach's *Die Auferstehung und Himmelfahrt Jesu*.[59] If the final chorus, like Finzi, turns to Psalm 47 and is really a celebration of divine power with its elaborate contrapuntal writing, the rest of the piece leaves us in no doubt that it is as a man that Christ has triumphed. It is perhaps Olivier Messiaen, though, in the twentieth century who best captures the two aspects. His 1932 work *L'Ascension*, originally scored for orchestra but also available for organ, consists of four mediations, three on words from John's Gospel and the fourth on the collect for the day. The last of the four has a melody that ascends gradually,[60] and it is this notion that forms the basis for the parallel piece in his more famous work, *Quatuor pour la fin du Temps*.[61] Written and first performed while he was imprisoned at Görlitz in 1941, an earlier section uses cello and piano to portray the eternity of the Word, while this final section has violin and piano gradually ascend, finally disappearing into silence.

Conclusion

The themes treated in this essay have also of course been discussed by preachers and theologians and, as with the particular artists mentioned, sometimes with success and sometimes not. So, for example, although Bede in the eighth century is concerned to differentiate this ascension from all others, he also remains in no doubt about its implications for humanity.[62] He writes of the disciples: 'how sweet were the tears which they poured forth when … they discerned that their God and Lord was now bringing thither part of their own nature'. Indeed, Bede finds not only humanity thus exalted but implicitly all of creation: 'he lifted up this earth on the wings of the wind when he elevated what he had taken from the earth'.[63] By contrast, although Newman's sermons so often exhibit a mastery of prose style that includes striking image or phrase, it is with some disappointment that one reads what he has to say for successive years on this theme. There is plenty on Christ as our heavenly mediator, but only one sermon focuses on the image of ascent itself. It is unsurprising that mountains are drawn into the discussion, but I detected only one occasion when he showed a little of his usual fire, and even then he is somewhat apologetic. For, following the hints in John's Gospel, he observes: 'we may even say that, when our Lord was lifted on the cross, then, too, he presented to us the same example of a soul raised heavenwards and hid in God'.[64]

It is therefore something of a relief to turn to Austin Farrer's provocative treatment of the theme.[65] His starting point is the familiar ascension hymn:

> Hail the day that sees him rise
> Glorious to his native skies.

Initially the theology sounds fine, but further reflection, Farrer argues, suggests quite otherwise. Christ's divinity never had a birth, so the skies can scarcely be 'native' to him except in some highly metaphorical sense. But equally the skies – heaven – were not native to humanity prior to this point. As Farrer observes, 'the marvel is not that the celestial Son of God returns where he belongs, but that the earthborn Jesus rises into the native heaven of that divine life which had become man in him... [H]e is the man glorified, which each of us may hope by his grace to become.'[66]

Yet, that conceded, it still seems to me that the artists surveyed in this essay attempted for the most part something rather more. They did not simply echo what they had learnt from Scripture and Christian doctrine, they also tried to develop further some of its unresolved tensions, in ways that are sometimes illuminating and sometimes not. Thus in the encounter of Christ with Mary Magdalene the artistic tradition was clearly unhappy that her story should end on a note of rebuke, and so pursued how the exchange might still in its turn have produced a deepening of the relationship, not only for Mary but also for us in the transfiguration of our own bodily desires. Again, creative work on the ascent itself in art, music and poetry all alike struggled with what it might mean to say that Christ's humanity continued into a quite different, new reality. If clear answers are not always given, there is a stronger insistence than is usually noticeable in contemporary preaching and theology that it must be a glorified human being that survives the transformation, and not just an exalted deity. Rembrandt's chunky legs and Dalí's dirty feet promise the gradual, ascending rise of Messiaen's music for us also in a way that, for example, Gerard Manley Hopkins's beautified Christ does not. In a sermon of 1879 he had declared: 'for myself I make no secret I look forward to seeing the matchless beauty of Christ's body in the heavenly light'.[67] That image, though, speaks too much of a world utterly different from our own, whereas the encounter with Mary Magdalene and the flawed ascending body alike give us hope, for the absorption of ordinary and troubled humanity into that more wondrous reality.[68]

Notes

1 Luke 24:50–3; Acts 1:6–11.
2 The proposal (requiring only a small emendation of the Greek) of J. H. Bernard, *Gospel According to St. John* (Edinburgh: T&T Clark, 1928), II: 669–70.
3 Chrysostom, *Homilies on John*, 86; Augustine, *Tractates on John*, 121.
4 C. K. Barrett, *The Gospel According to St John*, 2nd edn (London: SPCK, 1978), 565.
5 Also sometimes known as the Arena Chapel because it was once the site of a Roman amphitheatre. For illustration, Bruce Cole, *Giotto: The Scrovegni Chapel, Padua* (New York: George Braziller, 1993), no. 36; Anne Mueller von der Haegen, *Giotto* (Cologne: Könemann, 1998), no. 95.
6 For illustration, Christopher Lloyd, *Fra Angelico* (London: Phaidon, 1992 edn), no. 29. The painting dates from 1441, Giotto's from c. 1310.
7 Christ's feet are crossed, with the right foot only just holding back the onward advance of the left.
8 I examine this development, and seek to defend it from its critics (from feminist theologians and from those who believe that historical accuracy must always assume primacy) in my *Discipleship and Imagination: Christian Tradition and Truth* (Oxford: Oxford University Press, 2000), 31–61.
9 Anselm, *Oratio*, 16 (my trans.).
10 For illustration and some commentary, David Ekserdjian, *Correggio* (New Haven: Yale University Press, 1997), 156–159.
11 For illustration, Marion Kaminski, *Titian* (Cologne: Könemann, 1998), 24.
12 Painted in about 1514 when Titian was somewhere between twenty-four and twenty-seven, Titian survived till 1576.
13 *Christ Appearing to Mary Magdalen*, now in Buckingham Palace. For illustration and some commentary, Christopher Brown, Jan Kelch and Pieter van Thiel, *Rembrandt: The Master and His Workshop* (New Haven: Yale University Press, 1991), 204–207.
14 1 Kings 7:21; 2 Chronicles 3:17.
15 Sermons for 1620, 1621, 1622: available in Marianne Dorman, ed., *The Sermons of Lancelot Andrewes* (Edinburgh: Pentland Press, 1993), II: 145–178.
16 Ibid., 1622; II: 171.
17 Ibid., 1620; II: 152.
18 Ibid., 1621; II: 159; Matthew 28:9.
19 For the importance of touch in John, note particularly 1 John 1:1; for metaphorical uses of touch, e.g. 1 Samuel 10:26; Jeremiah 1:9; Isaiah, 41:13.
20 John 6:62.
21 The painting, dating from 1896, is illustrated in Nancy Grubb, *Scènes de la vie du Christ* (Paris: Éditions Abbeyville, 1996), 137. The original is in the Musée du Prieuré, Saint-Germain-en-Laye. The Nabis (who also included Bonnard, Maillol and Vuillard) saw themselves as 'prophets' of a new, anti-naturalist style that stressed the flatness of the canvas and often engaged with symbolist concerns.
22 Édouard Vuillard's work is perhaps best known in this connection. In some of his paintings his mother and sister seem almost to merge with the wallpaper.
23 The Collection is now housed at Westminster College, Oxford.
24 A helpful survey of his more secular art is to be found in Maurice Fréchuret et al., *Sutherland: une retrospective* (Antibes: Musée Picasso, 1998).
25 The other is now in Pallant House, also in Chichester. Pamela Tudor-Craig compared the two in the *Church Times* (2 May 2003, 28), unlike me giving the palm to the version in the cathedral. Where she does seem right is in the better quality of the faces in the latter.

26 John 1:51, based on Jacob's vision at Bethel: Genesis 28:10–17. The Greek implies that the Son of Man is himself the ladder rather than simply at the foot of it.
27 For illustrations, Elizabeth C. Parker and Charles T. Little, *The Cloister Cross: Its Art and its Meaning* (London: Harvey Miller, 1994), viii and 88.
28 Acts 1:14 was used to deduce the presence of Mary.
29 Argued by Meyer Shapiro, *Late Antiquity, Early Christian and Medieval Art* (London: Chatto & Windus, 1980), 267–288. He dates its origin to about AD 1000.
30 For illustration from this Psalter, now in Glasgow University Library, see Parker and Little, *The Cloister Cross*, 90.
31 For a good example, John Plummer, *The Hours of Catherine of Cleves* (New York: George Braziller, 1966), no. 94 (part of the Hours of the Virgin).
32 Cole, *Giotto*, no. 37.
33 For illustration, Vittoria Garibaldi, *Perugino* (Florence: Scala, 1997), 45. Recently restored, one version is in the Cathedral of San Sepolcro. For a discussion of the painting and its restoration, Stephano Casciu, ed., *The Ascension of Christ by Pietro Perugino* (Milan: Silvana Editoriale, 1998).
34 Black and white illustration in Grigore Arbore, *Bellini* (London: Abbey, 1978), no. 21. The original is in the Gemäldegalerie in Berlin.
35 Titian was among the first to adopt the new form. For two examples from the 1520s and 1540s (the former adopted as the front cover for N. T. Wright's major book on the resurrection), Marion Kaminski, *Titian* (Cologne: Könemann, 1998), 39, 73.
36 Illustrated in Leo Bronstein, *El Greco* (London: Thames and Hudson, 1991 ed.), no. 23.
37 The extent of the success can be seen by comparing the work to an earlier attempt in Toledo: illustrated in Richard G. Mann, *El Greco and His Patrons* (Cambridge: Cambridge University Press, 1986), no. 5.
38 Illustrated in Francesco Valcanover, *Jacopo Tintoretto and the Scuola Grande of San Rocco* (Venice: Storti Edizioni, 1983), 66.
39 Ibid., 53.
40 Ibid., 80.
41 Indicated by scale and by the relative strength of the colours for the two realities.
42 Illustrated in Simon Schama, *Rembrandt's Eyes* (London: Penguin, 1999), 440, 444. Both are now in the Alte Pinakothek in Munich.
43 Schama's view, ibid., 441.
44 For two examples from the United States, James B. Simpson and George H. Eatman, *A Treasury of Anglican Art* (New York: Rizzoli, 2002), 128–129.
45 The work dates from 1992; illustrated in Ron O'Grady, *Christ for All People: Celebrating a World of Christian Art* (Auckland: Pace, 2001), 143.
46 Illustrated in Susan A. Blain, ed., *Imaging the Word* (Cleveland: United Church Press, 1995), II: 202.
47 Illustrated in Kenneth T. Lawrence, ed., *Imagining the Word* (Cleveland: United Church Press, 1994), I: 185. The sculpture is in St Mark's Lutheran Cathedral in Minneapolis.
48 In a private collection, it is illustrated in Dawn Ades, *Dalí's Optical Illusions* (New Haven: Yale University Press, 2000), no. 56.
49 Her features are borrowed from those of his wife, Gala.
50 Raymond Brown comments: 'from the moment that God raises Jesus up, he is in heaven ... if he makes appearances, he appears from heaven': *The Gospel According to John* (New York: Doubleday, 1970), 1013. F. F. Bruce takes a similar view: 'the resurrection appearances ... were visitations from that eternal

order to which his "body of glory" now belonged': *The Book of the Acts* (Grand Rapids, Mich.: Eerdmans, 1988), 37.
51 Acts 1:11.
52 From 'Ascention', in Herbert J. C. Grierson, ed., *Donne: Poetical Works* (London: Oxford University Press, 1933), 292.
53 Alan Rudrum, ed., *Henry Vaughan: The Complete Poems* (Harmondsworth: Penguin, 1983 edn), 245–246. For other poems on the ascension, 185–186, 243–245, 246–247.
54 For physical resurrection, cf. John Updike's 'Seven Stanzas at Easter' and Levertov's 'On Belief in the Physical Resurrection of Jesus'; the latter is available in her *Sands of the Well* (Newcastle: Bloodaxe, 1998), 115–116. The lines quoted are from Levertov's poem 'Ascension' in her *A Door in the Hive and Evening Train* (Newcastle: Bloodaxe, 1993), 207, and are used with grateful permission.
55 I discuss what might be entailed by that new context in the final essay of *God in a Single Vision: Integrating Philosophy and Theology*, ed. Christopher R. Brewer and Robert MacSwain (London and New York: Routledge, 2016), 181–190.
56 Anonymous 4, *1000: A Mass for the End of Time* (Harmonia Mundi, 2000). The chosen title seems to me unfortunate, but was chosen apparently to capture the apocalyptic fervour around at the time of the new millennium, and the ascension's promise of Christ's return.
57 The 'ordinary' is the fixed element in the mass, 'tropes' additional commentary, usually, but by no means always, biblical quotation.
58 Applied to the ascension in Ephesians 4:8 (quoting Psalm 68:18), the verse is being used to speak of Christ as victorious over all the forces of evil ranged against him.
59 First performed in 1774, Mozart actually conducted three performances in Vienna in 1788.
60 'Prière du Christ montant vers son Père'. There is a fine performance on the organ of Beauvais Cathedral by Jennifer Bate, personally endorsed by Messiaen (recorded in 1982 and available on the Regis label).
61 The conclusion of the quartet, VIII: 'Louange à l'immortalité de Jésus'. The contrasting earlier section is V: 'Louange à l'éternité de Jésus'.
62 *Homilies on the Gospels*, II, 15. I have used the translation by Lawrence T. Martin and David Hurst (Kalamazoo, Mich.: Cistercian Publications, 1991), 135–147, esp. 141, 143. Bede's Latin text seems to have spoken of Elijah being taken up 'as if into heaven': 145 (not the usual Vulgate reading).
63 Cf. Psalm 18:10.
64 John Henry Newman, *Parochial and Plain Sermons* (San Francisco: Ignatius Press, 1987), V: 15, 1306–1313, esp. 1308. For a mediatorial example, II: 18, 356–362.
65 'A New Creation', in *Austin Farrer: The Essential Sermons*, ed. Leslie Houlden (London: SPCK, 1991), 69–71, esp. 70.
66 Ibid., 70. Farrer also pursues a similar theme in 'Gates to the City', in *A Celebration of Faith* (London: Hodder and Stoughton, 1970), 96–99.
67 Sermon for 23 November 1879; W. H. Gardner ed., *Gerard Manley Hopkins: A Selection of his Poetry and Prose* (Harmondsworth: Penguin, 1953), 137–139.
68 Originally published as 'Ascension and Transfigured Bodies', in *Faithful Performances: Enacting Christian Tradition*, ed. Trevor Hart and Steven R. Guthrie (Aldershot: Ashgate, 2007), 257–272. Reproduced here with permission of the editors and publishers, with some minor emendations. I am grateful to Ann Loades for comments on an earlier draft. For some helpful reflections of her own on related themes, Heather Walton and Susan Durber, eds, *Silence in Heaven: A Book of Women's Preaching* (London: SCM, 1994), 9–13, 130–134.

9   Artists on the Trinity

Because Christianity is founded upon a written revelation, the danger has always been that the power of the word will be exaggerated. So, despite the continuing protests of mystics over the ages about the limitations of language, precisely the same kinds of test for doctrinal orthodoxy or linguistic propriety have come to be applied in areas where they are either less suitable or indeed quite inappropriate. This is in my view one of the major stumbling-blocks which has plagued the Christian appropriation of art. A verbal checklist is applied, rather than care being taken to ascertain what it is that the artist is trying to achieve. The element of imaginative engagement is thus missed, as too is the fact that, because artists have not the same freedom to qualify as have writers, their metaphors have to be at once more forceful as well as – inevitably – more easily subject to misinterpretation. Such contrasts, though, far from being a weakness, can have much to teach us about the explication of doctrine. The extent to which different sorts of issue are raised by the visual as distinct from the verbal is well indicated, I believe, by the various types of presentation to which artists have resorted in developing imagery to highlight the significance and relevance of the doctrine of the Trinity.

Over the course of the centuries, quite a number of different forms of allusion have been attempted. At the risk of over-simplifying, I propose in what follows to identify three main types of approach. Inevitably, to some degree any type of classification prejudges issues, detecting common lines where others may prefer to see none, but whatever faults the method may have, it at least enables us to avoid a purely chronological investigation. So I propose we look at artistic representations under three heads, what I shall call triadic, societal and incarnational images. Very roughly what I mean by each is as follows. By 'triadic' I shall understand those images which focus on symbols of threeness, whether abstract such as a triangle or semi-representational such as three identical heads. By 'societal' I mean those where the primary focus is on relationality,[1] with its personal character stressed, and so one is immediately conscious of some form of interaction taking place. Finally, by 'incarnational' I intend reference to those images where the primary idea involves some form of allusion to specific events in

Christ's life. As we shall observe, overlap is inevitable if characterisations of this degree of vagueness are used as our starting point, but the differences of emphasis are, I believe, significant and so worth highlighting. All three types have in fact been subject to severe criticism, but I shall contend that more often than not such criticism misses its mark because it judges by the wrong criteria. Precise theological statements have never been the aim, but rather visual metaphors that invite further exploration and involvement. In the process important theological concerns were voiced which, because judged by the wrong criteria, have too often been rejected rather than developed further.

Triadic Versions

I begin here because, though historically the least common, such images are also at once the most ancient and the most modern. Though not in general unsympathetic to modern art, I do want in this particular case to suggest that, initial appearances notwithstanding, it is the modern versions which are in general the less thought-provoking or profound. To see why, let us begin with modernity. Perhaps the problem has to do with motivation. For the almost universal preference in modern times for symbolic allusion seems to have been inspired less by enthusiasm for the general trend in modern art towards abstraction and much more by revulsion from traditional forms of representation. Derisive comments about the Father as an old man and the Spirit as a bird are commonplace. That the worries inherent in such a critique are misconceived, I shall argue in due course. What, though, also needs to be acknowledged is that modern abstract representation also carries with it its own set of problems.

The principal of these is that, while functioning as useful reminders of trinitarian doctrine, such images are seldom effective in inspiring any fresh reflection on the nature of the doctrine, far less any suggestion of its relevance to ourselves. Louise Nevelson's work in New York might be used by way of illustration. Columnar forms and wall configurations are made triadic, and as such defended as a way of evoking the Trinity without it 'accosting' us.[2] Such muted reference certainly reminds us that we are in a church, but scarcely carries us beyond that point. John Piper's tapestry in Chichester Cathedral is more direct, but still quite subdued. It is the symbols of the three persons that one notices first and only then the triangle that unites them. A level of subtlety is introduced by the way in which the intended reference of the three symbols as trinitarian only becomes retrospectively apparent as the triangle behind them finally forces such a reading.[3] So we are certainly offered aesthetic and intellectual pleasure as we explore the tapestry, but it would be harder to argue that there accrues any deepening of one's religious understanding.[4] A better contender might be the piece of sculpture commissioned from Stephen Cox for Newcastle Cathedral. Egyptian alabaster marked into three segments is the idiom employed, but this is combined with the piece as a whole being used to evoke the sense of broken bread and poured chalice, and so both the source of trinitarian doctrine in the life of Christ and of its continued significance in the worship of the Church.[5]

One modern image much discussed is Anselm Kiefer's 1973 diptych *Vater, Sohn und hl. Geist*.[6] The lower painting is of a dense forest with three trunks so named from which there emerges the log cabin that constitutes the frame of the upper painting. Within this cabin are three identical seats with flames of fire upon each, while through the cabin's three windows there is to be seen nothing except thick snow. It seems clear that Kiefer intended to say something about the tension between Germany's pagan and Christian inheritance, clear too that he is pessimistic about the ability of Christianity to communicate to the wider world.[7] But most relevant here is the way in which the painting takes up the theme of the Trinity also building upon pagan interest in triads,[8] for, if we are to understand why triadic images were once so popular in Christian art, we will need to come to terms with their pagan antecedents.

In the pagan Celtic world in particular the representation of divinity as three appears to have been extremely common.[9] Sometimes it took the form of three identical figures, sometimes one figure with three identical heads, sometimes small variations between them. There are also variations in what type is most popular in which location. For instance, in Germany two identical matronly goddesses are found flanking a younger third, while elsewhere one finds three identical figures distinguished only by what they hold. Again, the area round Reims has yielded particularly fine examples of identical triple-faced deities, while elsewhere we find differentiation not only of age but also sometimes even of sex.[10] Scholars are uncertain how far differentiation must go before we should speak of three deities rather than one, and indeed it has been suggested that there may even have been a comparable uncertainty in the worshipper's own mind.[11] What, however, does seem clear is that such repetition was intended to indicate intensifying power, the presence in the deity of the relevant attributes to an unparalleled degree. One can see a related way of thinking operating where animals are given an additional horn or three phalli. The triad was the Celtic way of indicating the presence of something rather more than natural power.

Why three should have been chosen rather than, say, two or four is hard to say. Suggestions have included a reflection of social structure, the notion of the divine as all-seeing or even an allusion to phases of the moon.[12] In the absence of any suitable literary evidence, only speculation is possible. What can, however, be asserted is that this use of repetition as indicating divinity continued well into the Christian era. Abstract triads are found, as in the seventh-century Fyvie stone where the device of three circles inside a larger circle is used, or again with the three eggs found inside a bird's nest sculpted on the magnificent ninth-century Kildalton cross.[13] Triple-faced heads were once also very common, but, sadly, almost all were destroyed at the

Reformation, though occasionally an inconspicuous location has preserved them, as is the case with an early fifteenth-century misericord at Cartmel Priory.[14] Nor was the phenomenon by any means confined to what had once been the domain of Celtic paganism. An early example from Rome itself is now in the Vatican museum. A sarcophagus telling the story of the fall and redemption opens with God as three bonded, bearded men creating Eve from Adam on the ground, while in the next scene God now as a young man addresses Adam and Eve, with his trinitarian character this time identified by three identical stars above.[15] Though Roman religion did have triadic elements, they were scarcely dominant,[16] and so it seems implausible to suggest this as the source; nor need we postulate a Celtic sculptor. More likely is the Christian dogma interacting in the sculptor's mind with the thought that the repeated unnatural figure would suggest something greater than human personality. If so, there is an important element of engagement with that part of the narrative for which such a representation is chosen. Adam, we all know, was made in the divine image, but the three heads underline for the observer at once both the similarity and difference thus established between creator and created: God is in our image, but then also so much more.

Somewhat surprisingly, the Renaissance brought both renewed interest in such images and their eventual condemnation. As the latter issue is the less complicated, we may note the attack first. This was initiated by the celebrated St Antoninus of Florence (d. 1459), well known for his writings on economic theory, and it is in the context of his discussion of the payment of artists that he makes his comments. Along with pictures of Jesus entering Mary's womb at the annunciation fully formed and the Child reading before appropriate years, the Trinity as a single person with three heads is condemned 'because it is a monster in the nature of things'.[17] Ironically, here we find Antoninus fully in accord with the naturalising tendencies of Renaissance art as it was to develop, and indeed giving it a further push in that direction. Yet, as we have seen, what had once most appealed about the image was precisely its unnaturalness as indicative of divinity. Definitive condemnation finally came in 1628 from Pope Urban VIII.[18] Even so the image did not entirely disappear. Not only did abstract triadic structures become an image of Catholic dissent in sixteenth-century England,[19] even as late as the nineteenth century we still find this particular variant of a triple-faced deity receiving veneration, though admittedly in the remoteness of the Tirolese Alps.[20]

How popular that image had once been is well indicated by the numbers that have survived despite papal condemnation not only from Antoninus' own time but even from his own archdiocese of Florence. Though by major artists, none could be classed as a major work in its own right, and this no doubt in part explains their survival. Even so, their range is worth noting. Probably the earliest Renaissance example to survive is Donatello's three-faced Trinity in the tympanum of the Guelph party niche in Orsanmichele, dating from the second decade of the fifteenth century.[21] From 1438 comes

134 *Artists as Theologians*

Filippo Lippi's representation of St Augustine's vision of the Trinity as a three-headed figure piercing his heart.[22] Pollaiuolo (d. 1498), who also employs a triangular arrangement of angels to link heaven and earth in his famous series for the Church of St Augustine at San Gimignano, uses a three-faced Trinity in his allegory of theology on the tomb of Sixtus IV (d. 1484).[23] Finally, from 1511 comes Andrea del Sarto's medallion of a three-faced head of the Trinity surrounded by four other medallions of saints. In this last instance encasement in a glowing sun is used to further underline the divine unity.[24]

None of these examples can, it seems to me, be assessed fairly without due account being taken of the thought of the time. The Neoplatonism of the Renaissance very strongly endorsed the notion of a common theology, that paganism should be seen as an anticipation of Christianity, and indeed this attitude was shared by St Antoninus himself.[25] The leading intellectuals of the movement, however, in particular Pico della Mirandola (d. 1494) and Ficino (d. 1499), carried the argument a stage further, in finding triadism in the world everywhere about them, and in seeing in this a reflection at one and the same time both of the triadic structure of God and of his ultimate unity.[26] A surprising but perhaps inevitable conclusion of such a line of thought was that even negative triads could be taken to point in the same direction. So, for example, appeal was even made to the existence of three-headed Cerberus in classical mythology, and this may explain in part why the same triple-headed image could be used of the Devil or of humanity in conflict with itself, no less than of God himself.[27] Perhaps Dante's use of both negative and positive trinitarian imagery should be seen as an anticipation of such attitudes.[28] Certainly, the simultaneous use of the image in opposed senses very effectively enabled the idea to be conveyed that the negative image need not have the last word; instead of ultimate division, there was the possibility of complete integration. This would seem to be the idea behind Titian's intriguing *Allegory of Prudence*, represented by a three-headed man with three animals beneath. The present time of the middle-aged face in the centre is given a lion below to indicate someone who has successfully integrated within his life both the ferocious determination of the wolf of the past (the youthful zeal of the face on one side) and the faithfulness of the dog of the future (the old man on the other). In other words, the idea is of a present reality in which past memory and future hope are suitably balanced and modified through present integration.[29] But undoubtedly of most significance for this line of thinking are the various figures of the three Graces, which were regularly taken to imply reciprocal relationships of love that bring an ultimate unity, and indeed this may well be an important factor behind so famous a painting as Botticelli's *Primavera*.[30]

In rehearsing this history my objective has been to challenge the supposition that modern triadic representations of the Trinity are subtle in their allusions to the doctrine, whereas three-faced heads are crude and naïve. Of course, from our perspective that is the way that they must appear, but that is not, I contend, how they would have been received at the time. Augustine's writings were used to justify not only the perception of an analogy of the Trinity within the human soul, but the detection of such analogies everywhere, with suitable reinforcement for the argument then provided by a revived Neoplatonism. It was such considerations that led so many Renaissance patrons and painters to believe themselves justified in reappropriating this particular image from the classical and pagan world. In doing so, however, the objective was no mere academic exercise. Rather, the thought appears to have been that the Trinity thus understood could bring unity to a world – and human beings – which, because it and they were in the divine image, already had the makings of such a unity. The irony is that the Church put an end to such representations not because of theological or philosophical objections to the underlying theology, but on apparently quite secular grounds: lack of naturalism. Yet if a unity that is not of this world is to be suggested, as God's surely must be, is lack of naturalism not precisely what is required of our imagery, and so the pagan intuition in this case correct after all?[31]

Societal Versions

Without doubt the most popular image for the Trinity today is the famous icon of Andrei Rublev, based on the appearance of the angels to Abraham at Mamre.[32] Because the faces of the angels are alike, there are obviously some connections with the previous section,[33] but I place it here because societal interaction has now become the principal theme. A continuous dialogue of love is taking place between the gaze of their eyes, a dialogue bonded by the circle that implicitly encases them. Their interrelation is further underlined by the complementary character of the various balance of colours that make up their robes. Yet, though the image is a powerful one, it only indirectly engages our involvement, through the link in their gaze being mediated by means of the chalice in the centre of the painting.[34] I talk of indirect mediation, because though the Eucharistic involvement of the Trinity is thereby indicated (and reinforced by the blessings offered by Father and Son), there is nothing explicitly to draw us into the picture. Indeed, none of the three angels offers even a partial gaze towards the viewer.

That fact makes it all the more surprising that this is the image to which appeal has so often been made by those who think the doctrine of the Trinity central to a proper understanding of society, among them Moltmann.[35] Such a notion seems to have been no part of the intention of the artist. Moreover, account must surely be taken of the huge contrast that exists between any such divine society, however understood, and its supposed human equivalent. It is one thing to say that human society can on occasion provide an analogy for what the nature of God might be like; quite another to argue the other way round, and suppose that human beings ought, so far as possible, to conform to this pattern. What the latter argument ignores is that human beings are still developing, and one of the main ways they do so is through contrast, in childhood through learning to differentiate themselves from their parents and in adulthood through alternative possibilities being opened up to them beyond any particular social group.

In Western Christendom we find an early adoption of the same image in the Church of Santa Maria Maggiore in Rome, but it never became very popular, in part because in the Middle Ages in the West Mamre became primarily an image of the virtue of hospitality.[36] Added to that was the Renaissance and Reformation retreat from reading the passage in question (Genesis 18) as in any sense the description of a trinitarian experience. Here one might contrast the treatment of the scene in Rembrandt and in Murillo. The latter by portraying three identical angels continues at least to allow the old reading, whereas Rembrandt leaves us in no doubt that he has discarded it,[37] as does Chagall in the twentieth century.[38] But here it is to Murillo's alternative societal image that I particularly want to draw attention.

Murillo was not the only artist to adopt the iconography known as the Two Trinities, but his representation is certainly the best known.[39] In this iconography what we have is the holy family linked to the divine Trinity through the infant Christ, who does duty as a figure both human and divine. An early attempt at such a pattern is provided by an illustration in the early eleventh-century Anglo-Saxon Aelfwine Prayerbook. On the right of the manuscript painting an almost identical Father and Son are gazing lovingly into one another's eyes, while on the left the Holy Spirit hovers over Mary, who holds the infant Christ portrayed as a smaller version of himself as adult.[40] Though heaven and earth are thereby interwoven, an obvious difficulty lies in the repetition of the figure of the Son. Moreover, there is no suggestion of an analogy of relation between heavenly society and earthly, whereas undoubtedly this is one of the main aims in Murillo's version. As with most of Murillo's art, nowadays there is a tendency to dismiss his achievement as mere sentimentality,[41] but this is to ignore his own family history and the wider background of Spanish society at the time. His native Seville was in a period of decline, to which the population were reacting with intense penitential fervour.[42] One finds this reflected in Murillo's series of paintings of the parable of the Prodigal Son, and indeed it has been suggested that in them the human father is deliberately made to look like contemporary representations of God the Father.[43]

But penitence was not the only issue, there was also acute suffering and the issue of God's response to it. The city had been subject to plague, famine and earthquake,[44] and the artist's own history was far from a happy one. He lost both his own parents early, while his wife and most of his own children were to precede him to the grave.[45] So, in considering his two representations of the topic, particularly the second completed towards the end of his life, it is important that we do not see a false idyll where there had been none. Rather, the suggestion appears to be that, as the holy family was threatened with anguish and sorrow but not destroyed, so our earthly families can be carried through death and tragedy to a new and deeper unity beyond the grave. If to this interpretation it is objected that it places too heavy a reliance on the artist's own special circumstances, let me once more underline that his experience was commonplace in the Seville of the time, and indeed it was, though admittedly to a less intense degree, the pattern in contemporary Europe as a whole. We need to transport ourselves back into a world where loss of wife and children was the norm rather than the exception; only that way will we remove the glaze from our eyes that sees only sentimentality, when something much more profound was in fact at stake.

Admittedly, there was a negative side. In the later Middle Ages, the extended family had been given a semi-trinitarian image, with Mary, while holding the infant Christ, also made to sit upon the knee of her own mother, Anna. Commonly known by its German name of *Selbdritt*,[46] the image was sometimes given reinforcement through the notion of one family endorsing another by including the Trinity in the frame. A case in point would be Fra Bartolommeo's version in San Marco in Florence, which has a three-faced Trinity hovering above.[47] While scarcely raising the same level of problem as the cases where statues of Mary opened up to reveal a Trinity, there certainly was a danger of too easy an equation between heavenly and earthly realities. That issue was to repeat itself in the case of the Two Trinities. As I have already tried to indicate, to use the human family to draw one into relation with something analogous is a quite different pattern of argument from suggesting that the Trinity itself provides the endorsement for some particular earthly institution or way of behaving. Yet there can be no doubt that the Counter-Reformation did sometimes resort to the latter type of appeal. This is perhaps most obvious in the way in which its use of Joseph as an argument for a greater sense of responsibility on the part of men in the moral and religious life of their families was allowed to expand into seeing Joseph as the analogue of a heavenly Father.[48] Even today, devotional books on the holy family sometimes attempt the comparison, and suggest that Joseph be seen as our point of access to the divine Father, and so the nearest present equivalent of someone rightly to be obeyed.[49] Such attitudes left the way open for Murillo's painting to be understood rather differently from the exposition I have given above, as simply providing the divine endorsement of family life.

Although Murillo's commissions certainly reflect the Counter-Reformation's interest in Joseph,[50] I do contest the fairness of imposing such a reading on his *Two Trinities*. The youthful painting could perhaps yield such an interpretation, especially once account is taken of the high prominence given to Mary and Joseph and of the way in which God the Father might be seen as an older version of Joseph. But with the later, definitive version, matters are quite otherwise. God the Father has been deliberately increased in scale and alertness, while both Mary and Joseph are positioned at a lower level than Jesus, with the result that Jesus' gaze heavenward and his parents' dependence on that gaze become the central perspective. I conclude therefore that, though both

138 *Artists as Theologians*

variants of what I have called the societal image of the Trinity have been used to endorse social trinitarianism and with it particular understandings of society, this is by no means an inevitable consequence of such art, and it should thus be judged by independent criteria.

Incarnational Versions

Here I have in mind the typical representations of the involvement of the Father and Spirit in the incarnational act of redemption, through portraying the former as an elderly father or Ancient of Days looking down from the sky and the Spirit as a dove hovering over the Son. The use of the latter symbol clearly derives from Christ's baptism, but the best known images of this type are in fact of the crucifixion, and indeed were to acquire a distinctive name from nineteenth-century German art historians: *Gnadenstuhl* or 'Seat of Mercy'. One of the earliest examples dates from 1132.[51] Though now applied more widely, the term was originally intended specifically to refer to those instances in which the Father is himself seated, and holding the dying or dead Christ.[52] In such cases, the allusion is clearly to the mercy-seat of the Old Testament, and the way in which this image is taken up in the New.[53] However, I do not wish to confine myself quite so narrowly here. Instead, what I want to reflect upon is the reasons why this and related imagery have been so frequently attacked. What I shall contend is that the grounds are misplaced, because more often than not they represent a misconception of what the artist was trying to achieve.

The attack in the English Reformation on this particular image is well known. What is less well known is that it seems to have been not just part of the general assault on images, but also strongly motivated by revulsion against the particular form of imagery employed in this case. As early as Wycliffe it is specifically singled out as leading to a debased understanding of God; Queen Elizabeth attempted to stem the tide of destruction, but again in an influential tract by Anthony Gilby it was this image which was to be highlighted; finally, by Act of Parliament in 1643 all remaining examples were consigned to oblivion.[54] But in response to the repeated contention that the image is unworthy and demeaning of God, the question must be raised whether the fault did not also lie sometimes in the viewer, in the failure to allow other than a very literal reading, and, if so, whether the attack should not be seen as part of a much wider cultural change, the retreat to a more literalist interpretation of Scripture that foreclosed the more multivalent possibilities of the past.[55]

However that may be, this has been by no means the only form of critique in modern times. Also requiring note is a resurgent Orthodoxy which claims that, while the incarnation legitimated representation of the Son, this remains precluded in respect of the Father.[56] As a matter of fact Orthodoxy is replete with such images,[57] but the modern Orthodox tendency is to regard them as degenerate, and as created under Western influence. Art historians would in any case contest whether Orthodoxy has ever been as free from external influence as it would like to see itself when at its best,[58] but here let us note a rather different form of objection, and that is whether to use this type of argument against artistic representation of the Father does not undermine the fundamental equality of the persons. In the original iconoclastic controversy the argument for legitimating imagery from John of Damascus and Theodore the Studite was that God in becoming incarnate had in effect drawn or painted himself and so repealed the Old Testament prohibition against portrayal of divinity.[59] But if one person, why not all? It is not as though the Son thereby revealed specific characteristics which the Father lacks, or that we are thereby portraying what the Son actually looked like. Orthodoxy of course sometimes does make that latter claim,[60] but even were this true, it still would not seem to me to establish the necessity for some absolute difference. Though one hesitates to make such a fundamental and divisive criticism, it is hard to resist the conclusion that such objections really stem from residual notions of the Father as in some sense superior to the other two persons in virtue of being their *arche* or source.[61] Perhaps however, rather than expressing it thus, the objection could be put more neutrally by saying that space must be left for God to be other than incarnate, and such a prohibition would at least preserve such an insight.

The question then becomes whether this is the only way of underlining that claim, or whether some of the criticised images, when correctly understood, do not make the point equally well. Take Masaccio's great painting on the subject, probably from shortly before his death in 1428 at the age of twenty-seven.[62] Art historians often wax lyrical over his naturalism and his innovating use of light and perspective, and it is indeed true that he gives us a sense of the Trinity being presented to our vision in a chapel whose arch vault recedes before our very eyes. What, however, is not always noted is that, while the naturalism of the donor with his ear pushed back by his cap is in one plane and the crucified Christ in another, the Father exists quite outside space altogether. Masaccio thus succeeds in conveying the idea that, while the Son entered our space-time horizons, the Father did not. In short, the Father is imagined rather than seen, and the structure as a whole thus takes us from the corpse at the bottom through crucifixion into a world totally beyond space and time.

Admittedly, the same claim cannot always be made for those who use the *Gnadenstuhl* image. Dürer in giving a papal tiara to the Father draws him forcibly back into our world, while Ribera's intention seems to have been to capture a single eternal moment renewed at each Eucharistic sacrifice.[63] But Masaccio is by no means alone in conveying the sense that the meaning of God is not exhausted by the depiction. El Greco's *Trinity* would be an outstanding example.[64] Not only is Dürer's papal tiara replaced by the headgear taken at the time to be indicative of the office of the Jewish High Priest and discrete cherubs used to indicate the throne, more importantly there is

140 *Artists as Theologians*

also a profound sense of movement from this world into that of the divine. Moreover, because it is the human body of the Son that is being drawn into this new world, the painting suggests the possibility of a similar transformation for ourselves.

This is not to say that the *Gnadenstuhl* image was without its problems. On the contrary, patrons and artists were alike aware of the difficulties, and that is no doubt why we find various alternative solutions being explored. Let me briefly note seven such alternative formats, taking them in historical order. As we shall observe, they achieve varying degrees of success. Roughly contemporary with Masaccio's *Trinity* is Van Eyck's famous polyptych *The Adoration of the Lamb* in Ghent Cathedral. In the lower painting Christ is portrayed as a lamb shedding its blood on the altar, while in the upper the Father is given a human form he never had, and the dove beneath at the top of the lower painting used to link them both. With symbolic forms of representation so prominent, one might detect a return to the more abstract formats that characterised earlier allusions to the Trinity, such as that in San Clemente in Rome, where originally, it is sometimes argued, each of the persons had only a symbolic representation.[65] Certainly, some art historians have seen this painting of Van Eyck's as essentially conservative in its approach compared with his later treatment of religious themes.[66] What, however, I find most interesting in the painting is the artist's treatment of the Spirit. The vertical axis of the three persons finds its strongest focus in the rays of light emanating from the dove which has been encased in a sun, the symbol, as we have seen, once used to indicate the presence of God in its totality. Thereby any demotion of the Spirit is avoided, while the fact that its arc is incomplete forces us to complete it through incorporating the Father above. At the same time the sheer scale of the Father prevents us from reading any of the images too literally.[67]

Towards the end of the same century Filippo Lippi gave the imagery a quite new context by applying it to Christ's nativity,[68] or rather an apparently quite new context, since there are significant overlaps once one probes more deeply. On its surface the painting can easily come across as a sentimental picture with none of Van Eyck's mystic depths, but closer inspection discloses a programmatic painting about prayer, sacrifice and denial. Initially we are attracted by the benign gaze upon the Child of the Virgin and heavenly Father, and think no more of the finger in the Infant's mouth until we look more closely at the landscape. Then we discover its invitation on the right to sacrifice with the pelican and stacked logs, and on the left to rocky steps which carry us beyond the young Baptist to a praying St Bernard. Thus, though a direct vertical links the three persons of the Trinity, the steps on either side imply the possibility for ourselves of sharing in that divine life, arduous though that might be.

Giovanni Bellini's *Baptism of Christ* dates from the beginning of the sixteenth century.[69] Unlike Piero della Francesca's more famous painting of the same scene, the Father is given a face, but like that other painting there are once more three angels in attendance, whose presence is almost certainly, in part at least, necessitated by the desire to hint at the trinitarian unity. But this is by no means the sole device used. Christ's loin cloth is tinged with the same pink as the Father's robe, while a more accurate reflection is indicated by the presence of the same complementary colours as those worn by the Father in Christ's upper garments which two of the angels hold in safe-keeping nearby. A quite brilliant device is adopted as a means of acknowledging the participation of the Holy Spirit in that same divine unity: a second bird is introduced at the forefront of the picture – a parakeet with exactly the same colouring. An additional purpose served by the angels is to indicate the possibility of our own involvement in the scene. The second is already kneeling, while the one nearest to the viewer is just beginning to embark upon the process. The intersection of heaven and earth is thus seen as having an impact on our world, with the angels functioning for these purposes at one and the same time as members of both sides of the divide.

Not much later Dürer completed his very different *Adoration of the Trinity*. Here we are closer to the *Gnadenstuhl* format, but with two major differences: first, the dove of the Spirit is made the summit of the painting, hovering as it is over Father and Son alike; second, a great host of humanity joins in the adoration. What is interesting, though, about the various groups, in contrast to those in Van Eyck's *Adoration*, is that, although heaven and earth are distinguished, the painter places himself alone on earth, with the Church, whether dead or alive, moved to heaven. The fact that this includes the donor and his son-in-law might seem like self-serving cringing on the part of the painter, but, significantly, both are shown needing the help of others to see the vision, in the one case from a cardinal, in the other from an angel. The question of which time-space realm the Church inhabits is thus set acutely before us.[70]

Titian's mid-century *Trinity in Glory* abandons the vertical, and places the Spirit at the centre, to preside over Father and Son on either side, each of whom is dressed in blue and holds a globe.[71] The change might be thought to make for a static composition, but far from it. There is much more a sense of movement than was the case with Dürer, and in fact the painting gives the impression of all humanity being drawn heavenwards. Also in contrast to Dürer, monarchs no longer wear their crowns. Emperor Charles V is plainly dressed in white, with his crown at his feet. Ecclesia is also much more prominent. In Dürer she appeared on the sidelines, holding a chalice; here in the centre of the painting she presents the ark that is the Church to the Trinity above. Of particular interest is the dove with an olive leaf in his beak perched on top. Such double representations of the dove are to be found in other painters,[72] and may have served the function of warning that imagery is being used here, and not any simple reality. In this case it would seem particularly apposite since the most common modern theory for the source of the imagery at Christ's baptism is that it derives from the story of the Flood and so alludes to the notion of baptism as a new creation.

Next, an example from the eighteenth century, Tiepolo's *St Clement Adoring the Trinity*.[73] This time, Father and Son are aligned, with the Spirit portrayed as flying from them towards the pope. Initially, though, the painting is a disappointment since it seems so full of suggestions of wealth and only the Father seems to engage the pope's eye, with Christ strangely distant. But closer attention suggests a rather different focus, with the axis of the Son with his cross raised aloft paralleling the cherub sitting beneath the pope and ready to hand him his papal cross. In other words, we have an argument to the effect that the Father sends the Spirit upon the pope to enable him to become Christ-like by taking up his cross, and so the initial distance in Christ's gaze is deliberate, in order to suggest that chain of events. Finally, as a rare example from the twentieth century, we might note the work of the German-born artist Hans Feibusch in the Church of St Alban, Holborn, in London, dating from the 1960s. This magnificent mural behind the high altar of *The Trinity in Glory* shows some interesting differences from the original sketch. Whereas originally the Father had dominated the picture,[74] now he recedes into the background with, most significantly of all, Son and Spirit roughly aligned and breaking the spatial bound of Alban's vision to enter our own space.

There are four main conclusions which I want to draw from this survey of incarnational imagery. The first is that the accusations that God has thereby been wholly naturalised are quite unfair, and caused by misreadings of the pictorial frame. Normally, there is some way of indicating that not all of the content belongs to this world, whether through the medium of where the horizon is placed (the usual convention), through the Father stepping out of the frame altogether as in Masaccio or through the subtle play of symbolism as in Bellini's angels or Titian's repetition of the dove. Unadulterated naturalism is thus more in the eye of the careless observer than any part of the artist's intention. Second, what is of interest to the latter is less the doctrine as such or the *raison d'être* of its unity and much more its relevance to us. So it is the point of access to the divine which is stressed, and with that its ability to carry us beyond the events of this world into the transcendent realm. That is why it is never enough simply to note the three figures in line but also how often the line intersects with a horizon to suggest contact, or else ascent invited by other means such as Filippo Lippi's two rock-hewn staircases. Third, of the three images it is the Father's which is consistently the least successful, though here it seems to me that the artist is less to blame and more the restraints of Scripture. For the requirement of fatherhood, particularly when reinforced by the image of Ancient of Days, seems to have inhibited further development, whereas the vagueness of the allusion to the dove at Jesus' baptism allowed more room for creative possibilities. The result is no ordinary dove in several of the paintings which we have discussed, with it in effect becoming a figure of the sun. Nor was this by any means the only option that was explored. In the early fifteenth-century *Rohan Book of Hours* the artist experiments with the Spirit as a curtain of wings and as a playmate of the Christ Child on the Father's lap, while in the sixteenth century we find the dove skimming the waters of the Jordan, or drinking from the chalice into which Christ's blood flows, thereby symbolising the source of our own sustenance.[75] Finally, one might note that the question of formal trinitarian relations is largely ignored and indeed to some degree subverted, not, I think, because of the conceptual difficulty of the issue but because of the way in which such considerations would have run foul of the visual impact of the imagery. Instead, every imaginable personal and spatial relation between the three seems to have been explored in artistic attempts to achieve dramatic and visual power. To judge matters on formal, doctrinal grounds would, it seems to me, be tantamount almost to a category mistake, for we have no reason to believe that the demands of the visual will always pull in precisely the same direction as doctrine or purely verbal imagery.

Conclusion

In Olivier Messiaen's great organ work, *Méditations sur le mystère de la sainte Trinité*, the three persons of the Trinity are each given clearly defined musical themes, which are heard both separately and interwoven.[76] The ear is thus allowed to hear both distinctness and underlying principles of unity. It is not true that there is no possibility of similar temporal developments and movement in art. Clearly there can be, as the artist invites from the viewer deeper exploration of his theme, and things come to be noticed that did not engage the eye at first glance. Movement can also be suggested by the position of the figures or by the direction of the gaze of figures within the frame. Even so, there is still this difference, that these kinds of dynamic are much less under the control of visual artists. There is therefore a greater need to make assumptions about anterior knowledge, as well as ensure that the first impression is decisive in eliciting further reflection. These are features which we have observed in respect of each of the three types of imagery which I have distinguished. Renaissance triadic heads and Murillo's *Two Trinities*, for instance, convey a rather different and more powerful meaning once they are placed in the historical context of their background assumptions. But that does not mean that all is therefore dependent on those background assumptions. On the contrary, artists have sometimes felt the need significantly to modify those assumptions in order to achieve the decisive initial impact. That proved particularly so in respect of the way in which the *Gnadenstuhl* image came to be modified.

Perhaps the greatest literary image for the Trinity is that which concludes Dante's *Divine Comedy*, but visually it is quite unappealing,[77] and much the same might he said of the images of the book with which the New Testament canon ends, which even a great artist like Dürer could only succeed in making at most, in my view, faintly comic. Our eye does not make quite the same demands as our ear or our intellect. In reading we can quickly decode metaphors into simpler language or else complement with alternative images.

144 *Artists as Theologians*

When a painting is set before us, this is something which we cannot do, and indeed part of the power of such images must lie in their refusal to be decoded and so fade from the memory. The tragedy of much of the history of Christian attitudes towards art is that simple verbal tests have been mindlessly applied to works of the visual imagination, with the result that instead of such images being allowed to feed the imagination and so deepen faith, they have been treated as faulty intellectual exercises. What is properly required of us is that such visual images first be allowed to stand in their own right, and then perhaps, so far from merely complementing verbal approaches, they will be able to offer their own critique of them.[78]

Notes

1. 'Societal' is used rather than 'social' in order to avoid any automatic association with a social understanding of the Trinity. As will become apparent later, though the two (art and model) are often connected, this is by no means requisite or inevitable.
2. In St Peter's Lutheran church. For illustration and commentary, John Dillenberger, *A Theology of Artistic Sensibilities: The Visual Arts and the Church* (London: SCM, 1987), 170–171.
3. It was commissioned in 1966 by that major patron of the arts, Walter Hussey, while dean. Against a wider frame of the four elements above and the symbols of the four evangelists beneath, a green equilateral triangle has superimposed on it a sun disc to represent the Father, a tau cross the Son and flames the Holy Spirit.
4. Much the same might be said of his design for the stained glass in the lantern of the Metropolitan Cathedral in Liverpool, where three primary colours interacting are used to evoke the doctrine.
5. Installed with the help of an Arts Council Lottery grant of £33,000 in August 1997. An ellipse made of porphyry is used to represent the tilted chalice.
6. For illustration and discussion, R. López-Pedraza, *Anselm Kiefer* (London: Thames & Hudson, 1996), 50–52; for a theological discussion, Mark C. Taylor, *Disfiguring: Art, Architecture, Religion* (Chicago: University of Chicago Press, 1992), 290–305, esp. 296, though, inexplicably, the plate (34) reproduces only half the painting.
7. The tension is suggested by the way in which the trees need to be destroyed for a log cabin to be made; the lack of influence by the fire having no effect on the snow outside.
8. The three trees are given Christian labels and grow into the three chairs.
9. For a discussion with some illustrations, Miranda Green, *Symbol and Image in Celtic Religious Art* (London and New York: Routledge, 1989), 169–205. For the occurrence of related imagery among other pagan European peoples, R. Pettazzoni, 'The Pagan Origins of the Three-Headed Representation of the Christian Trinity', *Journal of Warburg and Courtland Institutes* 9 (1946), 149–157.
10. Green, *Symbol and Image*, 174.
11. Ibid., 203–204.
12. George Dumézil in *Jupiter, Mars, Qurinius* (Paris: Gallimard, 1941) and in a number of later books argued that a general Indo-European pattern is to be found, and this reflects the way in which society was divided between priests, warriors and farmers. Wilhelm Kirfel, in *Die dreiköpfige Gottheit* (Bonn: Dümmlers Verlag, 1948), suggested a pattern of influence spreading from India through

Artists on the Trinity   145

Iran and Thrace to Greece and Rome and then still further west. But this fails to explain the huge variations in the popularity of the image, with it prominent in Hinduism and among the Celts but really very muted in the Classical world.

13 For discussion and illustration of the former, Marianna Lines, *Sacred Stones, Sacred Places* (Edinburgh: Saint Andrews Press, 1992), 11–13 (though unconnected, the parallel with Dante's final image in the *Divine Comedy* is worth noting). The latter remains in situ on the island of Islay. Its more famous face contrasts Cain's killing of Abel with Isaac's voluntary sacrifice; its Trinity occurs on its western side.

14 This variant is of a crowned king with three noses and three mouths. For illustration, J. C. Dickinson, *The Priory of Cartmel* (Milnthorpe, Cumbria: Cicerone Press, 1991), 59.

15 For illustration and discussion, Robert Milburn, *Early Christian Art and Architecture* (Aldershot: Scolar Press, 1988), 67, 68, 82, n. 15.

16 As Kirfel notes, archaeological survivals are limited to Hecate and Cerberus (*Die dreiköpfige Gottheit*, 181ff.). Cerberus has three heads, Hecate sometimes three bodies.

17 *Summa Theologiae* IV.8.iv.II: 'Reprehensibles ... sunt ... cum faciunt Trinitatis imaginem unam personam cum tribus capitibus, quod monstrum est in rerum natura.' For a discussion of his motivation, Creighton Gilbert, 'The Archbishop on the Painters of Florence, 1450', *Art Bulletin* 41 (1959), 75–87, esp. 81.

18 Constitution of 11 August 1628.

19 As in Rushton Triangular Lodge in Northamptonshire, built in the late sixteenth century by Sir Thomas Tresham, the father of one of the conspirators in the Gunpowder Plot of 1605.

20 For an illustration, Pettazzoni, 'The Pagan Origins', 16b. Late examples also survive from Russian Orthodoxy, varying in date from the sixteenth to the eighteenth century: Kirfel, *Die dreiköpfige Gottheit*, illus. 174–177.

21 Kirfel finds the oldest three-headed Christian Trinity in a manuscript of the *Chronicles* of Isidore of Seville (*Die dreiköpfige Gottheit*, 148). The oldest painting I have been able to discover is a wooden altarpiece, now in the National Gallery of Umbria at Perugia, by Ottavigno Nelli, and dating from 1403.

22 For illustration and discussion, Maria Pia Mannini and Marco Fagioli, *Filippo Lippi: Catalogo Completo* (Florence: Octavo, 1997), 29, 97–99. Done as one of the scenes on the predella of the altar in an Augustinian church, it balances an unusual annunciation to the Virgin of her death, where the choice of imagery may also be due to Augustine.

23 In the former case the unusual triangle of angels is held together by a chalice placed beneath the foot of Christ, who is crowning his mother: Nicoletta Pons, *Pollaiolo* (Florence: Octavo, 1994), 86.

24 For illustration and brief discussion, Antonio Natali and Alessandro Cecchi, *Andrea del Sarto: Catalogo Completo* (Paris: Bordas, 1992), 38–39. Donatello had also used the imagery of sun and rays, but his figure was crowned and considerably older. Kirfel speaks of an 'uralte Motiv' deriving from Egypt or still further east (*Die dreiköpfige Gottheit*, 149).

25 For example, *Summa Theologiae* IV.10.vii.4: 'De verbo eterno seu filio dei multa dixit Plato ... et satis clare.'

26 The influence of their ideas on the art of the time is pursued in detail in Edgar Wind, *Pagan Mysteries in the Renaissance: An Exploration of Philosophical and Mystical Sources of Iconography in Renaissance Art* (London: Faber and Faber, 1958), esp. 1–127 and 241–262.

27 For an illustration of a three-headed Antichrist, Bernard McGinn, *Antichrist: Two Thousand Years of the Human Fascination with Evil* (San Francisco: Harper,

1994), 148; for a three-way-facing figure as humanity in conflict, note the example in Hexham Abbey, and also that by Grünewald in Berlin.
28 The work culminates in a vision of the Trinity as three intersecting circles and colours, but on the way the three women who guide him seem to be treated as an image of the Trinity, while in hell the Devil and his minion, Cerberus, are alike portrayed as three-headed and as all God is not. For the role of Mary, Beatrice and Lucy, Dorothy L. Sayers, trans. and ed., Dante, *The Divine Comedy I* (Baltimore: Penguin, 1949), 328; for Cerberus, 104ff. (Canto VI.13ff.); for Satan, 286 (Canto XXXIV.28ff.).
29 For a discussion, with the Egyptian roots of this particular image stressed, Erwin Panofsky, *Meaning in the Visual Arts* (New York: Doubleday, 1955), 181–205.
30 Pico's claim that 'the unity of Venus is unfolded in the trinity of the Graces' is explored in Wind, *Pagan Mysteries in the Renaissance*, 113–127. Cf. also E. H. Gombrich, *Symbolic Images: Studies in the Art of the Renaissance*, 3rd edn (London: Phaidon, 1985), 31–81.
31 In a recent article the Christian doctrine of the Trinity has been described as 'an implicit disruption and subversion of the Indo-European ideology': John Milbank, 'Sacred Triads: Augustine and the Indo-European Soul', *Modern Theology* 13 (1997), 451–474, esp. 462–463. While some of the author's points hit their mark, it seems to me unlikely that Christianity's mission would have been quite so successful, had there not been already within the Classical world an existent Neoplatonic triad on which to build and within wider paganism the image of triads as a sign of intensifying power. The former already offered intelligibility as the second 'person', and the latter possibility of the absence of 'hierarchy and heterogeneity'.
32 Painted about 1411, it is in the Tretyakov Gallery in Moscow. The extent to which it is an advance on early representations can be observed through comparison with a Greek icon of the same scene from the late fourteenth century: Kurt Weitzmann, *The Icon* (London: Chatto & Windus, 1978), 131.
33 It would be interesting to reflect why this image has gained in popularity, as that of the Graces has declined. Could gender issues be involved?
34 Established Orthodox convention insists upon identifying the central figure with Christ, and sometimes argues in support the balance of his robes (indicating humanity and divinity). Against, though, is the fact that only the figure on the right gazes at the chalice and only his staff forms a cross with the fold of his robe.
35 He acknowledges this 'wonderful' icon as the inspiration for his social understanding of the Trinity and its implications for humanity in the preface to one of his books: Jürgen Moltmann, *The Trinity and the Kingdom of God* (London: SCM, 1981), xvi.
36 The mosaic in Santa Maria Maggiore was commissioned by Sixtus III (d. 430), and pictures three incidents connected with the story: for illustration, James Hall, *History of Ideas and Images in Italian Art* (London: John Murray, 1983), 88. Just a century later at San Vitale the figures are more sharply differentiated, and hospitality rather than trinitarian revelation may already have become the main point: Giuseppe Bovini, *Ravenna: Art and History* (Ravenna: Longo, 1991), illus. 19, 20.
37 In Rembrandt's etching (now in Melbourne) the much larger central angel is deployed to represent the divine promise with the two other angels bearing no obvious resemblance to him (this comment corrects what I said in an earlier version of this essay). By contrast, in Murillo's painting (National Gallery, Ottawa), though the wings are abandoned, the three figures are so alike and interacting with one another as to invite a trinitarian interpretation. In Tiepolo's version, both traditions are rejected in favour of a mystic vision: for illustration, Michael

Levey, *Giambattista Tiepolo: His Life and Art* (New Haven: Yale University Press, 1986), 34.
38 Chagall's version (in Reims Cathedral) is closest to Rembrandt's, with Abraham primarily engaged with one angel.
39 Zurbarán painted the theme twice, as did Murillo. The earlier and less successful dates from 1640 and is in the National Museum, Stockholm: for illustration, *Murillo* (London: Royal Academy of the Arts, 1983), 75. The later, dating at most seven years before his death in 1682, is in the National Gallery, London.
40 For illustration and discussion, Barbara C. Raw, *Trinity and Incarnation in Anglo-Saxon Art and Thought* (Cambridge and New York: Cambridge University Press, 1997), 152–160, cf. 148, ill. XVb.
41 In the eighteenth century, it was common to reckon him second only to Raphael.
42 All secular plays were banned in 1679, in part as a result of the penitential mission of the Jesuit Tirso González de Santalla.
43 Mindy Nancarrow Taggard, *Murillo's Allegories of Salvation and Triumph* (Columbia: University of Missouri Press, 1992), 9–66, esp. 23.
44 Half the population died in the plague of 1649, and there was a terrible famine in 1651. Plague returned in 1676, followed by torrential rains in 1677 and an earthquake in 1680.
45 Both his parents died when he was nine. In 1664 he lost his wife, and only three out of his nine children were to survive him.
46 *Heilige Anna selbdritt* – St Anne as herself the third.
47 Bartolommeo (d. 1517), who became a Dominican in 1500 under the influence of Savonarola, originally intended the painting for his large altarpiece in the Sala del Gran Consiglio. Savonarola, though, also endorsed the notion of trinitarian vestiges: *Triumphus crucis*, 3.3.
48 Émile Mâle, *L'art religieux après le concile de Trente* (Paris: Librarie Armand Colin, 1932), 313–325. 'C'est ainsi que fut glorifié saint Joseph qui, dans la Sainte Famille, apparaissait comme l'image de Dieu le Père' (Ibid., 325).
49 For example, A. Druze, *Discovering Saint Joseph* (Slough: St Paul, 1991), esp. 135, 187. Obedience to Joseph is a recurring theme, and, following Olier, used to endorse the authority of priests (Ibid., 69).
50 As in his various paintings which depict Joseph holding the Child or leading him by the hand. For examples, see Liudmilla Kagané, *Murillo* (St Petersburg: Aurora, 1995), 96–99, 124–125, 128–131.
51 A German portable altar, now in the Victoria and Albert Museum in London.
52 There are two excellent examples of this genre, both with the seat fully visible, in the National Galleries in Edinburgh and London. The former has Hugo van der Goes's Trinity altarpiece of 1479, originally intended for a collegiate church of that dedication in Edinburgh; the latter, a splendid anonymous one of about 1410 from Austria.
53 For example, Exodus 25:17–22. In the New Testament the imagery is taken up at various points, e.g. Romans 3:25; Hebrews 9:5.
54 Margaret Aston, *England's Iconoclasts*, vol. 1, *Laws against Images* (Oxford: Clarendon Press, 1988), 76, 78, 99; Richard Marks, *Stained Glass in England during the Middle Ages* (Toronto and Buffalo: University of Toronto Press, 1993), 232. For a rare example of a survival, ibid., 35.
55 Though hard to prove, another factor may have been resistance to portrayals of a passible Father, showing obvious signs of grief.
56 Leonid Ouspensky, *Theology of the Icon* (Crestwood, NY: St Vladimir's Seminary Press, 1992), 287–409. Condemnations by Muscovite Councils in the sixteenth and seventeenth centuries are noted, one of 1667 describing the image in question as 'altogether absurd and improper' (Ibid., 371).

148 *Artists as Theologians*

57 Including some that modify the image in interesting ways, as in an eighteenth-century example from the Greek monastery of Toplou, which places the dove in the middle perched on a globe of the world.
58 In its origins there are heavy borrowings from the pagan world, while in the case of El Greco it is now argued that he was already subject to Western influence long before he moved west from Crete. Cf. Robin Cormack, *Painting the Soul: Icons, Death Masks and Shrouds* (London: Reaktion, 1997), 167–217.
59 For examples of the argument, John of Damascus, *Orations on the Holy Icons*, esp. I.15, II.5, III.8 and 26. The *aperigraptos* had become *perigraptos* (circumscribed).
60 As in the story of the *acheiropoietos* icon, allegedly made by Christ himself in response to a request from King Agbar of Edessa.
61 Ouspensky talks of 'the unrepresentable divine essence' (Ouspensky, *Theology of the Icon*, 308). Some modern Russian theologians, though, have defended such representations: ibid., 385ff.
62 In Santa Maria Novella in Florence and only restored to view in 1861. For illustration and example of a treatment against which I am reacting, József Takács, *Massacio* (Budapest: Corvina, 1980), plates 25–27. Against my interpretation is the shelf on which the Father appears to stand; in favour is Massacio's failure, uniquely in this case, to use foreshortening.
63 In the Prado, Madrid. Shared conventions rather than direct dependence on El Greco is the favoured view: Pérez Sánchez, Alfonso and Nicolo Spinosa, *L'opera complete del Ribera* (Milan: Rizzoli, 1978), table XX, n. 98.
64 For a comparison of the work of El Greco and Dürer, Richard G. Mann, *El Greco and his Patrons* (Cambridge and New York: Cambridge University Press, 1986), 32–36, ill. 6–7.
65 Created before 1128, it shows a hand stretching down to a cross on which twelve doves are represented. The less impressive figure of Christ himself may be later. For illustration, C. R. Dodwell, *The Pictorial Arts of the West 800–1200* (New Haven: Yale University Press, 1993), 158.
66 So Craig Harbison, *Jan van Eyck: The Play of Realism* (London: Reaktion, 1991), 193–197.
67 Note also St Christopher, leading the pilgrims, out of proportion on the right.
68 For illustration and comment, Mannini and Fagioli, *Filippo Lippi*, 52 and 127. The painting is sometimes called *The Adoration in the Forest*, and hangs in the Gemäldegalerie in Berlin.
69 Rona Goffen, *Giovanni Bellini* (New Haven: Yale University Press, 1989), 163–167. The painting still hangs in its original location in Santa Corona in Vicenza, Italy.
70 The influence of Augustine has been suggested: Erwin Panofsky, *The Life and Art of Albrecht Dürer*, 4th edn (Princeton: Princeton University Press, 1955), 125–131.
71 In the Prado in Madrid. For an illustration, Filippo Pedrocco, *Titian* (Florence: Scala, 1993), 52.
72 For example, Crivelli's *Annunciation* in the National Gallery, London, where the dove of the annunciation is repeated in the dove in the background that brings news of the new status for the town of Ascoli Piceno.
73 William Barcham, *Tiepolo* (London: Thames and Hudson, 1992), 70–71. Unfairly, in my view, contrasted with another Trinity of his by Levey, *Giambattista Tiepolo*, 75–77. It now hangs in the Alte Pinakothek in Munich.
74 For the original sketch, David Coke, ed., *Hans Feibusch* (London: Lund Humphries, 1995), 72.

75 For illustrations of the latter two images, James Clifton, *The Body of Christ* (Munich: Prestel, 1998), 64–65, 116–117.
76 Messiaen provides a detailed commentary with the score on the 'language' he has employed and its relation to Scripture and Aquinas. This includes the marking of specific sections as *Père, Fils* and *Saint Esprit*: *Méditations sur le mystère de la sainte Trinité* (Paris: Alphonse Leduc), 1973.
77 For a visual example of the problem, see Charles H. Taylor and Patricia Finley, *Images of the Journey in Dante's Divine Comedy* (New Haven: Yale University Press, 1997), 264.
78 First published as 'The Trinity in Art', in *The Trinity: An Interdisciplinary Symposium on the Trinity*, ed. Stephen T. Davis, Daniel Kendall and Gerald O'Collins (New York: Oxford University Press, 1999), 329–356. It is here reprinted with permission in a slightly revised form.

Part IV
Meaning in Religious Architecture

Introduction

In this final part of the book I want to explore a number of issues related to religious architecture. Inevitably, a number of themes raised earlier will recur. One will be a continuing protest against the marginalisation of the arts, including architecture. Many, perhaps most, contemporary theologians continue to see their chosen professional area of competence as essentially revolving round a number of key intellectual questions, and so, even among those hostile to philosophy, it remains the case that it is something like the practice of philosophy that is seen as the most appropriate model, both in identifying legitimate questions and then in developing some sort of systematic relation between proposed answers. Yet, what is thereby circumvented is one fundamental feature of Christianity, and that is that it is a religion, where practice is no less important than theory, including thus of course the whole question of worship. But, if that is so, the buildings in which the community worships cease to be a relatively insignificant dimension but just as much part of what gives Christianity its identity as many a doctrinal formulation.

Those who might be inclined to dismiss such a claim as an absurd exaggeration need to reflect on the history of the Christian inheritance. So used are Christians to marginalising aspects of Scripture that it is easy to forget how central the Temple is in much of the Old Testament,[1] while even in the New it is important to recall that one way of reading Hebrews has been as a reassertion of the continuing importance of Old Testament insights as expressed through the worship of the new covenant.[2] Nor should there ever be forgotten the practical commitment given to such theology in the huge expenditure of effort once given by Christian societies to the building of churches. But, even if both Scripture and history were to receive summary dismissal, what cannot be challenged is the undoubted continuing subliminal influence of such buildings. Of course, such facts do not of themselves accord automatic endorsement to such approaches (they could be signs of human sinfulness). Even so, they do at least raise the question of the legitimacy of the present marginalisation of such concerns.

Not that issues of architecture in relation to religion are entirely ignored at present. A goodly number of books are currently available which consider the religious dimension to key historical styles. Sadly, though, the current interests of theologians in the built environment as a whole have entailed that rather less attention is given to contemporary architecture in its own right.[3] Indeed, it can sometimes seem as though more probing analyses of the religious dimension actually tend of come from architects themselves.[4] However, given the relative paucity of material, perhaps it is better not to generalise, except to observe that the essays that follow (only one of which is at present easily accessible) are offered here to a wider readership in the hope of securing for such issues more sustained theological reflection.

That contemporary attitudes, though, could possibly be changing is reflected in the fact that the first essay was first published in a philosophy of religion encyclopaedia. That background also explains the substitution of the term 'theism' in its title for a more explicitly Christian perspective. The requirement to write in such a way, though, was not without its advantages, as it brought fully to the surface my conviction that religious architectural styles, while capable of reflecting specific convictions within a particular religion or denomination, nonetheless ultimately derive from deeper roots, in, as it were, a natural philosophy of religion, a desire to express aspects of divinity that will be found acknowledged both across the historical religions and prior to any particular one of them. That is why I go on to suggest in the second essay that reflection on the roots of religious architecture could allow for a form of inter-faith discussion that traces underlying formal similarities in a way that would be less fraught than more traditional attempts at dialogue can sometimes be, where to enter into discussion at all might seem disloyal to the absolute authority of one's own particular tradition of divine revelation. Of course, it could be argued that, because the essay confines itself to the three Western monotheistic religions, it is surreptitiously drawing on elements already shared in their historical traditions that have nothing to do with architecture. However, I do not believe that to be the case. The narrower focus was simply a consequence; partly of the added complexity that would have been the result had the essay looked more widely; and partly of issues deferred, at least on my part, to another day. In the mean time, I hope I have shown not only the potential for such a dialogue between Judaism, Christianity and Islam but also some signs of it having already occurred, sometimes admittedly only implicitly, across the long history of these three religions.

Then, in the remaining two essays I turn to consider, first, what has often been the very fraught relation between politics and religious architecture. So far from viewing such interaction purely negatively as evidence of a lack of purity in architecture, I want to suggest that not only does it sometimes work to the benefit of both but also that in any case the message of the architecture tends to survive well beyond any temporary political influence. The final essay is then devoted to arguing for the importance of the contribution of architecture and art alike to the kind of worship that takes place in a particular Christian building. Throughout each of the essays I sought to emphasise how the meaning of the architecture varied according to the style deployed, whereas in this essay I especially underline how such messages cannot simply be ignored since a subliminal effect will remain, whatever the intentions of priest or minister and congregation. Putting it another way, there is thus a generous surplus of meaning available, however niggardly the attitudes of those who use the building might be; something that could be seen as part of the generosity of God since the address of the architecture is sometimes most clearly heard by the casual, even non-believing visitor to a church. As the agnostic poet Philip Larkin once observed, a non-believer could 'forever be surprising/a hunger in himself … and gravitating with it to this ground'.[5]

Notes

1. The Temple is absolutely central to the theology of Chronicles and Ezekiel, while it also plays an indispensable role in history as viewed by the Deuteronomic historians and Ezra.
2. For a classic in this way of appropriating the text, see John Edward Field, *The Apostolic Liturgy and the Epistle to the Hebrews* (London: Rivingtons, 1882, republished 2006).
3. A trend evident since at least Harvey Cox's *The Secular City* (London: SCM, 1965). For two more recent examples, Graham Ward, *Cities of God* (London: Routledge, 2000); T. J. Gorringe, *A Theology of the Built Environment* (Cambridge: Cambridge University Press, 2002). Gorringe has at least a chapter on the subject (ch. 8). For a theologian arguing strongly in one particular direction, Mark A. Torgerson, *An Architecture of Immanence* (Grand Rapids, Mich.: Eerdmans, 2007).
4. For an excellent collection, Renata Hejduk and Jim Williamson, eds, *The Religious Imagination in Modern and Contemporary Architecture: A Reader* (London: Routledge, 2011); for an architect analysing various case studies, Thomas Barrie, *The Sacred In-Between: The Mediating Roles of Architecture* (London: Routledge, 2010).
5. From his poem 'Church Going', final stanza.

10 Architecture and Theism

In what follows I proceed by three stages. The *introduction* indicates why modern attempts to reduce architecture to a purely practical art appear mistaken. The *historical section* then observes how deeply the connections between architecture and theistic belief once ran. While some of these are no longer tenable, the *contemporary section* identifies other pertinent questions that have continued to demand philosophical investigation.

Introduction

Architecture has been given considerably less attention in philosophical writing than, for example, either painting or music. There is an obvious reason for this: it is very easy to reduce its significance by treating it as merely one of the applied arts, and so more like furniture-making or music that serves some particular purpose such as military marches or dance music. Ironically, much of twentieth-century architectural theory in effect endorsed such a view with its repeated refrain that form should follow function, a slogan first coined by the American architect Louis Sullivan (1856–1924); in other words, that practical purpose should wholly determine building style. How far actual practice ever conformed is a moot point, since in so much modern architecture the desire for simple forms was often allowed to override practical functions;[1] hence the reason why so much modern housing was eventually abandoned. But there were in any case two basic faults with the slogan. The first is that function cannot in fact be so easily divorced from wider human concerns. Thus housing, for example, is unlikely to satisfy unless a much wider raft of interests are taken into account besides adequate space for eating, sleeping and relaxing. Also relevant would be environmental setting (including questions such as view, garden or ambient noise) and ease of access (both directly and in terms of neighbouring facilities such as shopping and entertainment). Similarly, shops need to take into account not just the ability to display the relevant wares but also such things as security of setting, and even confidence generated in the business by the sense of the building as one that is here to stay.

Architecture and Theism   157

From the examples just quoted it is easy to see how questions of function slip almost imperceptibly into aesthetic considerations, and so it will come as no surprise that classic writing on architecture had already broadened the list from simple fulfilment of function to include durability and aesthetic pleasure – the *utilitas*, *firmitas* and *venustas* of Vitruvius in his *On Architecture* (c. 25 BC). 'Utility' or suitability to function needs to be supplemented by a building that is not only sustainable in the long term (*firmitas*) but also gives pleasure (*venustas*) by its visual appearance as much in its wider context as in itself. However, it should not be thought that only *utilitas* is subject to this sort of criticism. Much the same could be said about Vitruvius' other two criteria. Durability, for example, would seem to be not just about eliminating any possibility that the building will collapse, but also a matter of expressing the lasting character and value of the activities that take place within; hence, at least in the past, the durability of banks, churches and schools. Equally, one key element in determining the aesthetic pleasure given by a building is the way in which the building matches its intended function, with signals of transcendence, for example, in the architecture of a church, of care in a hospital or of security in a prison. As Kant observed, 'the beauty of a … building (such as a church, palace, armory, or summer house) does presuppose the concept of the purpose that determines what the thing is meant to be, and hence a concept of its perfection'.[2]

With most non-theists willing to acknowledge considerable aesthetic merits in many a religious building, it might be thought that it is, therefore, through beauty that a connection with religious belief should be sought. But, despite beauty having been treated as one of the traditional divine attributes, beauty in architecture seems seldom to have been sought in its own right in churches or other religious buildings. Its emergence proves more a consequence of the pursuit of certain other values, in particular symbolism. What those values were is discussed in more detail below in relation to Christianity in particular. So here it will be appropriate to make some more general remarks on how the issue affects some other forms of theism. Hindu temples, especially in their south Indian form with their riot of gaudy colours and sensuous imagery, can often seem to the Western observer an exercise in bad taste, but this is to misread what the architecture is intended to convey. The aim is not aesthetic but religious, with the structure of the building intended to evoke a divine dwelling (often alluding to a sacred mountain), and the colour and imagery awesome expectation as the worshipper approaches the dark mystery of the innermost sanctuary, the *garbha griha*.[3] The latter point in particular is important, as the symbolism works quite differently from Western art with the details less significant than the overall impact. By sheer excess the imagery indicates the inadequacy of any particular image and so prepares viewers for their final encounter with an image in the central shrine that is often very worn and sometimes deliberately aniconic, as with Shiva's *linga*.

158 *Meaning in Religious Architecture*

By contrast, those same Westerners who take an instant dislike to Hindu temples may well be found giving unqualified praise to the mosques of a city such as Isfahan (in Iran) in which colour, geometry and calligraphy seem to combine to produce works of exquisite artistry. Yet here also it is all too easy to draw the wrong conclusion. The fact that of all versions of theism Islam lays the most stress on divine transcendence should make one hesitate over artistry as such as the aim. In fact, the usual intention was to provide worshippers with further signals of transcendence. Calligraphy provided an obvious reminder of the Qur'an as divine speech and as such its primary intention was not necessarily that it should be read.[4] Again, the perfection of the geometry in the way in which it is built up from simple patterns has sometimes been seen as a deliberate attempt to reflect the perfection of the world as a divine creation,[5] while others stress more an invitation to go beyond the instability of creation to contemplation of the absolute character of the divine will.[6] No doubt the emphasis varied, depending on which feature of the building one focuses on. For instance, the way in which *muquarnas* or stalactites hang from the dome of the mosque give the impression of a lightness and insubstantiality that it would not otherwise have. Although both approaches imply the subordination of beauty to other considerations, this is not to deny exceptions. This probably holds for some of the major mosques built in the twentieth century, where questions of national pride also played an important role, for example, with King Hassan II Mosque, Casablanca.[7] Again, until after the Second World War Judaism usually imitated contemporary Christian styles.[8] So it seems quite likely that synagogue construction was based on aesthetic considerations rather than on any of the symbolic arguments that were engaging Christians at the time.[9]

Such considerations suggest that, though it is possible to pursue connections between theism and architecture through questions of beauty, their interrelation with issues of symbolism cannot be ignored. Indeed, the way in which the symbolic vocabulary of the different major religions varies could be used to explore the question of whether it is a case of different symbolic systems generating different standards of beauty or of the same standard applying throughout but training being required to perceive how exactly this operates across different visual languages.

Historical Overview

Here I want to provide a much broader context for such symbolic considerations before eventually focusing more narrowly on Christianity. Admittedly, it is possible to analyse religious buildings of the past purely in terms of their social and ritual significance,[10] but no sharp distinction would once have been drawn between the 'sacred' and the 'secular'. Divine creation was itself viewed as a form of architecture that delimited different areas for one purpose or another ('secular' no less than 'sacred'), while it also provided specific patterns to be imitated. It is perhaps those modern writers on architecture who speak of walls as boundaries that best capture this former view.[11] Although only modern Hinduism strongly retains the notion of the home as sacred, with an internal shrine always present, such attitudes were once universal, and reflected the view that the divine demarcated an appropriate place for the home no less than for the temple.[12] It was, therefore, more a matter of degrees of sacredness rather than any absolute opposition.

So in noting that the Jerusalem Temple was built under divine instruction (1 Kings 6–7), it is important to note that it was seen as culminating at the centre of a series of boundaries (the world, the Holy Land, the holy city), each with specific purposes, and was even identified with both the original locus of creation and the Garden of Eden. It is perhaps, therefore, not altogether surprising that later Christianity not only continued to treat Jerusalem as the world's centre (e.g. in its maps) but also frequently claimed that its churches were built in imitation of the Temple. In practice, however, there was so much confusion about the Temple's precise form until modern times that in effect almost any style could be claimed as having the building as its inspiration, and was.[13] Thus, while it was a plausible assumption that the proportions between nave and chancel in Gothic churches matched those between the Holy Place and the Holy of Holies in the original, identification of the seventh-century Dome of the Rock as the Temple's continuation was well wide of the mark, as was Raphael's deduction of a Classical form in his painting of *The Marriage of the Virgin* (1504), or of Baroque parallels in the eighteenth-century Karlskirche in Vienna with its twin external pillars seen as imitating the strangely named Boaz and Jachin (1 Kings 7:21) in the original. Yet, the very fact that the claim was made demonstrates the continuing desire to see architecture as modelled on a divine original.

Of much greater significance for architecture generally, though, was the supposition that the divine creation of the world was itself like the construction of a building. All ancient cultures presupposed that in the process of creation the Creator had assigned different land areas for different forms of human activity, with some seen as most appropriate for human dwelling and cultivation, and others (such as forest groves or mountains) as places for divine encounter where heaven and earth might be more easily bridged. So, just as the Garden of Eden is presented as a defined area for Adam and Eve to dwell in (Genesis 2:8; 3:24), townships continued to be marked out formally by religious ceremonies, as in the Roman ceremony of the *pomerium* or boundary.[14] Equally, the way in which the land itself originally had the significance later assigned to the building placed on it is to be observed not just in the original meaning of *templum* as any marked area deemed suitable for consulting the gods but also even to this day in the same residual notion within Islam, according to which any area whatsoever marked in the sand or soil can function as a mosque, provided it is appropriately directed toward Mecca. Similarly, the Sanskrit word *vimana* means 'well measured', a reflection of the way in which within Hinduism the temple building was (and is) required throughout to model cosmology.[15]

It would be very easy to relegate such ideas entirely to the past, but it is worth observing that town planning and the creation of National Parks marks the re-establishment of such notions of appropriate boundaries, and so it is possible for the theist to view modern zoning practices as in fact a return to some fundamental theistic principles. Although to many readers the last sentence may seem like a rather desperate attempt to establish the relevance of theistic considerations, the connection of parks and gardens with both theism and architecture is in fact long-standing. Taking the latter first, as with the Persian word 'Paradise', 'garden' in all European languages means an enclosure, and so has that boundary character that we suggested was so basic to early ideas of architecture.[16] If for the most part gardening and architecture are now treated quite separately, even today the connection is sometimes acknowledged as in the decision to expand the fifth edition of *The Penguin Dictionary of Architecture* to include *and Landscape Architecture* (1998).

Once, no less central was the connection with theism. The way in which the four quadrants of some Muslim gardens were intended to recall the rivers of Paradise is well known.[17] Christianity too has had a long history of involvement in garden symbolism. So extensive was the application of symbolism in the medieval garden that it has been described as 'a kind of surrogate Bible'.[18] Discussion continued well into more modern times. Formal Renaissance knot gardens were premised on the assumption that fallen nature needed restoration; whereas landscape and picturesque gardens were much more optimistic about where God could be perceived.[19] Not that religion was by any means the only factor in such discussions, but the way in which such types of argument might continue to be of relevance can be seen in modern debates about preserving wilderness. Is God, it may be asked, most easily experienced in places untouched by human hand, or can that same human hand (whether in garden or in building) facilitate such possibilities? In other words, there is the general question of whether any form of mediation necessarily produces greater distance. Even in the case of human beings, one can sometimes learn more about them through their family or friends than by encountering them directly, for example if they are shy or reserved. So there seems no reason in principle why the mediated, bounded garden or building could not after all make the greater contribution.

But it was not just a matter of observing the right boundaries; human architecture also sought justification in imitation of specific aspects of the divine architecture of the world. Vitruvius had already observed that structures in the Classical style were elaborations of basic patterns already to hand in nature. The greatest theorist of the Renaissance, Leon Battista Alberti (1404–1472), carried that idea a stage further. Classicism could appeal to what he saw as 'the absolute and fundamental rule of Nature' in *concinnitas*, by which he meant harmonic ratios that generated symmetry and proportion.[20] In the nineteenth century a similar kind of argument was pursued in great detail by John Ruskin (1819–1900), but this time in defence of the revival of the Gothic style. For him not only are 'forms ... not taken from nature ... ugly', but 'every line and hue is ... at its best a faded image of God's daily work'.[21] For this reason, although straight lines are conceded to be essential to human architecture, they must be used only where they are 'consistent with the most frequent natural groupings of them that we can discover'.[22]

As Ruskin's own partial later retreat from such an approach indicates, such ideas are harder to sustain in a post-Darwinian world. Even those who continue to adhere to theistic belief are now less confident of quite so direct a link between the patterns of nature and what God might ultimately intend. But there is also an additional difficulty. The idea of legitimate human activity simply assisting natural processes has come increasingly under strain, as humanity has discovered its potential to go well beyond them. While endorsement of contraception is probably the best-known example of this phenomenon, the issue is equally apparent in the production of buildings through the use of computer-generated plans. Technology now surpasses what even the best human minds could envisage, using only their own natural resources. One of the great ironies of modern architecture is that greater honesty in public exposure of the utilities that help the building to function (e.g. Piano and Rogers's Centre Pompidou in Paris, 1977) has also gone with greater concealment of what secures its continuing existence (e.g. Frank Gehry's Guggenheim Museum in Bilbao, 1997). Yet it is not just those of conservative or Catholic sympathies that might resist such modern developments. Buildings that give the impression of being about to keel over are hardly conducive to individuals feeling at home in their environment: for an extreme example, consider Massimiliano Fuksas's Gymnasium Paliano at Frosinone in Lazio (central Italy) from 1985. Of course, for the non-believer such objections amount to no more than recognition of human needs as they have been generated by evolution. But the theist could add that, however generated, they still constitute an appeal to nature and thus also, implicitly at least, to the Creator. So perhaps this type of argument from nature is not so much defeated as in need of more complex formulation.

However that may be, there remains one version of such traditional claims to a relation that appears immune to our changing attitudes to nature, and that is the idea that one style of architecture is better at reflecting the divine nature than another. So Classicism could claim that its sense of order best reflects the divine order, Gothic the majesty of the divine in drawing our thoughts heavenwards or Baroque in stressing the element of exuberance and theatre in divine action. Best known are perhaps the views of Abbot Suger (c. 1081–1151), the creator of the abbey of St-Denis, then on the outskirts of Paris but now in its suburbs. For him the new use of light in Gothic 'illumines minds so that they go through the true lights to the True Light where Christ is the true door' and so can be translated 'by divine grace from an inferior to a higher world'.[23] Nor is it hard to understand the force of his argument. To the typical spire pointing heavenwards is added a building made to look physically as light as possible, not least through the amount of glass used and seemingly held in position by the slenderest of frames. By contrast, whatever symbolism may once have underpinned the Classical style in antiquity, there is no doubt that with the Renaissance and the Enlightenment the primary intention was to speak of order, including divine order. In the modern world rationalism and religion are so often set in opposition that it is well to remember that this was once the favoured style of Protestant churches. What was intended was endorsement neither of Renaissance art nor of Enlightenment critiques of religion but rather affirmation of the ordered character of the Christian life and its beliefs, seen most obviously perhaps in the systematic character of Calvin's own theology.

Of all styles most difficult to comprehend are perhaps the claims of Baroque, in part because it secured no defence by some great theoretician and in part because its attitudes are currently so out of fashion in Church circles. In rough, what it sought to suggest by its architecture was a sense of movement and so of divine involvement in and with the world. So the oval replaced the more static Renaissance circle (as in Bernini's approach to St Peter's), while ornate balconies were used to suggest heavenly observers of the mass as it was performed below as a form of theatre (as in St John Nepomuk in Munich). Further aloft false ceilings (*trompe l'oeil*) implied the dissolution of barriers between heaven and earth, as saints floated upwards and angels downwards (as in the Jesuit church in Rome). All these ideas – whether in Gothic, Classicism or Baroque – may seem to have died a natural death with Modernism, but a few recent architects continued to be willing to make such connections, as with Mies van der Rohe's willingness to trace his ideas on simplicity back to Augustine on divine simplicity. Again, Charles Jencks has argued that postmodernist architecture demonstrates connections both with Baroque and with a religious way of viewing the world.[24]

In the past, all such approaches were usually set in opposition to one another, but there seems no reason in principle why they could not be treated as complementary insights. The greater difficulty is to know how to treat such approaches in a society that is no longer fundamentally theist in attitude. There may seem an obvious answer: to confine such questions to religious buildings. But matters are not quite that simple. Such styles were originally commonly also applied to secular buildings with similar ideas in mind. So with the Classical style, civic order and divine order were seen as closely related, while even the application of Gothic to nineteenth-century railway stations had a religious element, in endowing travel with a high seriousness. Britain's oldest travel firm, Thomas Cook, for example, began in the organisation of temperance rail excursions. Perhaps theist and non-theist could unite in seeking the preservation of such buildings on grounds of respect for the past and its skills in craftsmanship, while the theist would continue to detect rather more. Whether non-theists can generate sufficient shared values to allow for such public expression in buildings is an issue to which I return below. In the mean time, it is worth noting that even theists by and large retreated from such notions in the twentieth century, as church buildings for the most part slavishly followed contemporary styles. Here, the issue was not just a matter of following fashion. Two further arguments were repeatedly voiced: first, that a church devoted to service of the community should not be ostentatious in its buildings and, second, that in any case the building must be primarily instrumental or functional, as God could be worshipped anywhere.

The Contemporary Context

These last comments have already trespassed onto the present. There are two further issues worth noting that are more distinctly contemporary.

The first concerns the possibility or otherwise of great architecture in a society not based on theism. For example, Gordon Graham contends that present secular society lacks the necessary impetus.[25] At first sight, the very question might seem strange since much good architecture continues to be produced in the modern world. But it is noticeable how in seeking to identify such architecture the almost universal response is to appeal to individual buildings and not streets as a whole, or particular districts. In other words, what appeals are individual architectural expressions that often sit ill at ease with neighbouring buildings. For example, Daniel Liebeskind's widely praised Jewish Museum in Berlin (1989) succeeds so well because it is carefully integrated with the Classical building which stands next door while its more controversial aspects are a distance from any other building,[26] whereas his proposals for the extension to the Victoria and Albert Museum in London were rightly contested, it could be argued, because his proposals would have resulted in a building radically discontinuous with its immediate neighbours.

In considering what more might be required some have argued that it is just a matter of good manners, to consider how buildings relate to their neighbours.[27] Others have argued for the rooting of architecture in psychological needs, and seen that as a way of securing an alternative objective foundation to religious ideas.[28] But the difficulty is that the postulated 'needs' seem hard to sustain as universals, and in any case to produce a corporate vision what seems required is something more social than personal. Nor does the rhetoric of 'truthfulness' help. Notoriously, in his defence of the revival of Gothic architecture, Augustus Welby Northmore Pugin (1812–1852) defended Gothic as more honest in exposing its flying buttresses than had been Sir Christopher Wren (1632–1723) in his Baroque cathedral of St Paul's where they had remained concealed.[29] But, as later with Modernism, that basic principle of honesty was not consistently applied. More importantly, it could not be, because architecture has aims other than such 'moral' ideas, whether implying respect for function and a proper use of materials or even the *Zeitgeist* of the time.[30]

More recently, in a sustained philosophical discussion that plays off Heidegger against Hegel, Karsten Harries has argued that architecture can indeed embody notions like 'the common good'. Picking up on a hint in Augustine's *City of God*, he suggests that Adam went willingly with Eve from the Garden of Eden because 'he would rather know Eve, working and facing an inevitable death together with her, than be in paradise without her'.[31] From that analogy, he draws the conclusion: 'I would like to suggest that such a leave-taking from God for the sake of a genuinely human community is the foundation of any genuinely human dwelling. It is this leave-taking, this fall, this expulsion into insecurity and uncertainty that alone lets us develop into responsible individuals.' Indeed, so worried is he by the possibility of 'a golden calf' that he is adamant that 'interpretations of ideal dwelling must acknowledge that they are finally no more than precarious conjectures'.[32] But the result is that, while he offers excellent arguments against judging architecture solely on form or function, where his wider political concerns might take us remains underdetermined.

So, arguably, what is still missing without theism is a corporate vision: the church or other public building at its end giving unity to the street as a whole. Concrete alternative corporate visions have of course been canvassed, but it is noticeable how the most determined in Nazism and Stalinism both resulted in bombastic and essentially derivative architectural styles. However valuable democracy may be politically, aesthetically it seems only to result in individualism, as is perhaps most obvious in contemporary art, though this may well be (and often is) subsidised by the state. Even those who seek to defend a more communitarian approach that makes no appeal to religion but still contains some objective standards seem in the end forced to rely on finding those standards in some earlier style, as in Roger Scruton's own support for Classicism.[33]

The other issue is quite different, and is modern only in the sense that it becomes clear as an issue once religious belief has itself come under challenge. This is the question of whether it is possible to distinguish aesthetic and religious experience of a building when both seem to be present. In the atheist's view, the latter is simply a particular aura given to what is essentially an aesthetic experience as a result of prior disposition on the believer's part. In questioning that account some theists would no doubt argue that the religious element in fact constitutes a supervenient property on the aesthetic, in much the same way as the attribute 'good' functions in relation to non-moral features of our world. Others, however, might prefer a quite different approach, since there seem good grounds for more sharply differentiating the two types of experience. The first consideration is that the quality of the aesthetic experience and that of the religious do not necessarily run in parallel. Almost any spire can evoke in the believer a sense of divine transcendence, whereas typically an aesthetic experience will heavily depend on the scale and quality of the workmanship involved. Then, second, an aesthetic judgment is usually an estimation of a building's visual impact as a whole, whereas the religious need not be. So, for example, the aesthetic evaluation is likely to take account of such things as the nature and quality of the ornament on the building, something unlikely to have a bearing on the religious view, which will probably be more narrowly focused. Of course, sometimes overall judgments of beauty will be involved in both cases, but not necessarily; so for example, one can have a general sense of order without noting any of the details of a building.

Some might be inclined to add a third difference: that the aesthetic experience is intrinsic to what is seen whereas the religious experience is in fact constituted by a pointer elsewhere, to how God is understood. But, while this no doubt correctly describes what sometimes happens, on other occasions the two scenarios seem more nearly parallel, in that the divine is apparently encountered in the actual seeing of the relevant feature of the building. At this point even some theists may be tempted to disagree, insisting that it is inappropriate or even meaningless to speak of God being experienced in this way, for what could it mean to encounter an infinite being in this way?[34] And yet in reply one may observe that the claim is not that the totality of God is encountered but only divinity under some partial aspect: transcendent, ordered, dynamic and so on.[35]

Notes

1 See further Gordon Graham, *Philosophy of the Arts: An Introduction to Aesthetics*, 3rd edn (London: Routledge, 2000), ch.7.
2 Immanuel Kant, *Critique of Judgement*, trans. W. S. Pluhar (Indianapolis: Hackett, 1987), 76.
3 For helpful discussions, Henri Stierlin, *Hindu India* (Cologne: Taschen, 1998); R. Champalakalaksmi, *The Hindu Temple* (London: Greenwich Editions, 2001).
4 M. Frishman and H.-U. Khan, *The Mosque: History, Architectural Development and Relational Diversity* (London: Thames & Hudson, 1994), 44–45; though for a different view, Gulru Necipoglu, *The Age of Sinan: Architectural Culture in the Ottoman Empire* (London: Reaktion Books, 2005), 106.
5 Keith Critchlow, *Islamic Patterns: An Analytical and Cosmological Approach* (London: Thames & Hudson, 1976).
6 Dominique Clévenot, *Ornament and Decoration in Islamic Architecture* (London: Thames & Hudson, 2000).
7 Ismail Serageldin, ed., *Architecture of the Contemporary Mosque* (London: Academy Editions, 1996). 96–97; Renata Holod and Hasan-Uddin Khan, *The Contemporary Mosque: Architects, Clients and Designs since the 1950s* (New York: Rizzoli, 1997), 55–61.
8 H. A. Meek, *The Synagogue* (London: Phaidon, 1995); Dominique Jarrassé, *Synagogues* (Paris: Vilo International, 2001).
9 In retrospect, what I originally wrote at this point seems too unqualified, for it is possible that Jews were also at times motivated by similar symbolic considerations in choosing one form of architecture rather than another. See further the next essay.
10 For example, Lindsay Jones, *The Hermeneutics of Sacred Architecture* (Cambridge, Mass.: Harvard University Press, 2000), 2 vols.

166 Meaning in Religious Architecture

11 For example, Christopher Alexander, *The Timeless Way of Building* (New York: Oxford University Press, 1979).
12 See further David Brown, *God and Enchantment of Place: Reclaiming Human Experience* (Oxford: Oxford University Press, 2004), 170–189.
13 William J. Hamblin and David Rolph Seely, *Solomon's Temple: Myth and History* (London: Thames & Hudson, 2007).
14 Brown, *God and Enchantment of Place*, 172–173.
15 Emily Lyle, ed., *Sacred Architecture and Traditions of India, China, Judaism and Islam* (Edinburgh: Edinburgh University Press, 1992).
16 John Dixon Hunt, *Greater Perfections: The Practice of Garden Theory* (London: Thames & Hudson, 2000), 19–20.
17 D. Fairchild Ruggles, *Islamic Gardens and Landscapes* (Philadelphia: University of Pennsylvania Press, 2008).
18 John Prest, *The Garden of Eden: The Botanic Garden and the Recreation of Paradise* (New Haven: Yale University Press, 1981), 23–24.
19 Filippo Pizzoni, *The Garden: A History in Landscape and Art* (New York: Rizzoli, 1997); Christopher McIntosh, *Gardens of the Gods: Myth, Magic and Meaning* (London: I. B. Tauris, 2005).
20 Leon Battista Alberti, *The Ten Books of Architecture* (New York: Dover, 1986), esp. Book IX, 194–200.
21 John Ruskin, *The Seven Lamps of Architecture* (New York: Dover, 1989), 105, 147.
22 Ibid., 108.
23 Erwin Panovsky, ed., *Abbot Suger on the Abbey Church of St-Denis and its Art Treasures*, 2nd edn (Princeton: Princeton University Press, 1979), 48–49, 65.
24 Charles Jencks, *The Architecture of the Jumping Universe* (London: Academy, 1997); Charles Jencks, ed., *Ecstatic Architecture* (London: Academy, 1999).
25 Gordon Graham, *The Re-enchantment of the World: Art versus Religion* (Oxford: Oxford University Press, 2007).
26 I correct here inaccurate observations made in the first version of this essay.
27 Trystan Edwards, *Good and Bad Manners in Architecture* (London: Tirranti, 1944).
28 Norman Crowe, *Nature and the Idea of a Man-Made World: An Investigation into the Evolutionary Roots of Form and Order in the Built Environment* (Cambridge, Mass.: MIT Press, 1995); Ralf Weber, *Aesthetics of Architecture: A Psychological Approach* (Aldershot: Avebury, 1995).
29 Augustus W. N. Pugin, *The True Principles of Pointed or Christian Architecture* (Leominster: Gracewing, 2003), 4–5.
30 David Watkin, *Morality and Architecture* (Oxford: Clarendon Press, 1977).
31 Karsten Harries, *The Ethical Function of Architecture* (Cambridge, Mass.: MIT Press, 1997), 365.
32 Ibid., 364
33 Roger Scruton, *The Aesthetics of Architecture* (London: Methuen, 1979).
34 For example, Brian Davies, *Introduction to the Philosophy of Religion*, 3rd edn (Oxford: Oxford University Press, 2003).
35 Apart from nn. 9 and 26 and the exclusion of recommended Further Reading this essay is reprinted as it first appeared under the title of 'Architecture' in *The Routledge Companion to Theism*, ed. Charles Taliaferro, Victoria S. Harrison and Stewart Goetz (London: Routledge, 2012), 55–63, and is used with grateful permission.

11 Interfaith Dialogue through Architecture

First reflections might suggest that using architecture to initiate dialogue between the three great monotheistic religions has little prospect of success simply because the architectural traditions of Judaism, Christianity and Islam just seem so different. After all, it may be said, what could there possibly be in common between the elaborate theatricality of a Christian Baroque church and Islam's sole requirement for a mosque, that it allow worshippers to be correctly oriented towards Mecca?[1] On the latter rule, strictly speaking, not even walls are required; a simple marking in the sand would suffice.[2] Even with walls accepted, all the imagery in Catholic churches could easily be presented as a further insurmountable barrier given Islam's stark iconoclastic stance. Again, it would not prove difficult to generate similar antipathies for Judaism.

What, however, I would like to suggest is that these first thoughts are in fact quite wrong, and in at least three respects. First, however simply each of the three religions may have begun, all three experienced pressures towards symbolic elements in their architecture with, as is now being increasingly acknowledged, such pressures existing even from a very early stage. Second, part of the explanation for this phenomenon lies in influences (usually implicit) from one to the other in each of the three cases. So dialogue has in fact been taking place through architecture for a very long time. Finally, these movements do rather more than just reflect changing architectural tastes in the wider culture. In effect, they embody various theological ideas that, if handled carefully, could actually encourage dialogue to continue today and at a deeper and much more explicit level. Let me, therefore, now consider each of these points in turn.

Architecture as Religious Impetus

It is still quite common to find the origins of all three religions presented in large part as a revolt against the notion of sacred space, with temples seen as being replaced by the ability to worship God anywhere. Islam's mark in the sand thus replaced pagan shrines. Christianity rejected pagan and Jewish temple alike in moving to the home and eventually, when larger structures were required, to the adaption of a purely secular building, the imperial law-court or basilica. Again, Judaism, even before the Jerusalem Temple was destroyed, had started to move to a purely functional building, the synagogue, which of course literally means just a community gathering place. But, I would suggest, these simple stories in fact belie a much more complex reality.

For a start, it is a mistake to think of the home in the ancient world, as most of us now understand the term, as purely secular. For pagan and Jew alike it remained a sacred sphere, and so it seems likely that, with no evidence to the contrary, such an assumption was carried over also into early Christianity. To see the difference, just recall for the moment how, at the time of Christ, entry to a large Roman villa would have been experienced. Passing through a narrow passage (the *fauces* or jaws), one moved through an open courtyard to enter the main room (the *tablinum*) where the head of the house would already be waiting (in the distance). This intervening courtyard was the usual place of religious observance. It was here that the household gods (the *penates*) were honoured and key ceremonies performed, such as the giving of the *toga virilis* to a boy on reaching adulthood or the abandonment of her dolls on marriage for a girl.[3] Nor were matters essentially different among the poor. Each apartment in the *insulae* or tenements of imperial Rome would have had its little cupboard or shrine for the household gods at which daily worship would have been offered. In fact, the situation in the ancient world was closer to modern Hinduism than it is to most of contemporary Christianity – in Hinduism the practice of a separate room or cupboard, depending on the family's relative wealth, is maintained to this day.[4]

Nor is the next stage in the adaptation of the basilica rightly understood, if it is interpreted as a move towards secularity. The point is that Christianity had initially no alternative but to turn to models other than temples for its worship, because it required the community to gather within its buildings whereas ancient temples were specifically designed to function only as dwelling places for the gods, with sacrificial offerings being reserved as an activity for outside the building. In this respect even the Jerusalem Temple was no exception. So, although an adapted secular building, symbolic features soon began to emerge in basilicas also. Nor were matters any different in the earlier use of houses. The oldest surviving house adapted for Christian worship corroborates this claim. Thus while the building at Dura Europos in Syria may not have external architectural features as such that would have distinguished it from any other house, internally there is extensive use of iconography on its walls.

Again, our understanding of early Judaism has been transformed in recent years by archaeological discoveries in the Holy Land. Quite a lot of synagogues, several dating, like Dura Europos, from the third century, have been exposed to view, and turn out to be very far from plain edifices. Allusions to the Jerusalem Temple are frequent, as are references to key elements in

Israel's history such as the *Akedah* or offering of Isaac. More surprisingly perhaps, astrological symbolism is also to be found, as in the common depiction of the signs of the Zodiac.[5]

The history of Islam may seem quite different, but here again there are a number of reasons for doubting this. First, there is the question of attitudes to the Ka'ba or sacred cube at the heart of Mecca.[6] According to Islamic tradition not only was it a house of prayer for Adam and Abraham, it is also now to be seen as the special locus for the divine presence in the way the Ark and Jerusalem Temple once were, which is why Muslims orient themselves in prayer towards it.[7] Although the divine presence is conceived more as emanating out from it rather than being contained by it, the Ka'ba is nonetheless treated with great reverence, as in the annual renewal of its embroidered cover or *kiswa*. Such sacralisation of space is of course reinforced by the elaborate rituals that take place each year in the same area with the annual *hajj* or pilgrimage, all of which are intended to enable the pilgrim to identify closely with key events in the Muslim's history of salvation, including actions by Abraham, Hagar and Ishmael.

It is against such a background that I suggest we interpret the basic rule for the creation of a mosque. It is not so much that anywhere will do as that sacralisation is still a necessary preliminary, as in the requirement for appropriate orientation towards Mecca and the need for ritual ablutions before such prayer. To any who object that the absence of walls means that we are still not in the territory of architecture, it may be pointed out that not only do some architectural theorists declare the creation of boundaries to be the most basic feature of architecture but also, arguably, this is what lies at the root also of any explicitly religious architecture.[8] Thus, as already noted in the previous essay, the origin of the Latin term *templum* in fact lies not in what we would understand by a building but simply as a bounded space, in particular one in which religious auguries could be taken. Similarly, a number of books in the Hebrew Bible present the Temple less as a building in its own right and more as the culmination of a series of bounded spaces (the created world as a whole, the earth, the Holy Land, Jerusalem, the Temple Mount, the Holy of Holies).[9] In fact, ancient cultures generally presupposed that the divine creation of the world was itself something like the construction of a building; so in the process the Creator had assigned different land areas for different forms of human activity, with some seen as most appropriate for human dwelling and cultivation, and others (such as forest groves or mountains) as places for divine encounter where heaven and earth might be more easily bridged. So, just as the Garden of Eden is presented as a defined area for Adam and Eve to dwell in (Genesis 2:8; 3:24), townships continued to be marked out formally by religious ceremonies, as in the Roman ceremony of the *pomerium* or boundary.[10]

So, in short, it is wrong in my view to suppose that these three religions only at some later point in their history take an interest in the religious value of architecture. That is a principle which is present in all three from their

170 *Meaning in Religious Architecture*

outset. Of course, once the interest becomes more explicit, their traditions then often vary. But even so once again I want to suggest some underlying points of comparison. However, before doing so, it will be worth noting the extent to which dialogue has been implicitly taking place already, through mutual borrowings and fertilisations.

Implicit Dialogue

As one might expect, Christianity did eventually borrow much from the construction of the Temple as described in the Old Testament. So, for example, the internal division of the Temple between the Holy Place and the Holy of Holies quickly came to be adopted in many churches, with the nave constituting, like the Holy Place, two-thirds of the church and the quire or chancel, like the Holy of Holies, the remaining third. Individual pieces of symbolism were also copied, as, for example, a giant menorah in Romanesque Essen or the two mysterious pillars, Boaz and Jachin, that were reduplicated outside the Baroque Karlskirche in Vienna.[11] But more often than not the borrowings were rather muddled, since until modern times no clear notion of what the Temple had once looked like had gained ascendancy. The result was claims to imitation from almost all the competing architectural styles that have characterised the history of Christianity.[12] Astonishingly, even Jews themselves are found supposing that the long-departed Temple must have resembled its Muslim successor, the Dome of the Rock.[13] That could easily be read as simply the result of a lack of historical consciousness but rather more was almost certainly at stake: the conviction that God would have built the Jerusalem Temple in accordance with the best architectural principles, and what might these be but how they were currently conceived?

But, if Christianity borrowed from Judaism, and Judaism from Islam however unknowingly, borrowings in other directions are also observable. Surprising as it may seem, it is only since the Holocaust that synagogues can be seen to develop their own distinctive form of symbolism in their external appearance.[14] Prior to the modern period such buildings almost invariably reflect the architectural preoccupations of the dominant culture, and so in Christian lands there are also Classical, Baroque and other types of synagogues.[15] The analogies, however, run much deeper than this, for, while there are some obvious differences in internal structure, for example in location of the pulpit, it is hard not to see also deeper parallels. Tradition requires a richly embroidered curtain and/or decorated door to be placed in front of the Ark containing the Scrolls of the Law (*Sefer Torah*) which will be read in due course from a *bemah* or platform, their current location indicated by a perpetually burning light.[16] While such a light will recall for those within the Catholic tradition the presence of a similar constantly burning light before pyx or tabernacle containing the reserved sacrament, any more general analogy with a Christian altar might seem slight. But explore what happens in practice, and one immediately recalls the reredos or screen behind so many Christian altars or else some great Christian tabernacle.[17] So, whatever the origins of the practice, the various elements in fact combine to suggest the Ark as a particular locus of the divine presence, a source of grace for the practising Jew.

Again, interactions between Islam and Christianity may be noted. One subject of continuing debate, for example, is the extent to which Christian Romanesque architecture developed under influence from the Muslim world.[18] The point is of course especially pertinent in Sicily, where the Norman rulers seem to have employed Muslim craftsmen in some of their building operations.[19] Much earlier, though, almost certainly the relation was the other way round, with Christian craftsmen being employed in the early years of Islam, in the creation of major buildings such as the Dome of the Rock in Jerusalem and the Great Mosque in Damascus.[20] In the latter fine representational art is to be found which, although in the history of Islam it was replicated in other contexts, was never again repeated in such a sacred building. Nor did the borrowing end there. The great architect of the mosques of Istanbul, Sinan, makes major use of domes to suggest the vault of heaven.[21] While the symbolism already existed within Islam, especially for tombs of the saints, it can scarcely be doubted that its development by Sinan in the mosques of Istanbul and elsewhere was derived more directly from the precedent already set in the city by Justinian's Christian church of Hagia Sophia.

Again, despite their present frequent hostility to one another, Judaism can certainly also be seen to have borrowed from Islam (sometimes consciously, sometimes not), in everything from the horseshoe arch to prayer rugs in buildings for worship.[22]

Underlying Theological Ideas

What I have said thus far could be interpreted as claiming no more than various shared practices in common. My contention, however, is that such common origins and mutual borrowings point to something very much deeper: elements of a shared theology. By this I certainly do not mean that the three religions are after all essentially the same. Rather, my point is one in natural theology: that, just as one can argue for the existence of the same God from shared underlying basic principles (contingency, design and so on), so there are certain fundamental aspects of the nature of the deity and of religion that make likely shared reflection of these ideas in the architecture of each of these religions.

In considering why this might be so, a first stab at a response might propose a shared pursuit of beauty as the answer. But, although it is possible to extract from the history of Christianity various aesthetic theories, this is much more difficult with the other two religions.[23] In Islam its best-known medieval philosophers adopted an Aristotelian theory of the *mimesis* or imitation of nature but without specific reference to architecture, while it is hard to determine the extent of the influence of more mystical theories that talk of hidden inner meanings.[24] Modern interpreters have on the whole, therefore, preferred a simpler approach. Instead of addressing beauty as such, it is seen as more a question of identifying symbolism and the likely meanings it was intended to convey about the divine nature and purpose. Although in what follows some attention will still be paid to Judaism, comparisons between Christianity and Islam are in many ways more interesting, as often quite different means are employed to achieve the same symbolic end.

Three points of comparison will be considered, beginning, first, with transcendence. In the case of Christianity, at its most basic this is provided through the height of the building, a height of course that runs counter to considerations of warmth and communal sociability. But with a style like Gothic many other features may also be noted, among them spires and the double use of light, not only in the scale and number of windows but also in the attempt to suggest a building so physically light that it could almost be blown heavenwards. It is a symbolism that is extensively discussed not only in the Middle Ages in the writings of Abbot Suger, the style's founder as creator of the abbey of St-Denis, but also in nineteenth-century writers such as A. W. N. Pugin and John Ruskin.[25] It is, however, not the only way within Christianity in which the objective is achieved. Classicism prefers the dome with the vault symbolising the need to go beyond the building to heaven's vault or, in other words, the universe as a whole.

If, as we have seen, Islam also uses the vault and also its own equivalent of the spire in the minaret, there are also less familiar methods.[26] Two in particular are worth noting. First, there is the use of texts from the Qur'an to cover some of the mosque's walls, both internally and externally. Given that they are quotations from Allah's communication to humankind, it might be thought that they point more towards the world rather than away from it, but this would be ignore Islam's very high doctrine of the status of the Qur'an, much higher than the Bible bears within Christianity. It is essentially an other-worldly document, words straight from heaven, as it were, and so quite appropriately used in architecture to connote the otherness of God. The beauty of the calligraphy provided an obvious reminder of the Qur'an as divine speech and as such its primary intention may not necessarily have been even that it should be read.[27] So already even on the Dome of the Rock the writing proves difficult to read, even for those with a good knowledge of Arabic. Not only is it often too high to be easily read, but the stylised Kufic script with a minimum of diacritical points to distinguish the various letters adds to the difficulty.[28] So the issue in such cases seems to be less what the text says and much more what it represents: the wonderful and mysterious gift of divine speech in the Qur'an, with transcendence as the dominant theme.

My second example is rather different, the *murquanas* or stalactites that are found hanging from the ceilings of some mosques.[29] Their lightness and delicacy seems to be used to convey the apparent insubstantiality of the building, and so with it the pull to something beyond. Intriguingly, in modern Jewish architecture, that pull is in fact frequently represented through reference to Judaism's central revelation on Mount Sinai, with synagogues often alluding to Moses' mysterious encounter on the holy mountain.[30]

Given that immanence is commonly presented as at the opposite extreme to transcendence, it might be thought that they could not meaningfully occur in the same building, but this is to ignore the way in which symbols, and metaphors for that matter, function. On the literal level something cannot of course both transcend ('go beyond') and be immanent ('remain within'). But since God does not have a physical location, the objection does not apply. He is at one and the same time both beyond our world and all our imaginings and active within it. So, even the Christian style that places most emphasis on transcendence (Gothic) also has strong immanentist elements. Indeed, one way of reading Gothic churches is to see the style's immanent art as a deliberate counterpoise to its transcendent architecture, as seen not only in its Eucharistic symbolism (tabernacle lights and so forth) but also in the humanist character of its art (Romanesque hieratic figures replaced by Jesus as playful infant or suffering body on the cross, with even angels smiling, as at Reims).

In theory all a Muslim requires for prayer is the *qiblah* that indicates the direction of Mecca, and indeed this is sometimes provided by a decorative device on an outside wall that can be seen from a distance without even entering the mosque. In keeping with such thought, earlier versions of the prayer niche inside (the *mirhab*) often consisted of no more than a simple stone. Significantly, though, the *mirhab* does seem to have come to function in some ways like the Christian altar, not least because it was seen to mediate the divine presence through the intimate link it thus provided with the Ka'ba in Mecca. That is no doubt why in established practice the architecture at this particular point in the building, while still giving clear direction signs, yet also adds an element of mystery in what precisely is being conveyed. Against such a background, the Eucharistic light can be seen to have its obvious parallel not only in the light burning before the *mirhab* but also in the common quotation of the so-called 'Light verse' from the Qur'an either on the lamp itself or noted nearby.[31]

Again, some symbols seem intended to attempt to speak of both transcendence and immanence at the same time. Thus the way in which the top step of the *minbar* or pulpit is reserved for Muhammad could be taken to refer to his transcendence of any particular place now that he is in heaven, but it could also be used to speak of his continuing influence here on earth in each and every mosque. Equally, the elaborate housing of the Scrolls of the Law in a Jewish synagogue that we have already noted could be taken to refer to the immanence of such laws now within the Jewish community, nourishing it, or such reverence could be taken to imply the way in which the Law is never exhausted by human endeavour, given its transcendent origins on Mount Sinai.

174 *Meaning in Religious Architecture*

A third form of symbolism (in addition to transcendence and immanence), particularly associated with the Classical architecture of the Renaissance and subsequent revivals, is that of order. Among the various Renaissance treatises on the subject, Alberti's is perhaps the best known. He spoke of an 'absolute and fundamental rule in nature' in *concinnitas*, by which he meant harmonic ratios that generated symmetry and proportion.[32] So, recurring themes of order, balance and proportion are used to emphasise a good God who has produced a harmonious world suitably designed for human habitation.

Similarly, then, in Islam there is extensive use of recurring patterns often drawn from the natural world that reinforce a sense of order and design in that world. Some scholars suggest a deliberate contrast with the barrenness of a surrounding desert landscape, and so the aim is to give reassurance of 'a fearful and primitive world ... tamed and cultivated'.[33] If that is so, the parallel might be more with the Muslim tradition of Paradise gardens, reflecting the believer's ultimate destiny. But there is of course no reason why the symbol should not be multivalent, that is, carry more than one meaning. Much the same might be said about the quotations from the Qur'an. Earlier I noted their capacity to convey transcendence. But the way in which the text becomes a pattern could also be used to argue for a similar attempt, as in the floral and abstract patterns, to give a sense of a good divine purpose to the world in which God has placed us.[34] Indeed, the practice of combining text and floral patterns is very common. Even so, still more common is the treatment of writing as itself an abstract form, and so order is in fact indicated less by a connection to nature and more through the quality of its geometry.[35]

I began this essay by contrasting the elaborate character of Christian Baroque churches with the simplicity of the basic rules for a mosque. I want, therefore, to end by suggesting that even Baroque might have its parallels in these other two religions. Admittedly, finding parallels for the theatricality and playfulness of Baroque in Jewish architecture is difficult, but its liturgy is quite another matter. Think, for instance, of the riotous behaviour in Jewish synagogues during the feast of Purim with its elaborate and detailed playacting in remembrance of deliverance from persecution from Haman under Esther. Islam, however, does appear to offer some direct architectural parallels. Occasionally we find sunbursts to rival the typical Baroque monstrance.[36] More commonly, however, as in Baroque's whirling curves and *trompe l'oeil*, so wild arabesques are used in some Muslim architecture to suggest that only a dazzling divine miracle keeps our world in place.[37]

Conclusion

My aim here has been a strictly limited one: to demonstrate that, despite initial appearances to the contrary, the architecture of the three monotheistic religions draws on very similar themes. Although radically different symbols are sometimes used to make the same point, it seems clear that such symbols seek to explicate essentially the same God: one who, though totally beyond our adequate conceptualisation, is fully active in our world and in a way that suggests the goodness of a providential design. Of course, no doubt the relative weight put on any particular element will vary across the religions, but what I hope I have shown is the possibility of fruitful and creative dialogue between them through exploring further the symbolism embodied in their buildings. In sum, then, my hope is that I have given enough examples to suggest that it is not just formal arguments for God's existence that the three religions might share in common. Equally, one could explore the lived character of the three faiths and find in their actual practice of architecture shared elements in their approach to worship of, at least in some respects, the same God.[38]

Notes

1 For illustration of a modern application of this simple rule, in the grounds of a hotel in Pakistan, see Martin Frishman and Hasan-Uddin Khan, *The Mosque* (London: Thames & Hudson, 1994), 33.
2 *Masjid* literally means 'a place for bowing down'. For an example of the continuing requirement for simplicity, see Maulana Muhammad Ali, *The Religion of Islam: A Comprehensive Discussion of the Sources, Principles and Practices of Islam*, 6th edn (Columbus, Ohio: Lahore Institute, 1990), 281, 286–287.
3 For more detail, see John R. Clarke, *The Houses of Roman Italy 100 B.C.–A.D. 250* (Berkeley, Calif.: University of California Press, 1991), esp. 1–29.
4 See further David Brown, *God and Enchantment of Place: Reclaiming Human Experience* (Oxford: Oxford University Press, 2004), 170–189.
5 For illustrations from Dura Europos and Hamas, see Dominique Jarrassé, *Synagogues* (Paris: Vilo International, 2001), 39, 42; for illustrations from sixth-century Beth Alpha, see H. A. Meek, *The Synagogue* (London: Phaidon, 1995), 81.
6 For illustration, see George Mitchell, ed., *Architecture of the Islamic World: Its History and Social Meaning* (London: Thames & Hudson, 1978), 17.
7 Thus it can even be described as 'the main temple of the Muslim religion' because it 'embodies the divine presence and inspiration', with its alternative names as House of God (*Bayt Allah al-Haram*) and Sacred House (*Bayt al-Haram*): Malek Chebel, *Symbols of Islam* (New York: Assouline, 2000), 60.
8 For example, Christopher Alexander, *The Timeless Way of Building* (New York: Oxford University Press, 1979).
9 Ezekiel is an obvious example.
10 Brown, *God and Enchantment of Place*, 172–173.
11 Cf. 1 Kings 7:21.
12 For discussion and illustrations, William J. Hamblin and David Rolph Seely, *Solomon's Temple: Myth and History* (London: Thames & Hudson, 2007).
13 As in a fifteenth-century Jewish manuscript of Maimonides. This is one of a number of examples, from different historical periods and styles, given in Dan Bahat and Shalom Sabar, *Jerusalem Stone and Spirit: 3000 Years of History and Art* (New York: Rizzoli, 1998), esp. 101.
14 As, for example, in the repeated use of the Star of David on the façade of the Synagogue de la Paix in Strasbourg (1958): for illustration, Jarrassé, *Synagogues*, 232.

176 *Meaning in Religious Architecture*

15 A good example of the use of Classical architecture is the Scuola Grande Tedesca in Venice (1528–1529), illustrated ibid., 101.
16 The requirement for a curtain comes from Exodus 26:31–34; the light an allusion to the menorah: Exodus 27:20–21; Numbers 8:1–4.
17 See e.g. the Baroque Ark from Vittorio Veneto and that from the main Roman synagogue in Meek, *The Synagogue*, 135, 185.
18 For example, George Zarnecki, *Romanesque* (London: Herbert Press, 1989), 8; Andreas Petzold, *Romanesque Art* (London: Weidenfeld & Nicholson, 1995), 13–14, 150–155.
19 Note the influence from *murquanas*, for example, in the ceiling of the twelfth-century Palatine Chapel or their presence in the Fountain Room (both in Palermo).
20 See Oleg Grabar, *The Shape of the Holy: Early Islamic Jerusalem* (Princeton: Princeton University Press, 1996), e.g. 65–68 on an unusual inscription.
21 For a helpful discussion of Sinan, see Gulru Necipoglu, *The Age of Sinan: Architectural Culture in the Ottoman Empire* (London: Reaktion Books, 2005).
22 For Jewish use of horseshoe Moorish arches, see illustration from Toledo of former synagogue, Santa Maria la Blanca, Meek, *The Synagogue*, 106; for a seventeenth-century prayer rug that once hung in a Turkish synagogue, ibid., 119; for a Moorish style synagogue, ibid., 187.
23 There are very few books on aesthetics in Islam, but see Oliver Leaman, *Islamic Aesthetics: An Introduction* (Edinburgh: Edinburgh University Press, 2004) and Valerie Gonzalez, *Beauty and Islam: Aesthetics in Islamic Art and Architecture* (London: I. B. Tauris, 2001). Judaism has only explicitly engaged with the issue relatively recently, e.g. Zachary Braiterman, *The Shape of Revelation: Aesthetics and Modern Jewish Thought* (Stanford: Stanford University Press, 2007); Melissa Raphael, *Judaism and the Visual Image: A Jewish Theology of Art* (New York: Continuum, 2009).
24 True of the philosophers Ibn Sina (Avicenna), Al-Ghazzali and Ibn Rushd (Averroes). For some mystical approaches, see Henry Corbin, *Temple and Contemplation* (London: Islamic Publications, 1986).
25 As Suger puts it, the new use of light in Gothic 'illumines minds so that they go through the true lights to the True Light where Christ is the true door' and so can be 'translated by divine grace from an inferior to a higher world': Erwin Panovsky, ed., *Abbot Suger on the Abbey Church of St-Denis and its Art Treasures*, 2nd edn (Princeton: Princeton University Press, 1979).
26 Unlike the spire, the minaret has of course a practical function, in calling the faithful to prayer, but this should not be taken to preclude the existence also of a symbolic function.
27 So Frishman and Khan, *The Mosque*, 44–45.
28 See the comments of Richard Ettinghausen in 'The Man-Made Setting', in *The World of Islam: Faith, People, Culture*, ed. Bernard Lewis (London: Thames & Hudson, 1976), 57–88, esp. 61. For some illustrations, 73–74.
29 For examples from Isfahan and Samarqand, Frishman and Khan, *The Mosque*, 61.
30 Ironically, a trend set by a Christian architect, Frank Lloyd Wright; for illustrations of his 1955 Elkins Park Synagogue, Meek, *The Synagogue*, 222–223. Born into a Baptist family, as an adult Wright attended various Unitarian churches.
31 Qur'an 24:35, with its central metaphor of God as like a lamp burning olive oil.
32 Leon Battista Alberti, *The Ten Books of Architecture* (New York: Dover, 1986), 194–200.
33 Ettinghausen, 'The Man-Made Setting', 70.
34 For a similar argument, see Keith Critchlow, *Islamic Patterns: An Analytical and Cosmological Approach* (London: Thames & Hudson, 1976).

35 See, for example, the quotation from the fourteenth-century writer Muhammad ibn Mahud al-Amuli, in Richard Yeomans, *The Story of Islamic Architecture* (New York: New York University Press, 2000), 19.
36 For a couple of examples, see colour plates B and J in Eva Baer, *Islamic Ornament* (Edinburgh: Edinburgh University Press, 1998).
37 For such an interpretation (though without reference to Baroque), see Dominique Clévenot, *Ornament and Decoration in Islamic Decoration* (London: Thames & Hudson, 2000). For good illustrations of arabesque with and without text, ibid., 136–137 (nos. 190, 192). For set in relation to the text 'only God endures', ibid., 152 (no. 212). Note too Dalu Jones's comment: 'Islamic decoration covers buildings like a mantle; its purpose is to conceal the structure rather than reveal it', in 'The Elements of Decoration: Surface, Pattern and Light', in Mitchell, ed., *Architecture of the Islamic World*, 144.
38 This essay was first delivered as a lecture at a conference (Un Ponte tra le Religioni) that constituted part of the *SoleLuna* festival in Palermo in Sicily in 2011 and was subsequently published by one of the University of Palermo's journals: *Mediaeval Sophia* (2013), 1–11. I am deeply grateful both to the organisers of the conference and to the journal for helping to make this research possible.

12 Tensions between Politics and Religious Symbolism in Architecture

In the modern Western world it is usually the positioning of mosques that most frequently creates conflict. Their distinctive architecture is seen by non-Muslims in the neighbourhood as a threat to their own sense of belonging and self-identity. It is easy to suppose such conflicts essentially new, and generated by the negative esteem that current Islamic political extremism has brought on the religion more generally. That is far from being the case. Interaction between politics and religious symbolism runs deep throughout the course of human history. However, so far from the impact upon religion and its symbols always being negative, it is possible to identify a more complex and nuanced reality under which the politics is found to be, more often than not, transient when contrasted with the lasting impact of religion's symbols. To illustrate that point, I want to offer a brief survey of politics and religion interacting, initially in the Classical world within which Christianity came to birth, and then at two significant points in that religion's subsequent history. Then, at the end of the essay, I shall draw some tentative conclusions.

Politics and Religious Architecture in the Ancient World

Where opportunity presented itself, the most important religious building in Classical cities was usually on a prominent mountain or hill, as is true of Athens, Rome and Jerusalem. The measure was practical as well as symbolic: practical in that, if the city was attacked, religious rites could still continue to be performed on such an acropolis, but also symbolic, as indicating the importance of the gods concerned in the flourishing of that city: with Jerusalem it was Yahweh, with Athens Athene, and with Rome it was Jupiter.[1] Athens's Temple, the Parthenon, is the best known if for no other reason that it survived the vagaries of history.[2] That politics was integral to its foundation there seems no reason to doubt. Built at a time (447–432 BC) when Athens's own empire was under threat, the principal frieze is commonly taken to allude to a procession in honour of the goddess in which those who fell at Marathon defending Athens against the Persians are seen to be taking part.[3] So implicitly the temple is a prayer for the continued protective gaze, as at Marathon, of the goddess upon her city. Again, although the reliability of the details of the earlier history of the Temple at Jerusalem which would date it to the tenth century BC is subject to dispute, there seems little reason to contest the claim that it was used as a means of unifying a disparate people who had originally worshipped at a number of competing shrines across Israel.[4] Indeed, so strong was this identifying principle that from the time of the Second Temple (its rebuilding in the fourth century) even those Jewish groups (such as Qumran) who refused to obey its injunctions nevertheless defined themselves in relation to it.

But perhaps ancient Rome provides the best example of such intimate interweaving of politics and religion. Although the temple of Jupiter Optimus Maximus had been founded on the Capitoline hill by the last of its kings, the Roman Republic not only maintained the pre-eminent place for this temple in its life but even much of the regal terminology that had become associated with it.[5] Again, although Roman polytheism's natural tolerance of other religions is often favourably contrasted with Christianity, this contrast is undoubtedly overdone. In the introduction of new cults such as the Great Mother (Cybele) or Isis, careful control was exercised, and indeed new temples could only be built either with the assent of ancient prophecies known as the Sibylline Oracles or else as a result of vows made by commanders on military campaigns, and even then further authorisation was still required from the governing Senate.[6] If under the empire imperial autocracy meant a larger say for the whims of particular emperors, even here it is possible to detect at times strong political motives. So, if the second largest temple ever built in Rome – by Emperor Septimius Severus (193–211) to Liber and Hercules – reflected a desire on his part to honour the gods of his local native city of Lepcis Magna in north Africa, the largest, by Hadrian (117–138) to Venus and Rome, is more typical: Rome effectively declared part of the divine order along with the goddess Venus whom Virgil had celebrated as giving the city its birth.

The Christianity that gained power in the later empire was no less political. It is difficult to determine how genuine Constantine's conversion was. What cannot be disputed is the political advantage he gained in issuing an edict of toleration for Christianity throughout the empire in 313, for, although perhaps by this stage still only about 10 per cent of its population, Christians had become an increasingly influential minority and, as the modern world illustrates, minorities can be highly effective in supporting autocrats in power.[7] Even so, it was not till the end of the fourth century that Christianity became the only permitted religion. In the meantime successive emperors continued the church-building programme that Constantine had inaugurated. In a few cases this was to include the adaptation of existing temples, most famously with the Parthenon at Athens and the Pantheon in Rome, but for the most part this was not so. From that relative infrequency one might choose to infer that Christianity in principle objected to such adaptation to alternative use as pollution by association. But Paul's claim that eating meat offered in pagan sacrifice was a matter of indifference, or Pope Gregory's encouragement of the adaptation of pagan temples in England, demonstrates the ready availability of alternative arguments.[8] But in any case such rejection had little to do with the pagan worship for which such temples had hitherto been employed, and everything to do with the practicalities of Christian worship. The Latin word for church (*ecclesia*) means gathered assembly, and that is precisely what most temples could not provide. Their *cella* or core had been built small, simply to house a statue of the god or goddess concerned. As an alternative, Constantine and his successors turned to an already existing state model: that of the *basilica*, used for law courts and other administrative state purposes. The immediate consequence was a strong equation of Church and state, since where the judge or other state official once presided in the arch or apse at the building's head, the bishop now took his place.

Neither the earlier history of Rome nor of Christianity had made such a trajectory inevitable. The Roman Republic might have tolerated the new faith, whereas the decision of the empire from Augustus onwards to make worship of the emperor a test of civic loyalty inevitably not only threw the two on a collision course but also meant increasingly that Christianity saw itself in terms of Christ as an alternative emperor. It took the genius of Constantine to attempt a synthesis. But equally the earlier history of Christianity had been more open. So, Luke, for example, presents the early community as continuing to worship in the Jerusalem Temple, while in his description of Paul's sermon on the Areopagus hill in Athens he suggests that Paul not only quoted pagan poets but also made a favourable allusion to one altar nearby, dedicated 'to the unknown god'.[9] By contrast, the author of the final book in the New Testament, the Apocalypse or Book of Revelation, is unremittingly hostile. Particularly interesting is the short address (2:12–17) he gives – from the mouth of Christ himself – to his fellow Christians in Pergamum.[10] Not only does he adopt a more extreme attitude than Paul to meat that had been consecrated to pagan gods,[11] he also has an implicitly hostile allusion to the most famous temple there, the temple of Asclepius (if so, our only reference in the New Testament to pagan religious architecture).[12] Entirely ignoring the many healings that were attributed to work on this site, he describes Pergamum as a centre of Satan probably because of the symbol most commonly associated with Asclepius and indeed doctors in the ancient world, the caduceus or stick with serpent entwined. For the author the serpent can only point to the Devil, whereas for the pagan world it represented the possible transformation of a sick individual who too, like the snake, hoped to slough off his old skin. Asclepius' shrine was at the foot of Pergamum's acropolis but no doubt, had he been asked, the author would have returned a no less negative verdict on Zeus's temple on the summit. It is still possible to experience something of that latter temple's former magnificence from what has been preserved of it in Berlin.[13]

Politics and Religion in Architecture 181

This brief survey could be taken to imply that temples and churches alike were subservient to political ends, and indeed that was essentially the *raison d'être* for the support or otherwise that they received. But it is one thing to acknowledge the entanglements, quite another to speak of a stranglehold. Certainly, pagan piety divorced from political considerations was quite widespread. Evidence for this comes from the impressive range of religious poetry that has survived, semi-autobiographical material such as from the novelist Apuleius and the orator Aristides, and a not inconsiderable amount of archaeological evidence in votive offerings from particular temples.[14] Even in the minds of emperors piety was not always absent. Augustus' rebuilding of Rome appears to have been religiously motivated, while emperors are found wanting initiation into the Eleusinian mysteries just as much as private individuals.[15]

Again, it would be quite wrong to contrast purity of motive in the author of Revelation with a temporising Luke. While it may be true that Luke deliberately sought not to antagonise the Roman authorities by the way in which he presented the gospel story, it is equally true that he shows the incipient community still mixing with Jewish worshippers in the Temple despite what Jesus had done there just before his death.[16] In other words, we can see Luke in effect acknowledging a more complex world in which the bad in temple worship should not be allowed in and of itself to discount the good.

But it may be objected that, even if this other side is true, such influence still does not stem from the architecture. Again, I beg to differ. There is good evidence to suggest that quite a few of the original elements in Classical architecture had disturbing origins in allusions to sacrifice. So, for example, triglyphs probably found their original *raison d'être* not as a balance to the metopes but in an allusion to the logs necessary for the sacrifices that sought to maintain the political status quo,[17] while the myths in the pediments and friezes more often than not endorsed the politics of conflict and wars. Yet there is no doubt that the aesthetics implicit in that style (proportion, balance and so forth) eventually reflected back upon the religion of the time, as Vitruvius well illustrates.[18] Equally, if at one level the basilica made the church conform to patterns of imperial authority, the influence also went the other way, in Christianity rediscovering its own roots in Jewish law and ritual, and, perhaps more significantly, then seeing those laws as more binding than those of the state, as, for example, in Bishop Ambrose's famous confrontation with Emperor Theodosius.[19] In other words, the political hope in adapting the basilica might have been to suggest subordination to imperial authority but, once placed where emperor or his representative had stood, the bishop now saw himself in God's stead, not the emperor's.

As perhaps might have been expected, the interaction of politics and religious symbolism continues into the Christian centuries. Christians often express regret at such lack of purity of intention, but to my mind the more interesting question, as with the Classical world, is whether religious

182 *Meaning in Religious Architecture*

symbolism in the end achieves its purpose, whatever primary influence may initially have come from politics.

Politics and Religious Architecture in the Christian Era

Two periods subsequent to the collapse of the Roman Empire may be used to illustrate the complexity of the relations between politics and Christian architecture: eleventh-century Norman England and nineteenth-century Scotland. As will become clear, I want to suggest that despite politics clearly initially making the major determinative contribution towards the adoption of the two styles of religious architecture involved, in each case in the long term their various implicit religious meanings are seen to have won through.

First, then, something on the Norman-French invasion of England, and its introduction of Romanesque architecture in the large number of abbeys and cathedrals that were built in its immediate aftermath. While there were the necessary monastic and other clerical vocations to support the move, it would be foolish to suppose that the very large financial expenditure involved was for purely religious motives. These buildings helped undergird French control of the country, not least because celibate clergy had none of the family loyalties of the married clergy whom they were replacing. In addition, the sheer scale and positioning of these churches ensured that a clear message was delivered to the local Anglo-Saxon population: that they were now firmly subordinate to a new earthly power as well as a different ecclesiastical one. The result can be seen in a place like Durham Cathedral in the north-east of England, where a cathedral church already existed on its local hill. This was demolished and all the Anglo-Saxon married clergy expelled to be replaced initially at least by French Benedictines.[20] The bishop also became abbot of the monastery, and was known as Prince-Bishop of the area until the beginning of the nineteenth century, so extensive were his powers locally.

Yet that heavily political slant is not at all how the story or the building's symbolism is commonly read today, nor indeed has this been the case for most of English history. The fact that the Normans were foreigners has long since been forgotten, as indeed the fact that French remained the language at court for a further three centuries until the reign of Edward III.[21] Even the term Norman architecture is still proudly used as though it were quite distinct from its Romanesque cousin on mainland Europe. Of course, such change in attitudes has partly been helped by parallel changes in the landscape. The river banks surrounding cathedral and castle are now wooded, and so do little to suggest their primary original purpose of fortification, initially against the local population and then in subsequent centuries against the Scots. So ask most local north-easterners today (whether Christians or not) and they will speak with great pride of Durham Cathedral as their own, not a foreign imposition. The symbolism of an overwhelming divine presence has thus almost completely overridden its more troublesome origins: Romanesque religious architecture thus mediating its primary meaning of a rooted divine presence despite a contested political history that sought to convey something quite different.[22]

As my final example, I turn to nineteenth-century Scotland, and the revival of Gothic. In marked contrast to its present demography, in 1800 Scotland was an overwhelmingly Protestant country, indeed Calvinist and Presbyterian. Episcopalian worship had been banned as a result of widespread Episcopalian support for the Jacobite cause, while Roman Catholics were also likewise prohibited and were in any case a tiny minority. However, the late eighteenth and early nineteenth century saw not only a gradual relaxation of such penal laws but also a steady and substantial inflow from Ireland of poor but practising Catholics in search of work.[23] One of the first Catholic churches to be built to meet the new situation was the present Roman Catholic Cathedral of St Andrew in Glasgow, completed in 1816. The Catholic community was only allowed to build the church at a distance from the city centre, by the River Clyde in the city's industrial dockland. Even so there were public protests, and attempts to demolish the building were only finally thwarted by placing permanent guards on the building site. Many factors contributed to such opposition, but important among them was the fact that the new building was seen as representative of not only an alien religion but also an alien building style, for the then unfashionable Gothic was chosen when all existing city-centre churches were Classical in design.[24] Gothic had been chosen to suggest continuity with the forms of worship that once held sway within the medieval Gothic cathedral, itself now lying on the edge of the centre as the city moved westwards.[25] So in this case there can be little doubt that architecture had contributed to the strength of the conflict, though the majority did have their revenge, inasmuch as one traditional feature of Gothic was forbidden to the new building (a spire or tower) on the grounds that the alien religion should not be allowed to advertise its presence more widely by protruding on the skyline.[26]

Very different was public response to the first major building from the Episcopalians. Here a different social class was involved, a fact accentuated by the way in which many wealthier citizens chose to educate their children at English public schools, where daily attendance at Anglican worship was compulsory. The result was the kind of influence that could secure a major building site in the country's capital city of Edinburgh, and indeed on one of its major thoroughfares, Princes Street.[27] Here St John's Church was built at roughly the same time as Glasgow's Roman Catholic cathedral.[28] Again, the unfashionable Gothic was chosen but for quite different reasons, since the model was definitely English (in the Perpendicular style) and with a ceiling modelled on Henry VII's Chapel in Westminster Abbey.[29] Thus, whereas St Andrew's Cathedral in Glasgow had sought a political statement in terms of continuity with Scotland's medieval past, here the message was of a British identity allied with the monarchy that easily surpassed in its splendour anything that was available within Scotland itself.[30] Episcopalian wealth was to ensure prime building sites and the Gothic style for the rest of the nineteenth century, the most spectacular example being St Mary's Episcopal Cathedral in Edinburgh's West End, which proved to be the largest church built in Scotland since the Reformation.

Yet once again such political motivations have long since receded from public memory, and their place taken by the religious meaning of the architecture, even for those who still worship in the two buildings concerned, as could be demonstrated from the various modifications made to the building since.[31] Nor is it hard to comprehend why this has happened. The later nineteenth century saw two major advocates of the religious significance of Gothic in its thrust heavenward, A. W. N. Pugin and John Ruskin, who indeed argued that Gothic was the only appropriate Christian style of architecture. But allied with those arguments was also an unparalleled church-building programme within Scotland itself. Because of disputes over how church appointments were made, by 1850 Scotland ended up with three major competing denominations, the continuing Church of Scotland, the Free Church of Scotland and the United Presbyterian Church.[32] The latter two embarked on extensive building programmes, with Gothic in effect becoming the favoured style even though it was actually less well suited to Presbyterian forms of worship than the Classical box where sermons would be more easily audible.[33] However, at the time, even though religious symbolism played a part, there was also a strong political element in that choice since Gothic spires and towers not only pointed heavenwards to God but also were able to dominate the skyline in contrast to existing Church of Scotland buildings. An obvious case in point is New College (originally the new training college for Free Church clergy, now the Divinity School of the University of Edinburgh), that still dominates the Edinburgh skyline on the Mound. Yet, that said, today it is only the religious symbolism of Gothic that survives in the consciousness of most Scots.

Conclusion

What I have sought to suggest in these reflections is that, whatever the political origins for the use of a particular architectural style such as Romanesque, Gothic or Classical, the religious meaning that might be attached to the corresponding aesthetics has usually eventually won through. Not that this is particularly surprising given that politics is essentially a short-term art, negotiating temporary human aspirations and conflicts, whereas religion has more long-term aims. Nonetheless, it is worth emphasising the fact because it helps to provide a more adequate, wider context within which to set current discussions both about conflicts generated by the arrival of new religious forms of architecture in Europe and about disputes within Christianity itself about the purity of its buildings. I shall take each topic in turn.

In respect of the appearance of new religious styles for non-Christian places of worship, perhaps most important to note is the fact that we are still in essentially untried waters since until the Second World War other religions usually adopted one of the architectural choices available within Christianity. Thus, to take the obvious example, Classical and Romanesque synagogues are in fact commonplace.[34] Although there is no reason in principle why former churches might not be used (Islam in particular having no essential requirement apart from worship being in the direction of Mecca), naturally enough Hindus and Muslims like reminders of the lands from which they have come.[35] In Scotland (where I live), this has meant that, although some native elements may be incorporated into non-Christian places of worship, these are usually of a secular kind such as the type of stone or Scottish turrets. The result is, therefore, still a predominantly foreign feel to the building. Muslims have tried to counter this by holding open days at the mosques concerned. But largely because of the relatively small numbers involved, Scotland has in any case encountered few of the problems that have befallen some of the cities of England and of continental Europe.[36]

Such problems are of course as much cultural as religious, economic as social. Even so, it is worth pondering whether, insofar as religious forms of architecture do contribute to the problem, that might in the long term resolve itself by common elements in a shared symbolism eventually being recognised: that is, a convergence of styles takes place with similar underlying religious meanings acknowledged. Indeed, it is possible to detect this already happening in a few cases, as with some recent building projects, where the architecture for minaret and spire seem already to have evolved in the same direction. Thus considered in the abstract, the spire of the new Cathedral of the Northern Lights at Alta in Norway or that of the Martin Luther Church at Hainburg in Austria is virtually indistinguishable from minarets such as those on the Islamic Cultural Centre in Cologne or at the Al-Furkan mosque in Glasgow.[37] The point is that once Muslims and Christians become more relaxed in their relations with one another, this symbol of transcendence and summons to prayer could come to be seen as shared, however much the two religions continue to differ in other respects.

So far as debates within Christianity are concerned, as its influence continues to decline within the Western world one tempting strategy is to set the religion over against the rest of society as its critique. In one sense that is exactly right, and something that lies deep within the Judaeo-Christian revelation. In the Hebrew Scriptures there is the witness of the prophets, while in the New Testament there is no doubt that most of its writers saw themselves as set over against the rest of pagan and Jewish society. Nonetheless, to concede unqualified authority to this view would seem to me a major mistake. Prophet rightly challenged priest and scribe but it was the latter two groups who had to effect some sort of political action. In a similar way the New Testament community could hold up a marvellous social ideal but it remained untested on an imperial scale, while it proved problematic even within as small a community as the typical New Testament church gathering.[38]

186 *Meaning in Religious Architecture*

The solution then is not to pursue the impossible ideal of the small, perfect Christian community or even to suppose that it could be set as an ideal against which society in general could measure itself,[39] but rather to recognise that politics necessarily brings compromise and mixed motives, and that this is the world within which God has called us to live and to fulfil our vocations. The author of the Book of Revelation unfortunately failed to see the sin in his own heart even as he condemned the magnificent religious architecture of Pergamum and the conduct of imperial Rome in general. This is not to say that Augustus was a wholly good man, but it is to claim that his motives in ordering the improvement of religious architecture in Rome were mixed. In a similar way, the Norman Benedictines displayed real concern for the flourishing of the Christian religion in the new Romanesque architecture, even as they confused the interests of Cuthbert (Durham's resident saint) with their own. Likewise, St Andrew's Roman Catholic Cathedral in Glasgow and St John's Episcopal Church in Edinburgh may have had their origins in petty attempts at triumphalism. Nonetheless, their architecture now speaks to those who visit the two churches of the transcendent glory of God.[40] In short, God can be seen to work through the complexity of tensions between politics and architecture in such a way that in the end the message implicit in the architecture becomes made known, in making possible a sense of divine presence and its purposes. The way forward is thus in interacting with that complexity, not in its denial.[41]

Notes

1 Though with accompanying *cellae* or shrines within the same temple to his wife and daughter, Juno and Minerva.
2 A plausible complete reconstruction, including of the goddess's huge statue, can be visited at Nashville, Tennessee.
3 This to follow the interpretation offered by John Boardman, 'The Parthenon Frieze', in *Parthenon-Kongress, Basel*, ed. Ernst Berger (Mainz: Zabern, 1984), 210–215. Even those who challenge his account still tend to offer patriotic explanations: e.g. E. B. Henderson, 'The Web of History: A Conservative Reading of the Parthenon Frieze', in *Worshipping Athena: Panathenaia and Parthenon*, ed. Jenifer Neils (Madison: University of Wisconsin Press, 1996), 198–214.
4 Among them Shiloh, Nob, Kiriath-Jearim, Liash-Dan and Bethel.
5 See Mary Beard, John North and Simon Price, *Religions of Rome*, vol. 1, *A History* (Cambridge: Cambridge University Press, 1998), 59–60.
6 For detailed discussion of the rules, see Eric M. Orlin, *Temples, Religion, and Politics in the Roman Republic* (Leiden: Brill Academic Publishers, 2002). Worship of Cybele (known as Magna Mater at Rome) was first allowed in the city *c*. 204 BC but even then carefully controlled, with processions confined to her Palatine temple and only Oriental priests allowed to participate. Again, as with the cult of Bacchus, that of Isis also endured periodic persecution e.g. in 59, 58, 53, 50 and 48 BC, and probably for similar reasons: a personal cult that eschewed easy political control (Beard *et al.*, *Religions of Rome*, 161).
7 Seen e.g. in Iraq under Saddam Hussein or in Syria under the Assads (father and son), in the latter case, for example, Alawites and Christians, and Shias

Politics and Religion in Architecture 187

more generally. Within half a century Constantine's toleration had become Theodosius' official religion, in 380.
8 1 Corinthians 8: only the weak conscience will be defiled by such eating (v. 7); for the contents of Pope Gregory's letter to Abbot Mellitus urging that idols be destroyed but not temples, see Bede, *History of the English Church and People*, I.30.
9 Acts 2:46; Acts 17:23 and 28.
10 Near Bergama in modern Turkey.
11 Revelation 2:14. Contrast Paul in 1 Corinthians 8.
12 Generally assumed to lie behind Revelation 2:13.
13 In the museum not surprisingly named after it, given the impressive reconstruction of its altar.
14 *The Homeric Hymns* and Pindar provide two early examples of piety in poetry. The final book of *The Golden Ass* of Apuleius reveals a deep commitment to the worship of Isis, while the *Sacred Tales* of Aelius Aristeides are full of the praises of Asclepius and what the god achieved for Aristeides' own health in his temples. For a survey of pagan temples that takes their religion seriously, including archaeological evidence, see Robin Lane Fox, *Pagans and Christians* (Harmondsworth: Viking, 1986), esp. Part I.
15 For positive estimates of the piety of Augustus, see Paul Zanker, *The Power of Images in the Age of Augustus* (Ann Arbor: University of Michigan Press, 1990); Diane Favro, *The Urban Image of Augustan Rome* (Cambridge: Cambridge University Press, 1996); for my own brief assessment of the evidence, *God and Enchantment of Place: Reclaiming Human Experience* (Oxford: Oxford University Press, 2004), 173–175. Emperors who were initiates in the Eleusinian mysteries included Augustus, Hadrian, Marcus Aurelius and Commodus.
16 An early sign of Luke avoiding suggestions of conflict with Rome is the fact that he alone records John the Baptist giving moral instructions to Roman soldiers that includes them being content with their wages (4:14). Then on the Jewish side, there is both the cleansing of the temple (19:45ff.) and worshipping in it thereafter (24:53).
17 Triglyphs are the three vertical grooves in a Doric frieze that divide the rectangular spaces between, known as metopes and often adorned with sculpture. For some of the speculations, see George L. Hersey, *The Lost Meaning of Classical Architecture* (Cambridge, Mass.: MIT Press, 1988).
18 See Vitruvius, *Ten Books of Architecture*, esp. Books III and IV.
19 Ambrose excommunicated Theodosius I for a massacre he had ordered at Thessalonica in 390, with the emperor responding in penitent submission. Ambrose displayed a similar freedom in his dealings with two previous emperors, Gratian and Valentinian II.
20 For the latest scholarship on the relation between the two churches, see David Rollason, 'The Anglo-Norman Priory and Its Predecessor', in *Durham Cathedral: History, Fabric and Culture*, ed. David Brown (New Haven and London: Yale University Press, 2015), 27–38.
21 English formally replaced French as the official language of the country in 1362, and Edward III's own practice is often said to have been determinative of that change. But some historians (e.g. Michael Prestwich) argue that even as early as Edward I England had a king fluent in English.
22 While the intended religious meaning of Gothic is beyond dispute, and indeed was already firmly entrenched at the time of the style's origins with the writings of Abbot Suger of St-Denis, there is no comparable work for Romanesque. So one might argue that it too was concerned with pointing heavenward, not least given the scale of such buildings, but any such notion was surely secondary to

188 *Meaning in Religious Architecture*

the sense of a rooted divine presence afforded by the massive pillars that were commonly deployed, as for example in Durham or even more obviously perhaps at Gloucester. For more detailed consideration of Durham, politics, and architecture, see my article 'Durham Cathedral and the Jerusalem Temple: Let Sacred Buildings Speak', *International Journal for the Study of the Christian Church* 16.2 (2016), 93–107.

23 The Roman Catholic population of Glasgow at the turn of the century was about 450, whereas by 1814, the year in which the future cathedral was built, it had had already risen to 3,000.
24 Or simplified Baroque, as with St Andrew's and St George's Tron.
25 The principal street of the medieval city (the High Street), at the head of which the cathedral stood, gradually degenerated into a slum, with the resultant marginalisation of the cathedral and the migration of the university buildings to the opposite end of the town.
26 The result of continuing restrictions embodied in the Relief Act of 1791. Complete Catholic Emancipation was only finally achieved in 1829.
27 At this time still second in importance to George Street, though by the twentieth century it would eventually gain the primacy it now holds. Agreement to the building only narrowly succeeded, as an Act of Parliament was used to secure the rejection of all subsequent building on the south side of Princes Street.
28 It was completed in 1818. Ironically, the architect of St Andrew's Cathedral in Glasgow was the initial choice for St John's also. But, although James Gillespie Graham was an Episcopalian, he was eventually passed over in favour of William Burn a Presbyterian.
29 All William Burn's previous work had been in the Classical style. Although elements of Gothic revival had already come into existence in the late eighteenth century, it is hard to see anything other than a consciously English motive at this stage: cf. Dianne M. Watters, *St John's Episcopal Church, Edinburgh* (Edinburgh: RCAHMS, 2008), 15–19.
30 Strictly speaking, the building was actually intended for an English congregation that was already in existence, one of the so-called Qualified Chapels that were permitted by the Scottish Episcopalian Act of 1711 to those willing to swear allegiance to the Hanoverian monarchy. Although the Toleration Act of 1746 and the Penal Act of 1748 had limited Episcopalian worship to not more than four gathering among those who refused such allegiance, by this time the issue was in effect a dead letter since Bonnie Prince Charlie had died in 1788 and the Penal Act had been repealed in 1792.
31 Particularly noticeable in the case of St John's, which initially lacked a proper chancel.
32 The Free Church was created by the great Disruption of 1843; the United Presbyterians in 1847 by the union of various churches that had participated in earlier splits.
33 As a result of such competition, the nineteenth century saw a huge building programme, with the Free Church building over 700 new churches by 1847. The established Church of Scotland, mainly in response, increased its number of churches from 924 in 1843 to 1,437 by 1909.
34 For more information, see the previous essay in this volume.
35 For example, one mosque in Dundee is a former church, while another Muslim community in Aberdeen actually uses a local Episcopalian church (St John's) for its daily prayers. The invitation was first issued in 2013 to the adjacent small mosque (Syed Shah Mustafa Jame Masjid), which had run out of space, by the rector, Isaac Poobalan, who had grown up alongside Muslims in Southern India. For examples of, and contests over, shared space, see further Margaret

Cormack, ed., *Muslims and Others in Sacred Space* (Oxford: Oxford University Press, 2013).

36 In London eighteen years of conflict over the proposed Abbey Mills mosque (Masyid e-ilyas) finally came to an end in 2015 when the final court of appeal in the national government also rejected the proposal.

37 For illustrations, see Chris van Uffelen, *Sacred Architecture + Design: Churches, Synagogues, Mosques* (Salenstein, Switzerland: Braun Publishing, 2014), 18–21, 80–83, 214–217.

38 As the various disputes within the Corinthian church bear witness.

39 One of the common themes running through Stanley Hauerwas's approach to Christian ethics, as in what is perhaps still his best-known work, *The Peaceable Kingdom* (London: SCM, 1984).

40 Both have been beautifully restored in recent years. Under the inspiration of Archbishop Mario Conti, St Andrew's Cathedral underwent a major restoration in 2008–2010 that included much new art work, though still in keeping with the church's Gothic principles.

41 This essay took its origins from an invited contribution to a cross-disciplinary colloquium on 'The Politics of Urban Religious Architecture' at the Royal Netherlands Academy of Arts and Sciences held in Amsterdam in October 2014. I am most grateful to the organisers, Oskar Verkaaik of the University of Amsterdam and M. G. Valenta of Radboud University, for their help and encouragement, and permission to publish it here.

13 Worshipping with Art and Architecture

So used are Protestant Christians to thinking of Christianity as a religion of the word that they often treat the place in which they worship and its internal decoration as matters of little or no importance: the wallpaper of faith, as it were. Even as cultured a scholar as C. S. Lewis allowed himself to fall foul of just such a fault when he contrasted the truth that could be found in a building and its art.[1] Not that Roman Catholics are necessarily any better. Prior to the Second Vatican Council (1962–1965) the strongest focus was usually on the reserved sacrament and statues of particular patron saints rather than the building as a whole, whereas in more recent years the stress has tended to move to community experience rather than any sense of the impact of the building or the artworks contained within it. Part of the problem lies in a misunderstanding of what good religious art is trying to achieve, and that is the issue I will tackle in the first part of this essay. Thereafter, however, I want to move to the impact of the building as a whole, both in its own right and in relation to the art contained with it. Not only are worshippers often unaware of the subliminal effect that they will experience, however indifferent they pretend to be, but also of how opportunities will thereby be lost that might otherwise have effected a fully integrated experience in worship. For the truth is that art, architecture and worshipper will all fight against each other unless some basic principles are observed.

Experiencing Christian Art

Of course Christian churches with paintings or sculptures are the exception rather than the rule, but, even so, almost all have stained glass. So, to that extent the issue arises for everyone, though it must be conceded that with stained glass there seems to be an even greater tendency to treat it as no more than background decoration, warm, reassuring patterns but without further interest. Such a misconception cannot be blamed on the quality of the art, for even in its nineteenth-century forms it would now be widely recognised to be of much higher quality than was admitted for most of the twentieth century. A more general problem is the common assumption that such art was never intended to be more than illustrative, and so, once the topic is known, it requires no further reflection.

To counter that assumption, let me therefore first consider art more generally, and in particular two familiar paintings, one the most commonly reproduced image of Christ in twentieth-century America, Warner Sallman's *Head of Christ* (1940), and the other what is probably now the best-known painting of the crucifixion, Matthias Grünewald's early sixteenth-century Isenheim Altarpiece. Both intended more than simple representation. The artists concerned rightly wanted to encourage viewers to engage with the significance of Christ. But what makes Grünewald's work by far the greater painting is the way in which various layers have been introduced to the presentation to ensure continuing further reflection. Thus, once you have noted the light on the face and the upward look you have got all that Sallman has to tell us about Christ,[2] whereas with Grünewald's Isenheim Altarpiece there is still much to interact with even after you have been shocked by all the horrors the crucifixion must have involved, painted here in all its gruesome detail. John the Baptist, though dead, is there, for instance, to indicate the eternal significance of the event; Mary Magdalene made smaller than the other figures, not to belittle her but to remind us of ourselves, for the convention was to make donors of paintings this size, and so she kneels there as one of us, her ointment jar of repentance ready to restore our own relationship with Christ. Again, the Temptations of St Anthony of Egypt find their place in one of the accompanying scenes, to propose to our imaginations that the lacerations on Christ's body are like the lacerations that could be on our own, as indeed they were on the patients in the hospital chapel where this painting once hung, in a place that treated those suffering from ergotism or St Anthony's Fire, which produced boils just like these. In short, it is a painting that makes Christ's suffering one with our own anxieties and pains.[3]

Currently, many feminist theologians take exception to paintings like Grünewald's that treat Mary Magdalene as the representative sinner on the grounds that it is both unfair to women and in any case historically improbable. But, while such questions are important in their place, it would seriously misrepresent the artist's intentions if such considerations were given central place in understanding this painting, and in appropriating what the artist is trying to convey to us. This can be seen from the fact that John the Baptist's presence is equally symbolic rather than historical, where the artist could have been in no doubt that the Baptist was long since dead. The point is that in art sometimes symbol is more important than historical fact or, to put matters more accurately, other types of fact are given precedence. As Henry James observed in response to his fellow novelist, Anthony Trollope's claim that the novelist is essentially engaged in make-believe: your comment 'implies that the novelist is less occupied in looking for the truth than the historian, and in doing so it deprives him at a stroke of all standing room'.[4] So, similarly, this is how we should understand matters here with

Grünewald. We can see what significance Christ might have for us more clearly, precisely by exploring those figures of partial make-believe, Mary Magdalene and John the Baptist.

This is not to say, though, that there is only one way of expressing such significance. Contemporary theologians and preachers are often quite snooty about Renaissance religious art. In their view the story is all too prettified, with beautiful Madonnas and crucifixions where Jesus seems to suffer scarcely any pain. After all, was Jesus' mother not an ordinary peasant girl, and crucifixion among the most horrific of tortures invented by the Romans? Yes, and it is possible to draw meaning out of both facts. But again that need not be the only way of engaging with the significance of Christ. So, keeping to the theme of crucifixion for the moment, the danger in simply stressing the horror is that we forgot that Christ came to the world to do rather more than just suffer and die. He came also to catch us up into the new life that God can provide. That is one reason why Eastern Orthodox theologians, so far from admiring Grünewald, actually condemn the work as bad Christian art.[5] I certainly would not wish to go down that road but equally I want to acknowledge alternatives that can supplement what Grünewald has to say to us.

Raphael was a contemporary of Grünewald's but unlike Grünewald was part of the High Renaissance and so did not share the same Northern Gothic assumptions that had inspired Grünewald. At first sight, the way Raphael paints the crucifixion may well seem shallow by comparison. Thus in the Mond Crucifixion of 1502 no obvious signs of pain are present on the Saviour's beautiful body, whilst angels dance beneath the arms of the cross to catch his blood for their chalices.[6] But the key point of course to bear in mind is that beauty is now being used to suggest that suffering and death will not have the last word. Moreover, Christ's victory over death brings continuing aid and sustenance to disciples in every age, as the scene of the angels gathering the blood from the cross for the Eucharist is meant to indicate. But perhaps the kind of appeal this sort of art makes can be seen even more effectively if we turn to the work of Raphael's teacher, Pietro Perugino.

Perugino's version of the crucifixion was Michael Ramsey's favourite painting and it therefore stayed with him through most of his life, indeed through nineteen house moves.[7] Finally, he left the work to Nashotah House in Wisconsin – a copy of course, for the original hangs in the National Gallery in Washington, where it has been ever since it was sold by Stalin, having previously been confiscated in the Russian Revolution from the Galitzin family. Known therefore as the Galitzin Triptych, as with Raphael's image it may still repel, and for similar reasons: an aesthetic beauty that seems to discount all the horror that was undoubtedly involved. But not so for Michael Ramsey, so it is intriguing to ask why. The point is that, as with Raphael's version, clearly modelled on Perugino's work which was done about twenty years earlier, there is a beauty to Christ's body and a calm on his face that encourages us to believe that even suffering and death will not have the last word, just as was so in this case with Christ.

But there is also a deeper message, and this may have been what particularly attracted Ramsey, for we are in effect told how such beauty may be brought into our lives. Unlike Raphael's Mond Crucifixion, it is a triptych, with two side panels, the one on the left devoted to Jerome and the other on the right to Mary Magdalene. Significantly, if we look at the open gateway behind Mary Magdalene, in effect we find an invitation to reach such serenity through a penitential and trusting relationship, with a similar message conveyed more humorously on the other side, where Jerome's lion invites us to turn round with him and ascend jointly towards the cross and Christ's beautiful body, and the beautiful landscape against which it is portrayed. Christ, we are being told, will lead us on our path but equally for this to happen penitence is required on our part, since Mary Magdalene's ointment jar is there on the one side and Jerome beating his breast with a stone on the other. So beauty is certainly a powerful symbol of what can be achieved through Christ, but not without neglect of the demands that must first be met before this can be achieved.

Given that very few churches will be lucky enough to have paintings such as these on their walls, it may have seemed an unnecessary diversion that I have begun by discussing major works of art. But there remains a twofold relevance. First, given the general willingness to visit public galleries, great art can provide an easy point of access to explain what motivates art in churches, not least since much of the latter was in fact intended for specific churches, including the works of Grünewald, Perugino and Raphael just mentioned. But, second and more pertinently, stained-glass designers will almost certainly have adopted similar conventions from the history of art, and so, once certain principles are identified in the wider art world, the same assumptions can then be applied specifically in the case of stained glass. Even so, this should not be interpreted as simple copying, still less as art now reduced to mere education.

Pope Gregory the Great's comment on art in churches is often thought to apply particularly to stained glass: 'what Scripture is to the educated, images are to the ignorant who see through them what they must accept; they read in them what they cannot read in books'.[8] But in actual fact even in medieval times when illiteracy was at its highest some of the iconography would have been too difficult to interpret without help, which is why the existence of written guides is sometimes suggested.[9] But in any case there was usually a subtlety to the chosen imagery that did far more than simply illustrate the biblical text. In the twelfth-century ancestors of Christ window at Canterbury Cathedral, for example, it might be thought that nothing more is at stake than the recording of the infant's genealogy, but it looks as though the commissioning monks deliberately opted for Luke's version over the hitherto preferred Matthew in order not only to lessen the tie with monarchy (a contentious subject at the time),[10] but also to give more obviously christological anticipations, with Adam portrayed putting on skins to work the land just as God the Son was eventually to put on human flesh.[11] Again, apparently uncomplicated narratives like the parable of the Prodigal Son can take on a logic of their own, when artists are asked to extend the narrative to as many as thirty scenes.[12]

So it was not simply a matter of copying existing assumptions, whether these were scriptural or current traditions within art. Not only was a degree of creativity possible but also in some ways essential, precisely because of the different medium that was now being employed. To draw attention to itself in relatively small frames, for instance, more incidents were required in a parable like the one just mentioned. But also the sheer size of the windows meant that more attention had to be given to fit with the architectural environment. One question was strength of colour and complexity of design. Too little colour in a large space in effect meant no impact at all, as can be seen in the interesting changes that took place many centuries later in Henri Mattise's three successive sketches he attempted for the larger of the windows he was asked to do at Vence.[13] Too much, though, might well conflict with still allowing sufficient natural light to percolate through. Light was after all not only one of the principal symbols for divinity in Scripture but also one of the main *raisons d'être* for Gothic. So it is perhaps not altogether surprising that the later medieval period seems to have simplified both colours and design in an attempt to lighten the building as a whole. Finally, one might note the need for integration of the windows with one another. By that I do not mean that they must share the same iconographical programme, still less the same artist, but that they work also towards the unification of the building. That could be seen as purely an aesthetic requirement, but also involved is how both window and building may most effectively speak of God. If the window jars with its surroundings, it can of course still speak, but what it says will be, initially at least, heard as discordant with what is being said elsewhere, for that is the subliminal message being conveyed. Sometimes of course that might be a good thing, but if the various messages (building and window) are all ultimately compatible it will be a pity if disunity is implied when none is in reality present. That is why on my view at least a window must be pronounced less than successful however fine its design, colours and content if it speaks only by being heard in isolation, and otherwise rather jarringly.[14]

Although it is always hard to quantify these things, it is probably stained glass that these days continues to fare the worst of all the arts in relation to Christian worship and practice. One problem is that what survives comes overwhelmingly from one particular historical period, the nineteenth century, while also, unlike the other arts, it has very few secular equivalents. It is thus from what remains very largely an unpopular period for art,[15] and is also not a medium that is constantly encountered elsewhere. Yet such a fate in neglect need not be inevitable. We know, for example, that in the Middle Ages occasionally prayer requests were set before particular windows because of the saints or biblical scenes in them.[16] Again, the twentieth century has witnessed new life injected into stained glass through a range of conspicuously gifted artists specialising in the medium as well with those coming from the arts elsewhere.[17]

Yet it may be objected in my approach to stained glass, as to religious art more generally, that I am missing the point. It is not that such windows and other art should engage us and deepen understanding of our faith. It is enough that they are there to summon us to worship. It is a point that has recently been made by Nicholas Wolterstorff against my favouring of Renaissance art over icons.[18] Icons, I have suggested elsewhere, failed in their iconography to move with the times, and so now propose a quite different and possibly alien world rather than allowing the world of Christ and his saints to interact with our own.[19] So, for example, in icons the Virgin Mary at the annunciation is always presented as either spinning or drawing water from a well, whereas Western Renaissance art showed her praying or reading, and so engaged with contemporary arguments about female education. In this case one could of course argue that the former is better because it is both more likely to be historical and demonstrates identification with the poor. Even so, that would still leave numerous cases where Orthodoxy seems simply to have frozen tradition, in everything from representation of a spirit in the water at Jesus' baptism to the mysterious figure with a cloth at Pentecost.

However, perhaps it may be suggested that I am missing the heart of objections such as Wolterstorff's. Icons are at their most effective when they are experienced simply as a call to worship, as typically happens with the sort of icon that is overlaid with silver or gold, and which worshippers venerate by kissing. Here the content has clearly become quite secondary. If so, I would make two observations by way of reply. By no means all icons are like this, and indeed among those most frequently encountered in non-Orthodox churches in the West it is those with content that exercise the most appeal. Under those circumstances there is certainly a similar kind of interaction as in Western art, even if it is usually induction to another world, as in the way saintly figures are deliberately placed on platforms so as not directly to touch the earth, and thus suggest the inhabiting of another reality. No doubt that otherness also draws the viewer into worship but it includes interaction just like Western art, even if the latter is conceived quite differently, of God coming close to us, and inviting a response.[20] A good example of the latter would be Hans Memling's diptych in the Sint-jan Hospitaal Museum in Bruges in which a young man (Maarten van Nieuwenhove) is praying in the right-hand panel to a Virgin and Child in the left-hand one, with Mary's robe deliberately allowed to invade the right-hand panel and indeed even step into the viewer's space, with some of the same material found on the frame itself. Thus we as viewers are invited into prayerful worship, just like the young man.

So it is simply not true that reflection on content necessarily works to the exclusion of worship; on the contrary it can lead to its enhancement.

Nor need it be a staged pattern, with one type of approach succeeding the other. Worship could come first and then deeper understanding, or repeated interactions between the two. For example, it is unlikely that a viewer will discover an incarnational reading of the Canterbury depiction of Adam on first viewing, but repeated viewing of the form of Adam's representation (strong and confident) and of others in the same window (for example, Elijah ascending to heaven) should gradually lead to this conclusion.

These comments should not be taken to indicate hostility to icons, only that greater fairness is needed in comparing and contrasting their role and function as compared with Western art. Non-Orthodox churches now often introduce them to produce a more meditative or 'holy' atmosphere but there is no reason why a similar result could not have been produced through re-educating congregations on the aims of Western religious art. However that may be, if they are to be introduced, careful attention needs to be given to their placement, to ensure that they function as augmentation to the religious message of the building as a whole rather than as an admission of its presumed failure to achieve a sense of the holy on its own. It is worth recalling that in the Orthodox tradition the desired effect is achieved not by one or two icons but by a complex scheme that includes, together with painted walls and cupola, the building in its entirety witnessing to a single vision of the Orthodox account of the Christian faith.[21] Occasionally, this has been achieved in a Western church when it was first built, but in the main there is not only considerable variety of approaches across such buildings but also quite often an amalgam of different styles and approaches even within the same building. So significantly different questions are raised about the integration of art and architecture in the typical Western church, and it is to that issue that I therefore now turn.

Congregation and Art in Its Architectural Setting

So far, I have been exploring only individual paintings or windows, and not how they relate to the church building as a whole. Again, as with the treatment of stained glass as wallpaper, my worry would be that the building may be seen by priest or minister and parishioners alike as simply a place to meet, with the view taken that any other suitable building would do just as well, preferably, though, perhaps less expensive to heat! Such attitudes are widespread. When the new Coventry Cathedral was being built, the then dean infuriated the architect, Sir Basil Spence, by remarking that 'whether they were Gothic or just tin shanties, the essential purposes of a cathedral could be proved in any context'.[22] Admittedly, there is a clear sense in which this is true, but there are also other equally clear senses in which the architecture does make a difference. Indeed, in the nineteenth century, this was a matter of passionate debate, with defenders of the revival of Gothic like John Ruskin and Augustus Welby Northmore Pugin arguing that Gothic was the only legitimate Christian style.[23] There is not space to go into the competing arguments here, except to note that each of the major styles has a language and meaning that we ignore at our peril because the building will almost certainly subliminally communicate something, and to most people, even though they may well not be properly aware of what is happening.

Very roughly speaking, Europe witnessed four major styles of architecture which historically succeeded one another: Romanesque at the turn of the first millennium, Gothic, which dominated the high Middle Ages, Classicism, which attempted to recover the architectural styles of ancient Greece and Rome, and finally Baroque, a style particularly associated with the Counter-Reformation that is essentially Classicism modified to engage more effectively with the drama and wonder of the Christian story. All experienced revivals from the eighteenth century onwards. So, especially in a country as young as the United States, it is possible to find representatives of all these styles within a short compass, such as in New York City and Washington, DC.[24]

Such variety might suggest indifference in the choice of style at the point of commissioning, and so the inappropriateness of any proposed restraints on what kind of art that might be subsequently introduced into the building, or in the style of liturgy and preaching deployed. But in fact each of the styles has its own particular logic, and so, even if the subsequent traditions of the Church move in a different direction, this does not mean that such divergence is an uncomplicated matter. In fact, the wider architectural environment will continue to have an impact, in implicit messages that may effectively either support or undermine what is said or done. Some examples should make the point clearer. Suppose the preacher is in a Gothic church and urges the congregation to find Jesus entirely or even chiefly in this world and not in the next. Whether such a message is appropriate or not, it is certainly the case that the building will be seen to advocate a quite different response, for the thrust of Gothic architecture is all heavenward, with its pointed arches, tall spires and so on. The result is that, whatever may be said, the congregation will view what the preacher says in support of such a this-world message with a measure of scepticism for, to put it bluntly, the building tells them to think quite differently. Or again, think of a church in the Classical style and of a preacher enamoured of a perspective on the gospel of the type advocated by Tertullian or Kierkegaard as going well beyond what the world regards as reasonable. In the words of Tertullian, 'I believe because it is absurd', or Kierkegaard on paradox, 'A thinker without a paradox is like a lover without a passion.'[25] No matter how powerful the preacher's rhetoric is for the rejection of reason, the congregation will find him or her odd and unconvincing for the beautiful proportions and balance of the building in which they are sitting will tell an altogether different tale, of the eminent reasonableness of Christianity.

While one might conclude from such reflections that clergy and worshippers are effectively trapped by the particular building in which they happen to worship, that is not at all my intention. My point is simply that in anything one says or does it is important to take account of the logic of the building. So, if one wants to run counter to the building's own internal logic, this needs to be faced rather than ignored, since the congregation will be receiving subliminal messages to the contrary that arise naturally from the setting, even if they have never previously been brought explicitly to the surface. However, this does not mean necessarily attacking the building as such. This is because, taking a broader historical perspective, it is possible to observe such conflicts occurring in the past, and means being found for their resolution. Indeed, so far from seeing the four major styles as inherently and implacably opposed to one another, another way of reading them is to view them as introducing one aspect of the divine reality that then needs somehow or other to be complemented by its opposite. That is because Christianity wants to affirm that God is both transcendent and immanent (both Gothic and Romanesque, as it were); and both simple and ordered as well as playful and mysterious (Classical on the one hand and Baroque on the other). In other words, each style addresses some aspect of our standing before God, and so the trick is to discover how to present such complementarity in a way that takes seriously the existing appearance of the building, and the meanings already implicit in its forms.

Probably then the best way of accessing an appropriate technique for achieving such an aim and so resolving the tension is to look to history. Certainly, both Romanesque and Gothic architecture did in fact seek to complement the building with a quite different sort of art: that is, with the building allowed to pull in one direction and the art in quite another. Thus all that Gothic upward thrust was complemented by a strong emphasis on Christ's immanence in the Eucharist, nowhere seen more conspicuously than in the central moment of the medieval mass, in the elevation of the host and the priest's declaration, 'Behold the Lamb of God': in other words, God now come down rather than us having to be pulled up. But it was not only the Eucharist that was used to make this point, equally art was harnessed to the same aim. That is why Gothic religious art is so humanistic and empathetic. The Christ Child, for instance, rather than interrogating us with a forward-looking hieratic glance (as in earlier art) instead interacts with his mother, playing, for instance, with her veil. Indeed, even angels are given a human smile, as at Reims. Nor is this balancing act an accident, for central to the medieval vision was a two-way traffic, to and from heaven. And that complementarity is also exactly what you would expect if sufficient attention is paid to the meaning of the two main descriptive words in this case, transcendence and immanence, for of course they are not real opposites, since God as a being not limited by space can be at one and the same time both active in our world (immanent) and beyond it (transcendent).

So it should come as no surprise that Romanesque adopted a similar strategy, though in reverse. Whereas Gothic architects did everything to try to make their buildings soar (which is why they so often fell down!),[26] Romanesque architects were so relieved that the world had not come to an end in AD 1000 that their stress was instead on a massive stability, heavy buildings obviously meant to last with a great downward thrust, with huge piers, for example, often compared to oaks and the building's ceiling to the sky. But with that downward thrust went an art that, unlike Gothic's, soared: bodies unnaturally elongated that looked as though they were seeking to soar heavenwards. The contrast with Gothic is well illustrated in France's most famous body of Romanesque art, in the cathedral at Autun in Provence. Gislibertus, the artist, leaves us in no doubt of a reference elsewhere, to a world beyond our own.[27]

So, if wise choices have been made in the decoration of the interior the preacher can have it both ways, using the architecture to draw an otherworld reference, and the art, a this-world. Equally the same would be true for Romanesque, though in reverse, with the art this time pulling upwards and the architecture back to earth. Romanesque, however, is often thought to be a more difficult case since, while Gothic and neo-Gothic artefacts survive in profusion, the passage of time has not treated Romanesque art nearly so well. Even so, even today there are contemporary artists working in this tradition. A conspicuous example is Peter Eugene Ball (b. 1943), who has achieved huge popularity in England through his re-creation of Romanesque-type sculptures.[28] However, if something looking rather more modern is preferred, it is salutary to observe that the greatest artist of the twentieth century also acknowledged his debt to Romanesque and indeed kept in his studio one such Spanish painting.[29] So, although Picasso's own religious paintings are disappointing, there is no doubt that some of his many styles could be adapted for the purpose. Indeed one of his most famous early paintings clearly evokes just such a style.[30]

In the case of Classical buildings there was no such tradition of an accompanying opposing art, but that does not mean that one could not be created, though careful consideration would need to be given to how this might be achieved. One possibility is some form of abstract art, though by no means all. Jackson Pollock, for instance, with his arbitrary and rough casting of the paint on the canvas would only badly jar. But the work of many another, perhaps especially the two Americans, Barnett Newman and Mark Rothko, could work well. Thus it is no accident that some of their works are to be found in modernist buildings that followed the so-called International style, where simplicity and proportion is again the chosen ideal as with Classicism, though of course expressed quite differently from the earlier style in the materials chosen, concrete and steel. The point is that whereas the European abstract simplicity of Piet Mondrian had been used to suggest the underlying simplicity of all reality, Rothko and Newman both wanted to hint at mystery, the simplicity being employed to suggest something rather more.[31] So it would be not so much a matter of deploying the oppositions inherent within the two major medieval styles, as of thinking at a tangent, using a continuation of the same style, the simplicity and proportions of abstract art used to open out onto something more.

Indeed, even during the heyday of Classicism it is sometimes possible to find a similar way of lateral thinking. Note, for instance, how in Protestant Ireland, the Classical cathedral at Waterford was given in 1779 a reredos that automatically suggested an element of mystery since it has the divine Tetragrammaton as happened also (but less successfully), at about the same time with St Martin in the Fields and St George's, Bloomsbury.[32]

Finally, there is Baroque. This is a style more familiar in southern Germany or Poland than in the English-speaking world, though Sir Christopher Wren's St Paul's Cathedral in London offers a moderate example. Indeed, until the interior redecoration by Sir James Thornhill it must have been quite hard to see what the building shared with more theatrical representatives of this type, like St John Nepomuk in Munich, where wonder, drama and playfulness are to be found to exuberant excess. Baroque well illustrates how it is not just preachers who can err in relation to the logic of a church building. Even professional liturgists can go badly wrong, as any holiday in continental Europe subsequent to the reforms of Vatican II immediately confirmed. Following the injunctions of the Council, simple westward-facing, rectangular altars were introduced but immediately jarred in a building that was otherwise dominated by curves and meandering lines. Yet clergy were surprised by the resultant hostility of congregations. Fortunately, in more recent years greater sensitivity is now being shown on this issue. Yet even in a country like Poland, where people and clergy are still unusually close,[33] a new form of the problem has emerged. To encourage congregational singing, words are projected onto a screen, but lurid rectangular white ones are deployed without any thought given to how they might be made to fit better their environment. The glaring black and white looks totally out of place amidst the riot of curve and colour elsewhere. The example could be taken to argue that unlike the other three styles, Baroque does not easily yield to complementarity: that, in short, its natural position is one of extremes. Yet this does not seem to me to be necessarily the case. Traditional Baroque liturgy, for example, could scarcely be described as simple, but it could plausibly be upheld as a model of order. Indeed, it is its very control and order that allows the sense of mystery to reach its proper culmination, with, for example, everyone carefully placed at the elevation of the host. In a similar way, then, it would be possible to envisage a screen that still conveys the necessary information but which was set, for example, within curved borders and softer fabric that thus linked the words on the screen with the same God proclaimed by the building as a whole. It is probably also in any case worth reminding readers that Baroque is not in principle opposed to order, but instead in many ways builds upon it since it grew out of Classicism. The point is thus getting the right dynamic between intricacy and movement on the one hand and balance and order on the other, well illustrated in architecture like Versailles or music like that of Johann Sebastian Bach.

So I end by appealing to my fellow Christians to take more seriously the logic of the building in which they worship. We all like our homes to be comfortable and to express something of ourselves. Historically, temples were conceived as homes for the divinity concerned. While that is not the right way to think of a church, it is true that, whether we like the image or not, the building and the art it contains will say something of the God who is worshipped there. So we need to pay heed to our surroundings and the implicit messages they contain, no less than the words heard from the pulpit or the other acts we perform within the building's confines. A church is not simply a space to gather in but one which reflects the totality of who we are as Christians, one in which our eyes and bodies should be responding no less effectively than our minds.[34]

Notes

1 In the Preface to *Mere Christianity* he writes that one 'must be asking which door is the true one, not which pleases you best by its paint and panelling'. Of course, pleasure is an inadequate motive, but in assuming that to be the reason, Lewis implicitly deprives art of any ability to contribute to truth.
2 Sallman's work is given extensive consideration in David Morgan, *Visual Piety: A History and Theory of Popular Religious Images* (Berkeley: University of California Press, 1998). For the actual image, which sold in the millions, 2, fig.1.
3 For an excellent discussion of the painting, Andrée Hayum, *The Isenheim Altarpiece: God's Medicine and the Painter's Vision* (Princeton: Princeton University Press, 1989). The painting, which was once housed in the Antonite Hospital at Isenheim (in Germany), is now in the museum at Colmar (France).
4 'The Art of Fiction', in Henry James, *The Art of Fiction and Other Essays* (New York: Oxford University Press, 1948), 3–23, esp. 5–6.
5 This is, for example, the view taken by Michel Quenot, *The Icon: Window on the Kingdom* (London: Mowbray, 1992), 72–83, esp. 80. Similar sentiments are expressed by Paul Evdokimov in *The Art of the Icon* (Redondo Beach, Calif.: Oakwood, 1990), who is even prepared to declare that 'once past the middle of the 16th century the great painters ... painted images with Christian themes but with a total lack of religious meaning'. Bernini is numbered among the condemned: 73–95, esp. 74–75.
6 The painting is now in the National Gallery in London.
7 For a detailed discussion of the painting, see my 'God in the Landscape: Michael Ramsey's Theological Vision', *Anglican Theological Review* 83 (2001), 775–792.
8 A fuller version of the context can be found Gesa Thiessen, *Theological Aesthetics* (London: SCM, 2004), 47–48.
9 See Richard Marks, *Stained Glass in England during the Middle Ages* (London: Routledge, 1991), 61. Ignorance of the meaning of the images at Canterbury Cathedral is emphasised by one of the stories added to *The Canterbury Tales*. See *The Tale of Beryn* (Early English Texts, extra series, vol. CV, 1909), 6.
10 Thomas Beckett had been recently martyred during the reign of Henry II.
11 See Madeline Harrison Caviness, *The Early Stained Glass of Canterbury Cathedral* (Princeton: Princeton University Press, 1977), 107–115. For Adam illustration, no. 6; for precedents in Origen, 111.
12 This is the argument of Wolfgang Kemp as applied to windows at Chartres and Bourges in *The Narratives of Gothic Stained Glass* (Cambridge: Cambridge University Press, 1997), 22–33; 91–101. Controversially, he suggests that expanding the narrative becomes the primary motivation, and indeed boldly talks of the stained-glass version as 'at a far remove from the Bible story and

totally uninfluenced by theological commentaries' (ibid., 29). That would seem to me an exaggeration, even if of necessity visits to brothels and gaming assume a much larger role.
13 Xavier Barral I Altet, *Stained Glass: Masterpieces of the Modern Era* (London: Thames & Hudson, 2007), 136. For further details, see M. A. Couturier, *Henri Matisse: The Vence Chapel: The Archive of a Creation* (New York: Skira, 1999).
14 Sadly, this is a common problem when contemporary glass is commissioned for a historic church. All too often no thought is given to how the window will relate to its immediate environment (which will include other windows). An excellent example of an artist conscious of the wider surroundings is Tom Denny's Transfiguration Window (2010) in Durham Cathedral. I had the privilege of negotiating with the artist on behalf of the cathedral, and was very favourably impressed by his spontaneously volunteering such considerations in relation to his own project.
15 With some conspicuous exceptions such as the Pre-Raphaelites in England and the Impressionists in France.
16 Marks, *Stained Glass in England*, 59.
17 My favourites in the former category include Evie Hone and Douglas Strachan. Thanks to the patronage of Fr Marie-Alain Couturier in France the number in the latter category is surprisingly large, and includes Bonnard, Braque, Chagall, Leger, Matisse and Rouault. In Britain there are examples by Chagall, Paolozzi, Piper and Morocco, while in 2007 Gerard Richter produced a major window for Cologne Cathedral.
18 In a review of Robert MacSwain and Taylor Worley, eds, *Theology, Aesthetics, and Culture: Responses to the Work of David Brown* in *International Journal of Systematic Theology* 17 (2015), 473–475.
19 David Brown, *God and Enchantment of Place: Reclaiming Human Experience* (Oxford: Oxford University Press, 2004), 37–83.
20 That interaction in both cases is one reason why I find Wolterstorff's aligning of my position with the 'contemplation' of the famous art critic Clive Bell (d. 1964) so odd. I certainly do not think that one should remain purely passive before the art. Conversation rather than contemplation is what I had in mind.
21 With a sense as much of heaven brought to earth as of us caught up to heaven: see my comments in *God and Enchantment of Place*, 261–262.
22 Quoted in Louise Campbell, *Coventry Cathedral: Art and Architecture in Post-War Britain* (Oxford: Clarendon Press, 1996), 241–242.
23 Pugin in writings such as *The True Principles of Pointed or Christian Architecture* (1841), Ruskin with works such as *The Seven Lamps of Architecture* (1849) and *The Stones of Venice* (1851–1853).
24 So, for example, in Manhattan there is St Paul's Chapel, Broadway (Classical, 1766); Trinity Church, Wall St (Gothic, 1830); St John the Divine (Gothic, 1897); St Bartholomew's (Romanesque, 1902); St Jean Baptiste (Baroque, 1910); Riverside (Gothic, 1930).
25 With Tertullian, the usual paraphrase for *De carne Christi*, V, 4; Kierkegaard, *Philosophical Fragments*, ed. H. V. Hong and E. H. Hong (Princeton: Princeton University Press, 1985), III: 37.
26 Beauvais is perhaps the best example, with the collapse of its choir in 1284 and of its tower (planned as the tallest in the world) in 1573. William Golding's novel *The Spire* (based on Salisbury) centres on such vaulting ambition.
27 The impact of the elongated figures of Gislibertus and other Romanesque artists, and the contrast with the heavy nature of the architecture, is well brought out in Benedetta Chiesa, ed., *Romanesque Art* (Florence: Scala, Visual Encyclopedia of Art, 2009).

Worshipping with Art and Architecture 203

28 As well as in numerous parish churches, there are sculptures of his in the following cathedrals: Chelmsford, Lichfield, Portsmouth, Southwell and Winchester.
29 A copy of Christ in Majesty by the Master of Taüll from St Clement's Church, Taüll, in Catalonia.
30 His masterpiece of 1907, *Demoiselles d'Avignon*.
31 As can be seen, for example, in the Rothko Chapel at Houston, Texas, and in Newman's *Stations of the Cross* in the National Gallery in Washington, DC.
32 Illustrated in Sam Hutchinson, *Towers, Spires and Pinnacles: A History of the Cathedrals and Churches of the Church of Ireland* (Bray: Wordwell, 2003), 25. The ones in London are much less conspicuous, in the ceiling.
33 By way of illustration of the contrast from the rest of Europe, on a recent visit to Gdansk I saw an advertisement featuring a young priest in jeans used to advertise one particular brand, surely counter-productive in most of the rest of Europe.
34 These reflections took their origin from an invitation to deliver the DuBose Lectures in 2014 at the University of the South in Sewanee, Tennessee. I am grateful to my various hosts on that occasion, in particular to Neil Alexander and Robert MacSwain. The *Sewanee Theological Review* also plans to publish this essay in due course.

Index

Adam and Eve 72, 106, 133, 159, 164, 169, 194, 196
Aelfwine Prayerbook 136
aesthetics 5, 11, 15, 27, 29, 59, 75, 131, 157–8, 164–5, 181, 184, 201 n.7; in Islam 176 n.23
Alberti, Leon Battista 160, 174
analytic theology 31, 36 n.27; *see also* theology
analytic philosophy 29, 54; *see also* philosophy
Andrewes, Lancelot 117
Angelico, Fra 103 n.2, n.4, 115
angels 39–41, 73–4, 92, 102, 105–12, 114, 120, 122, 141, 192
Angers tapestry 9–10
annunciation 40, 46, 47 n.8, 105–7, 109, 111, 111 n.10, 145 n.22, 195
Anselm 32, 36 n.28, 115
anthropology 11, 54, 57–8
Anthony of Egypt 191
Antoninus of Florence 33, 133–4
Aquinas 26–7, 61, 72, 90–1, 93, 97 n.41, 149 n.76
architecture 10, 12, 14–15, 29, 70, 78, 81, 87, 90, 151–203; Baroque 14, 159, 161–3, 167, 169–70, 174, 198, 200; Classicism 160–4, 170, 172, 174, 176 n.15, 181, 183–5, 188 n.25, 197–200; Gothic 14, 76, 87–90, 159–63, 172–3, 183–4, 194, 196, 197–9; Romanesque 87, 170–1, 182–5, 197–9
Aristotle 27, 54, 90, 171
Arnold, John 107, 111 n.7
art 7, 13, 18, 23–4, 31, 38, 40, 54, 78, 81, 101, 113, 124, 130, 190, 195; literary 8–9, 70, 113; visual 7–9, 23–4, 56, 101, 130

art history 16, 38, 54, 69, 139
artists as theologians 99–150
ascension 113–29
Athanasian Creed 33
Athanasius 32
atheism 38, 41, 43, 164
atonement 32, 36 n.30
Augustine 15, 52, 57, 65, 90, 97 n.39, 114, 134–5, 145 n.22, 148 n.70, 162, 164
Augustodunensis, Honorius 71

Baal 86
Bach, C. P. E. 125
Bach, Johann Sebastian 10, 16, 38, 200
Bacon, Francis x, 13, 41–2, 48 n.34, 118
Ball, Peter Eugene 199
Balla, Giacomo 91–2
Balthasar, Hans Urs von 109, 112 n.15
baptism 51, 59, 65–80, 94, 138, 141–2, 195
Barrett, C. K. 114
Barth, Karl vii, 14, 16, 30
Bartolommeo, Fra 137
Becket, Thomas 57–8
Bede 125
Begbie, Jeremy ix
Bellini, Giovanni 120, 140
Benedict, Rule of 71
Benedictine monasteries 182
Bernard 72, 108, 111 n.12, 140
Bible *see* Scripture
biblical criticism 13, 31, 110, 119, 122
Birgitta of Sweden 89–90, 94
blood 51, 58, 63 n.15, 123; Christ's 25, 68, 140, 143, 192
Bonaventure 72

Bonhoeffer, Dietrich 14
Bosch, Hieronymus 66
Bostridge, Ian 43
Botticelli 134
bread: *see* Eucharist
Brecht, Bertolt 13–14
Bridget *see* Birgitta of Sweden
Broadbent, Stephen 70
Butler, Joseph vii

Calvin, John 32, 56, 162
Caravaggio 90, 102
Cassirer, Ernst 59–60
cathedrals: Chichester 118–19, 131; Christ Church, Oxford 106; Durham 15, 77, 106–7, 182; Ely 118; Newcastle 131–2; Northern Lights, Alta 185; St Andrew's, Glasgow 183, 186, 188 n.28; Salisbury 27, 43
Cézanne 44–5
Christ: divinity 31, 118–19, 121–2, 124; gardener 116–17, 119; humanity 41, 121–3, 109, 139; lamb imagery 55, 62, 68, 140; miracles 9, 37, 55, 69; suffering of 8, 41–2, 191; wounds of 68, 116, 191
Chrysostom, John 114
Cistercians 71
Cloisters Cross 119
cloud imagery 85–6, 113
Cloud of Unknowing 85
Coakley, Sarah 33
Coltrane, John 45–6, 48 n.31
Constable, John 27, 43–4
Constantine 73, 179–80
Correggio 116
Counter-Reformation 102, 137
Cowper, William 89
Cox, Stephen 131–2
creation xi n.23, 3, 8–9, 14–15, 28–9, 57, 59–60, 66–8, 70, 82, 84, 91–2, 125, 133, 141, 158–9, 161, 169
creeds 33, 42, 53, 81, 109; *see also* Athansian Creed; Nicene Creed
criteria ix, 13, 15, 24, 131, 138
crucifixion 13, 21 n.49, 33, 41, 45, 52 n.2, 74, 76, 80 n.49, 111 n.2, 138–9, 191–2

Dalí, Salvador 92–3, 122–3, 126
dance 10, 14, 91, 118, 122, 156, 192; ballet 25
Dante 95, 134, 143, 145 n.13

Darkness, as symbol 81–97
David, King 10, 84
Davies, Brian 20 n.34, 29, 35 n.11
deism vii–viii, x–xi n.4
Denis, Maurice 118
Denys 85, 87
Desmond, William ix
Dickens, Charles 13, 65–6
Dickinson, Emily 13, 19 n.9
Dillard, Annie 28
Dionysius 85
Donatello 133, 145 n.24
Donne, John 123
Douglas, Mary 58
Drury, John 40, 43, 106
dualism 24
Duccio 107–8, 111 n.9
Dürer 10, 139, 141, 143
Dura Europos 168
Dyer, George 42

Eckhart (Meister) 85
Edinburgh: New College, University of Edinburgh 184; St John's Church 183, 186
El Greco 36 n.36, 72, 121, 139, 148 n.58
Eliade, Mircea 57, 60
Eliot, T. S. 25
Enlightenment 30, 59, 162
Ernst, Max 41, 110
Eucharist 15, 43, 51, 53, 56, 68, 72, 74–5, 117–18, 135, 173, 198
experience, religious viii, ix, 14–18, 190–203

Farrer, Austin 31, 38, 126, 129 n.66
Feibusch, Hans 142
feminist theology 191
Ficino 134
Finzi, Gerald 124–5
Fischer-Dieskau, Dietrich 43
Flavin, Dan 93–4
Flood 67, 71, 141; *see also* water
Friedrich 27
Ford, David F. 45–6
Fuksas, Massimiliano 161
Futurist Manifesto 91, 94
Fyvie stone 132

Garden of Eden 9, 66–8, 159, 164, 169
Geerten tot Sint Jans 90
Gennep, Arnold van 57

Giotto 114–17, 120
Gogh, Vincent van 14, 44–5
Golgotha 106
Gombrich, Ernst 54
Good Samaritan 37
Gormley, Anthony 77
Graham, Gordon 163
Granlund, Paul 122
Gregory of Nazianzus 84
Gregory of Nyssa 84–5
Gregory the Great 115, 180, 193
Grünewald, Matthias 191–2

Habermas, Jürgen 30
Hagia Sophia 171
Hajj see pilgrimage
Hardy, Thomas 66
Harries, Karsten 164
Hamann, J. G. 59
Hegel 59, 164
Herder, J. G. 59
Hick, John vii
Hindu temples 157–9
Holy Spirit 8, 18 n.3, 33, 56, 71, 73, 113, 121, 131, 141–2
Hopkins, Gerard Manley 27–8, 109, 126

iconoclasm 7, 55, 139, 167–8
icons 7–8, 72, 194, 196
idolatry 7–22
Ignatius Loyola 9
image 7–22, 29–34
imagination 11, 18, 24–5, 31–2, 103, 130
imitation 71, 171–2
incarnation x, 3, 7–8, 12, 15–16, 21 n.49, 38, 44, 109, 124, 130–1, 142
inter-faith dialogue 167–77
Islam 167–77; *see also* Mecca; mosques

James, brother of Christ 109
James, Henry 13, 191
Jerusalem 10–11, 70, 83, 117, 159, 178; *see also* Temple
Jesus *see* Christ
Jesus Christ Superstar 115
John the Baptist 65, 73, 192
John of Damascus 7–8
John of the Cross 85
Joseph 38, 89, 110, 137

Ka'ba *see* Mecca
Karlskirche 170
Kamba Luesa, André 122
Kant, Immanuel 11, 31, 157
kenosis 16, 31
Kiefer, Anselm 132
Kierkegaard 197
Kildalton cross 132
King's College Chapel, Cambridge 89
Kussudiardja, Bagong 122

Langer, Susan 59–61
language, openness of 24–5, 27, 32, 54, 60–1, 67, 76, 78, 94, 103, 130
Larkin, Philip 155
Last Supper 74; *see also* Eucharist
Led Zeppelin 15–16, 21 n.40
Leeuw, Gerard van der 11
Levertov, Denise 124
Lévy-Bruhl, Lucien 59
Lewis, C. S. 190
Liebeskind, Daniel 163
Light, as symbol 81–97
Lippi, Filippo 107–8, 133–4, 140, 142
liturgy 3, 51, 55, 58–9, 65–6, 73–6, 78, 79 n.40, 80 n.53, 174, 197, 200
Logos 8, 84; *see also* word
Luther, Martin 19 n.24, 32, 56

Maistre, Roy de 118
Margaret of Antioch 17
Martin Luther Church at Hainburg 185
Mary Magdalene 113–20, 126, 127 n.13, 191–3
Mary, mother of Christ *see* Virgin Mary
Masaccio 36 n.36, 139–40, 142
Matheson, George 86–7
McGilchrist, Iain 26
Mecca 159, 167, 169, 173, 184
Mellers, Wilfrid 29
Memling, Hans 195
Messiaen, Olivier 125, 143
Michelangelo 102
Milton, John 88–9
mimesis see imitation
Mirandola, Pico della 134
Moltmann, Jürgen 135, 146 n.35
Moore, Henry 62
Moses 69, 82, 84, 104 n.9, 173
mosques 158–9, 167, 172, 178; Dome of the Rock 19 n.19, 159, 170–1
Muhammad 55, 70, 173

Murquanas 172–3; *see also* mosques
Murillo 136–7, 143, 146 n.37
Murray, Les 26
music xi n.18, 7, 10, 12, 19 n.24, 21 n.37, 23, 38–9, 42, 60–1, 102, 113, 124, 156; Gregorian Chant 12; jazz 45; pop 21 n.40
mystical theology 84–5, 130, 140, 171–2

narrative 9
National Parks 160
natural theology x, xi n.18, xii n.27, 14, 16, 23, 44, 57–9, 69, 154, 171, 174; *see also* theology
Neoplatonism 55, 134–5; mysticism 55
Nevelson, Louise 131
Newman, Barnett 93, 125–6, 199
Nicene Creed 81
Noah 71; *see also* Flood

O'Siadhail, Michael 45
Origen 84
Orthodox Christianity 40, 63 n.4, 73, 138–9, 145 n.20, 146 n.34, 192, 195–6
orthodoxy 8, 15, 38, 130

Pacheco, Francesco 72
paganism 37–48, 111 n.1, 132–3, 167–8, 179–81
painting 8, 11, 13, 16, 18, 27, 29, 31, 33, 40, 62, 75, 102, 114, 116, 135, 141, 156, 190
Palestrina 19 n.24, 39
pantheism 14
Parthenon 178–9
Pattison, George ix
Pearl 68
Perugino, Pietro 120, 192
Peter 69, 72
Peter of Celle 71
Pfitzner, Hans 39
philosophy vii–ix, 5, 8, 11, 23–4, 26–7, 29–30, 32, 34, 59–60, 83, 135, 153, 156
Piero della Francesca 13, 74–5
pilgrimage 57, 169
Piper, John 131
Plato 8, 61, 90
Platonism 24, 28; *see also* neoplatonism

poetry 9, 11, 23, 25, 28–9, 31, 42, 45, 59, 78, 83, 89, 113, 119, 124
politics 178–89
Pollaiuolo 134
Poussin, Nicholas 74–5, 107–8
prayer 8, 10, 15, 40, 57, 70, 90, 110, 118, 140, 169, 173, 176 n.26, 185, 188 n.35, 194–5
Presbyterianism 56, 183–4, 188 n.33
Prodigal Son 136
Pseudo-Bonaventure 9
Pseudo-Denys *see* Denys
psychology 11, 41, 163
Pugin, Augustus Welby Northmore 163, 184, 196

Qu'ran 55, 70, 158, 172, 174
Quine W. V. 54

Rahner, Karl 14, 20 n.33
Raphael 120, 159, 192
Reformation 12, 15, 18, 20 n.25, 26, 55–6, 132–3, 136, 184; *see also* Calvin, John; Luther, Martin
Rembrandt 16, 38, 44, 90, 117, 121–3, 136
Renaissance 62, 116, 133–6, 143, 160, 174, 192, 195
resurrection 43, 62, 89, 107, 113, 117, 120, 122
revelation vii–vii, 7, 15, 16–17, 31–2, 34, 38, 46, 61, 63 n.17, 103, 130, 146 n.36, 154, 185
Rice, Tim *see Jesus Christ Superstar*
Ricoeur, Paul 60
Rohan Book of Hours 142–3
Rohe, Mies van der 162
Rome 12, 37, 73, 133, 136, 140, 162, 168, 178–80
Root, Howard E. x
Rublev, Andrei 135
Ruskin, John 28–9, 88, 160–1, 172, 184, 196

Sacraments 24–5, 31, 55, 65, 75–6
Sallman, Warner 191
Salvation 9, 31–2, 37
Sarto, Andrea del 134
Schleiermacher, Friedrich 14
Schongauer 120
Schubert, Franz 42–3

Scripture i, 3–4, 7, 9–11, 13, 16, 23, 30, 32, 34, 37, 39, 46, 55–7, 67, 70, 75, 94, 101–2, 118, 122, 126, 137, 142, 153, 172, 185, 193–4; Acts 21 n.41, 78 n.1, 96 n.15, 112 n.13, n.14; 128 n.28, 1987 n.9; Colossians 70; Chronicles 10, 86, 95 n.4, 106, 111 n.2, 127 n.14, 155 n.1; Deuteronomy 10, 95 n.3, 155 n.1; Exodus 61, 79 n.22, 82, 85, 95 n.10, 147 n.53, 176 n.16; Ezekiel 82, 155 n.1; Ezra 155 n.1; Genesis 8, 19 n.8, 35 n.24, 67–8, 82, 128 n.26, 136, 159, 169; Hebrews 147 n.53, 153; Isaiah 18 n.4, 40, 47 n.3, 86, 109; Job 3, 5 n.2, 20 n.26, 28, 87; John's Gospel 7–8, 16, 42, 51, 65, 68–9, 84, 94, 109, 118–19, 125–6; Jonah 3, 67, 71; Luke's Gospel 5 n.3, 41, 96 n.15, 105–9, 113, 127 n.1, 180–1, 193; Mark's Gospel 19 n.7, 47 n.1, 62, 78 n.1, 105, 109; Matthew's Gospel 5 n.3, 37, 47 n.1, 65, 75, 78 n.2, 80 n.47, 96 n.15, 117, 127 n.18, 193; Psalms 10, 67, 81–2, 86, 124–5; Revelation 9, 68, 72, 180, 186; Song of Songs 62, 71–2
Scruton, Roger 164
shadow imagery *see* cloud imagery
sin 10, 15, 18, 41, 59, 65, 78 n.6, 116; original 51, 59–60, 65, 72, 74, 80 n.53, 108, 116
Solomon 10, 82
Spirit: *see* Holy Spirit
spirituality 3, 14–15
stained glass 87–8, 144 n.4, 190, 193–6, 201 n.12
Suger (Abbot) 161, 172
Sullivan, Louis 156
Sullivan, W. T. 92
Sutherland, Graham 118–19
symbol vii, ix, x, xii n.27, xiii n.38, 51–97, 106, 174, 178–90
synagogues 158, 168, 170, 174 n.14
Syrophoenician woman 37–8, 46

Tarkovsky, Andrei 77
Taylor, Charles 26
Temple 7, 10–11, 67–8, 70, 82–4, 106, 155 n.1, 168–70, 179–81; Holy of Holies 83–4, 86, 94, 159, 170
Tennyson 67, 69
Tertullian 197
theatre 13–14, 161–2
theology viii, ix, 3, 18, 23–36, 162; *see also* natural theology
Tiamat 67
Tiepolo 142
Tillich, Paul 14, 56, 88, 102
Tintoretto 121
Titian 116, 127 n.12, 128 n.35, 134, 141–2
transcendence 13–14, 16, 27, 31, 44, 57, 60, 84, 92, 95, 117, 142, 157–8, 164–5, 172
Trent, Council of 19 n.24, 39, 121, 197
Trinity 18 n.3, 32–4, 36 n.31, 95, 101–3, 130–50; *see also* incarnation
Trollope, Anthony 191
Turner, Denys 29
Turner, Victor 57
Turrell, James 92

universalism 45, 57
Updike, John 16, 92–3, 124

Van Eyck 68, 140
Vaughan, Henry 123
Vietnam War 55
Virgin Mary 13, 17–18, 38, 40, 62, 71–2, 89–90, 102–3, 106–11, 119–20, 133, 137, 192, 195
Vitruvius 157, 160, 181

water 8–9, 15, 25, 28, 51–2, 58–9, 65–80, 81, 84
Westcott, B. F. 83–4
Weyden, Rogier van der 76
Wiles, Maurice vii
Williams, Rowan 38
wine: *see* Eucharist
Wittgenstein, Ludwig 61
Witz, Konrad 69
Wolterstorff, Nicholas 195
Word 7, 9, 125; *see also* logos
worship 190–203
Wren, Christopher 163
Wynne, David 118